The Notion of the *A Priori*

Northwestern University

STUDIES IN *Phenomenology &*

Existential Philosophy

Mikel Dufrenne

Translated from the French and with an introduction by

Preface by

The Notion of the *A Priori*

EDWARD S. CASEY

PAUL RICOEUR

NORTHWESTERN UNIVERSITY PRESS
EVANSTON, ILLINOIS

Northwestern University Press
www.nupress.northwestern.edu

First paperback printing 2009

Printed in the United States of America

10 9 8 7 6 5 4 3 2 1

Library of Congress Cataloging-in-Publication Data

Dufrenne, Mikel.
    [Notion d'apriori. English]
    The notion of the a priori / Mikel Dufrenne ; translated from the
French and with an introduction by Edward S. Casey ; preface by Paul
Ricoeur. — 1st paperback printing.
       p. cm. — (Northwestern university studies in phenomenology and
existential philosophy)
    Reprint. Originally published: Evanston : Northwestern University
Press, 1966.
    Includes bibliographical references and index.
    ISBN 978-0-8101-2543-8 (pbk. : alk. paper)
    1. Kant, Immanuel, 1724–1804. 2. A priori. 3. Experience. 4.
Phenomenology. I. Casey, Edward S., 1939– II. Title. III. Series:
Northwestern University studies in phenomenology & existential
philosophy.
B2799.K7D83 2009
121.3—dc22

2008053861

Contents

Preface

THE NOTION OF THE A PRIORI is a book with a hard shell and a soft center: a continuous dialogue with all the philosophers who count, from Parmenides to Heidegger, this essay is inspired by a great intellectual and verbal agility, as well as by a constant concern for precision and proper nuance; it certainly is not addressed to the impatient reader, for the simplicity of its design is revealed only gradually. In fact, its apparent point of departure is somewhat exterior to this design; there *is* a vast Kantian philosophy of the *a priori* which itself derives from a prolonged philosophical debate and which in turn gives rise to a complex and contradictory history; Dufrenne inserts his own meditation into this tissue of controversies. Yet a strong and lucid thesis runs through this multiform altercation. My first task will be to reconstruct this implicit thesis by referring all later discussions to the original Kantian framework.

The traditional Kantian view of the *a priori*—a view which Dufrenne wishes to revise—is found in the following two points:

1) For Kant the *a priori* resides only in the knowing subject. Subjectivity constitutes all that is valid in the object of knowledge;

2) The *a priori* is the form of universality and necessity belonging to these objects. (Even if space and time are the *a priori* of sensibility, they underlie the construction of the mathematical sciences; thus we may conclude that for Kant all *a priori* are doomed to intellectuality.)

In opposition to the first point, Dufrenne proposes a dualistic conception of the *a priori:* on the one hand, it is a *structure* of objects which appears and expresses itself outside us, before us; on the other hand, the *a priori* is a virtual *knowledge* of these structures which is rooted in the human subject. In opposition to the second point, Dufrenne discerns a concrete meaning in such objective structures, which resemble countenances [*physionomies*] rather than intelligible relations, and a corporeal character in this subjective knowledge, which is nearer to feeling [*sentiment*] or immediate apprehension than it is to abstract intelligence.

Through this double reform of transcendental philosophy, Dufrenne introduces a remarkably original reflection proceeding from a certain number of themes, or better, from vivid experiences whose import is considerable.

I

TAKING THE OBJECT'S POINT OF VIEW FIRST, Dufrenne extends the limits of the *a priori:* to the Kantian "formal" *a priori* he adds the "material" structures of the great regions of reality described by Husserl, as well as the entire group of values, affective qualities, and even mythical significations which compose the categories of feeling or imagination. This extension necessarily plunges the *a priori* into experience; in its "primitive state" [*à l'état sauvage*]—an expression recurring often in the book—the *a priori* is "the immediate presence of a meaning."[1] Here one might ask: why not simply deny the existence of the *a priori*? Because there is no genesis of this immediately apprehended meaning: we cannot "learn" it; it is already there, preceding all learning and genesis; this "pre-historical" character of a certain kind of meaning authorizes us to retain the notion of the *a priori*, in spite of its conceivably limitless extension and its immersion in experience.

This radical position has a number of consequences; above all, we should no longer refer to the *a priori* as strictly formal or even as universal and necessary; the *a priori* is "the meaning immediately grasped in experience, and instantly recognized" (p. 59); thus we must realize that the universe imposes this meaning: here is where the most original necessity is found. Now, that which is imposed is not universally recognized; the objective *a priori* is transmitted by a history and a culture: "The necessity of the *a priori* is not necessarily felt" (p. 65). Hence Dufrenne, following the lead of Husserl and Scheler, prefers to compare the notion of the *a priori* with that of "essence" rather than "form,"

1. See below, p. 51. Hereafter all page references to *The Notion of the A Priori* will be placed in parentheses directly following the quotation. The reader will note that I have altered the translation in several instances for reasons of emphasis.—Trans.

although he is aware that it is not easy to "find a cutting-off point for our list of the various kinds of *a priori*" (p. 78).

Herein lies the difficulty of the undertaking: once the dam of formalism has burst, where should we stop in assessing experiences that yield the *a priori*? Dufrenne proposes a flexible criterion: the meaning is certainly *in* the object, but it *surpasses* any single incarnation: "Thus a playing child expresses youth, but youth is also expressed by one of Mozart's melodies or by springtime" (p. 82). Therefore, it is the possibility of correspondences, in the Baudelairian sense of the word, that determines the domain of the various *a priori* which we apprehend directly in objects. It is in this sense that the *a priori* is *constitutive,* not because we constitute it, but because it constitutes the meanings of things: "Thus joyfulness constitutes a Bach fugue, and the tragic pervades Van Gogh's paintings. . . . The same thing can be said for the values experienced by feeling or the meanings apprehended by the imagination: when the object appears as something good or evil, a value or a group of values constitutes its being; when the object appears as sacred, a mythical meaning is similarly constitutive: for the imagination, youth is the truth of springtime, just as happiness is the truth of the Enchanted Isles, and life the truth of fertile earth" (p. 105).

With the assurance of not allowing ourselves to be engulfed by the infinitude of the perceived, we can say that the *a priori* is perceived and thus arrive at an "empiricism of the transcendental" (*passim*). Here Dufrenne anticipates a conviction which will be brought out at the end of the book: all logic is solicited and provoked by the rich and overflowing presence of the universe that inspires reflection. This conviction animates his repeated refusal to admit a constitutive activity on the part of the subject: "The world makes itself known, reveals itself as world to someone capable of knowing it: this defines the *a priori*" (p. 100). In the final analysis, the metaphor of *expression* best embraces Dufrenne's position: expression manifests Being itself; it does not mean, it says; it adheres to the thing and renders it discernible and recognizable. Such is the nature of the *a priori*, which at once inspires our conception of the universal and our perception of the singular.

II

TURNING NOW TO THE SUBJECT, we can say that the *a priori of* the object is known *a priori by* the subject. The *a priori* is not learned, but known from the very beginning; we meet it in anticipation: "As subjective, the *a priori* is precisely this aptitude, this pre-given comprehension of the given, without which the meaning of the given would appear—as in the case of the *a posteriori*—only at the end of a more or less detailed investigation" (p. 122). But just as the objective *a priori* had to be wrested from its Platonic or Kantian cloud and thrust into the paste of the perceived, so the subjective *a priori* must also descend into the flesh of the perceiver. Part II of the book is devoted to this hazardous enterprise.

Hazardous, for we must discern that which knows no birth or chronology in the very fiber of the history of individuals, groups, cultures, and humanity considered as a whole; the always already known organizes the history of all discoveries, and from a position neither *outside* this history nor *within* it. Thus we must run the risk of sinking into psychologism or sociologism and confront their claim to explain the genesis of the entire human being in terms of an experience *learned* by the individual or society. The necessity of incarnating the *a priori*, with its attendant danger of ambiguity, inevitably entails this risk. Time is a destiny for consciousness, but the subject possesses "something nontemporal, as is attested by the unspecifiable anteriority of the virtual. This anteriority is unspecifiable because the past involved in knowledge is an absolute past" (p. 128).

In this connection, we must conceive of a memory, a "primordial" [*originaire*] memory which would be at once corporeal but more than the body, and historical without being a mere account; this memory of the virtual would be like "the echo of the world so far as I appear in it" (p. 131). But the full meaning of this statement will not become clear until the end of the book, when the two kinds of *a priori* are brought together. Let us say for now that, just as the objective *a priori*[2] constitute objects—though apprehended against the background formed by the world—so the subjective *a priori* constitute me: I *am* these virtualities.

There are important corollaries to this thesis: first, the transcendental subject is personal, empirical, and singular; secondly, this personal subject is a body, a body constitutive, as it were, of the body as constituted: a thinking body, the body understood as *lumen naturale*, as the virtuality of all of man's encounters with all of the world's appearances [*physionomies*]. This corporeal foreknowledge constitutes "a sort of pre-language, an original orientation of the body as still not speaking—an orientation by which

---

2. *A priori* may be singular or plural, depending on the context.—Trans.

consciousness becomes sensitive to certain experiences that language can later render explicit but that do not refer to any particular and namable objects" (p. 159).

Here Dufrenne is faced with a problem parallel to the one he had to face from the standpoint of the object: where does the list of corporeal virtualities end? And corresponding to the transcendence of the object by its meaning is the safety catch of "representation" in the subject: the only virtualities meriting the name of *a priori* are those possessing a recognizable "virtual knowledge [*savoir virtuel*] which can be made explicit and which is actualized in articulated knowledge [*connaissance*]" (p. 160); even in the body, "consciousness" is the transcendental factor.

But the body does not account for the entire domain of subjectivity. Dufrenne conceives of the subject in very broad terms: as not wholly individualized; he recognizes a certain detached, anonymous, communal, and yet human subjectivity. In this light, the social becomes homologous with the corporeal, and culture is seen as the transcendental element in those larger bodies represented by historical groups and by humanity as a whole.

And here we can be grateful to Dufrenne for avoiding the tendency in contemporary philosophy to dramatize the relationship of man to man by reducing it merely to struggle. The *a priori* possessed in common by men point precisely to the fact that other human beings are first of all similar to one another; they are different only because they are basically the same; the *a priori* "makes the similar similar" (p. 166). At the limit—a limit that remains a task—the transcendental is the imprint [*le texte*] of humanity in each person: "Communication is possible because the person is nourished by humanity" (p. 167). But Dufrenne avoids a too literal comparison of personal subjects and cultures; the latter are only quasi-subjects and should instead be compared to the body. Cultures are schemata permitting the virtual to be actualized; a certain culture or epoch affords an occasion for the realization of certain *a priori*, without preventing the actualization of others. Yet in the final analysis the virtual is neither the social nor the historical, but the transcendental element in both.

III

THESE THEN ARE the portals of the *a priori*: structure of the object and virtual knowledge in the subject. But why must we insist so much on the duality of the objective and subjective *a priori*? Here we discover the author's overall design in this work. The doubling of the *a priori* represents an attempt to treat openly as a problem—as an impasse—what remains hidden in Kantian philosophy: the fundament [*fondement*] of the accord existing between man and the world. That the *a priori* of the object is *for* us is amazing; and it is equally surprising that the *a priori* of the subject is *for* the world; we are astonished to recognize ourselves in a world that surpasses us on all sides. This astonishment is the real inspiration of the present book: all the previous discussions and analyses simply allow us to regain this starting point.

Our astonishment consists in the fact that the accord of man and the world is not a result of man's domination of the world—Dufrenne does not think in terms of intellectual or practical mastery—or of the world's power over man, such as we find in a purely naturalistic perspective. Instead, the relationship of man with the world is one of familiarity, and here we sense Dufrenne's own delight in existence and his feeling of harmony with his surroundings. Now, we must continually revitalize dualism to show the marvel of man's affinity with the world. This is why, through a final reinforcement of dualism, we shall no longer speak of the object, but of the world, in order to express the inexhaustible, the overwhelming [*le débordant*], the powerful, the young, and the tragic: "If the *a priori* constitutes objects, it is at the same time the herald of a world" (p. 192). This admiration for the world surrounding and including us lies at the basis of Dufrenne's protest against restricting the *a priori* to the subjective sphere: "the real is inexhaustible" (p. 200). The world is the source of the objectivity of objects. It is both inexhaustible and strong: for the very *power* [*puissance*] of the world is responsible for the fact that the *a priori* first of all *imposes itself* upon me as an objective *a priori*, as a sign addressed to me both from the very near and the very far. Thus, the world is revealed to me as world—science too is in the world and the imaginary itself appears only against the background of the real—not by active conquest or by the domination of thought, but by feeling. In feeling, Mikel Dufrenne sees the cosmic more than the private [*intime*]: or rather he discerns in it the inner resonance of the world's immensity. Through feeling, man considered even in his singularity finds himself *equal* to this immensity.

Consequently, having skirted the twin dangers of empiricism and psychologism in the first two parts of the book, the author now brings himself face to face with naturalism.

For the world to which [naturalism] gives primacy—the world that engenders man, the foyer of possibilities and the theater of individuations that
is always in operation—is *natura naturans* or the Being whose primary
predicate is reality. . . . Why should we fear a regression to a pre-Kantian,
pre-critical ontology? Perhaps it is the only viable one (p. 203).

Yet, on the verge of being swallowed up in the whole [*le tout*], we
are rescued by the memory of the subject, who is an origin-less
echo of this vast world. "The man who is born does not come into
the world as its product; he comes as its equal: every man is a
Minerva" (p. 205). Since he is himself the *a priori* subject, man as
overwhelmed by the world is in turn overwhelming and on equal
terms with it, with its immensity; the failure of any attempt to
engender man from something other than himself is the counter-
proof—one which needs to be constantly re-established—of this
truth: *man is born into the world as unengenderable.*

IV

WE ARRIVE THUS at the last of the book's peripeteia,
and we can now see what is at stake philosophically.

Given the accord of man and the world—their equality, or
better: their affinity—from what radical *origin* does this accord
proceed? Rejecting naturalism because of the subject and idealism because of reality, can we embrace the two aspects of the *a
priori*—subjective and objective—in a system more vast than either naturalism or idealism? Is there "an *a priori* of the *a priori*"
(p. 202)? Can we fit the reciprocal finality of the two facets of the
a priori into a rational theology—for example, the pre-established
harmony of Leibniz? Dufrenne does not believe that we should go
back beyond Kant, whose transcendental philosophy has made all
dogmatic metaphysics—all recourse to an accord *in-itself* [*en-soi*]
—impossible. Moreover, the unity that we seek incessantly produces dualities composed of heterogeneous terms, enveloped one
in the other according to incomparable modes.

This is why Dufrenne prefers to consider the compatibility of
man and the world as a *fact*, irreducible to any logic, dialectic, or
system: a fact that we can only *witness* (pp. 209, 218, 224–26,
233).

This is also why, though momentarily tempted by the Heideggerian siren to reject metaphysics for the "thought of Being" (p.
228–33), Dufrenne prefers to admit the ultimate failure of philosophy and to grant the poet the last word. For only the poet is a witness to the "fact which is a fundament" (p. 233), but which cannot

xvi / THE NOTION OF THE A Priori

be founded; only poetry expresses "the experience of a concrete reconciliation of man and Nature. . . . The intelligibility of Being
consists primarily in the inhabitability of the world" (p. 234). This
experience resists being pigeonholed in a system, for it is "its own
self-revelation . . . the poet seems to transport himself beyond
dualism in a leap exhibiting all the ingenuousness of innocence:
the world ceases to be the other; it is made to the poet's measure
and in his image" (p. 235). Poetry alone puts "power and grace"
within our reach, by revealing them as created in our image.

This is an admirable conclusion, if a perplexing one. Even the
author is left perplexed, since he declares in closing that the
uniqueness of the philosophical enterprise should be respected,
that "philosophy is reflection," and that "its proper tool is analysis,
and its peculiar virtue rigor" (p. 239). Is a philosophy of feeling
possible in these terms? If we cannot construct a system including, or a dialectic between, the objective and subjective *a priori*,
can we speak of a fact which is a fundament? Should we then
relate the shipwreck of philosophy to the manifestation of Being,
as Karl Jaspers has done?

The cumulative force of the book finally lays bare this very
difficulty.

Starting from this final problem, we may now point to two
major difficulties which are linked to the double confrontation
with Kant set forth at the beginning of this article.

First difficulty: once having abandoned the Kantian criteria of
the *a priori*, how can we be sure of being able to stop ourselves at
will on the slippery slope at whose base every empirical presence
would be an objective *a priori* and every psychological virtuality a
subjective *a priori*? Of course, the criteria proposed above are
quite flexible; only an attempt at the actual enumeration of concrete *a priori* could indicate the self-limiting character of the
enumeration; and if this character did not exist, the very problem
of the *a priori* would vanish altogether. But we know that Kant
struggled for a long time—at least ten years!—to discover the
"clue" (*Leitfaden*) to an enumeration itself *a priori* and self-limiting because *a priori*. Dufrenne's forthcoming book on the "inventory" of the *a priori* should illuminate this enigma.

The second difficulty is more serious: is it legitimate to split
the *a priori* into two parts? Can we describe as separate the

expression of things in the world and the virtualities of knowledge [*savoir*] in man? Does expression have a *meaning* independently of the power of apprehension in which it is given? And do the virtualities of knowledge exist by themselves and independently of the very appearance [*visage*] of things for which this knowledge is the meaning? By defining *separately* the world's appearances and our pre-comprehension of them, Dufrenne has perhaps created an insoluble problem and made the "in-itself" [*en-soi*] of the objective *a priori* incommunicable with the "for-itself" [*pour-soi*] of the subjective *a priori*. I realize that the initial intuition of this book is found in the perpetual oscillation—both toward and away from each other—of the power belonging to an inexhaustible reality and the anticipatory power constituting the human subject; the accord of man and the world must always be attained through a double discordance and a reciprocal envelopment. This is why the problem of the *a priori* is dissolved if the accord is granted too soon or too quickly. But we must also say that if the duality of the *a priori* is insisted upon from the beginning and if it is considered as a real duality, there is no *reason* why the affinity revealed by feeling should ever have a meaning.

Might not the final word be: there are two *meanings* of the *a priori*, yet only a *feeling* of their unity? But if this is the case, does the poetry expressing this feeling itself have a *meaning*?

PAUL RICOEUR

MIKEL DUFRENNE, a leading figure in contemporary French philosophy, is known to American readers through a single book, *Language and Philosophy*.[1] The following translation of *La Notion d'a priori* was undertaken to bring what Dufrenne considers his most representative work to the attention of an American audience. As we shall see, this is an essay occupying a pivotal position between his early aesthetic writings and his more recent sallies into ontology. In fact, Dufrenne's preoccupation with the *a priori* has spanned practically his entire writing career. But, beyond this, the reader might well ask: why a whole book on the *a priori*? Have we not already heard enough discussion of this equivocal concept in recent philosophy?

Yet there *is* a need for the present book if the *a priori* is understood in its full amplitude. Precisely one of Dufrenne's goals is to expand the notion of the *a priori* beyond the narrow confines within which Kant had left it to suffer in the merciless hands of contemporary philosophers. Not even Kant's idea of a synthetic *a priori*—itself often rejected today—does proper justice to the scope of the *a priori*, since Kant's criteria were only formal and were meant to be applied to the objects of mathematics and physics alone. What of the rest of experience? The body and society, history and art: do they not possess their own *a priori*, that is, their own characteristic structures or qualities? Phenomenology[2] has shown that this is indeed the case; its founder, Edmund Husserl, attempted to provide a definitive methodology for delimiting "essences" and "regions." Without rejecting Husserl's pioneering work, Dufrenne prefers the term "*a priori*" for two basic reasons: first, he wishes to retain the Kantian idea that

1. *Language and Philosophy*, trans. Henry B. Veatch (Bloomington, University of Indiana Press, 1963). These were the 1959 Mahlon Powell Lectures at the University of Indiana.

2. "I understand phenomenology in the sense in which Sartre and Merleau-Ponty have acclimated this term in France: a description aiming at an essence, itself defined as a meaning immanent in the phenomenon and given with it." (Mikel Dufrenne, *Phénoménologie de l'expérience esthétique* [Paris, Presses Universitaires de France, 1953], I, 4–5n.—hereafter referred to as "*Phénoménologie*.")

the *a priori* is somehow constitutive of experience—hence, as constituting objects, it is objective; secondly, there is a subjective connotation attached to "*a priori*" which is not found with "essence," "region," or even the Platonic "form." But the subjectivity of the *a priori* is not what Kant took it to be: the constitution of the objects of experience by a transcendental subjectivity; rather, it refers to the common notion that we "know certain things *a priori*." Dufrenne interprets this statement not in terms of Platonic reminiscence but in terms of our possession of a "virtual" knowledge *of* the *a priori* that is activated *by* the *a priori* as it appears objectively—i.e., as constituting objects, persons, worlds, and societies. We possess a predisposition to apprehend the meaning of certain experiences immediately, and the fact of this immediacy finds no adequate explanation in the learning theories of empirical psychology. Thus, when Jean Hyppolite once asked Dufrenne why he used the term "*a priori*," Dufrenne replied, "because the meaning revealed by experience constitutes the object—that is, founds experience—and because it is always already known, so that this knowledge constitutes the subject in turn." [3] It is the dual aspect of the *a priori*—its subjective and objective sides—that convinces Dufrenne of its philosophical fecundity. In brief, "the *a priori* is the something in common that permits communication between subject and object, without abolishing their duality in a dialectical fashion." [4]

Dufrenne was first led to attempt a delineation of the "field" of the *a priori* through his consideration of the nature of aesthetic experience. This should come as no surprise since it is in this kind of experience above all that "meaning" or "expression" is perceived immediately through feeling. But Dufrenne went beyond this observation to discuss the possibility of a "pure aesthetics." [5] In evolving such an ideal aesthetics, he isolated certain "affective categories" which are based upon "affective qualities," or better, "affective *a priori*." Such categories as "the tragic," "the noble," or even "the beautiful" function as the *a priori* of the world expressed by the aesthetic object; that is, they constitute such a world as tragic, noble, or beautiful. As constitutive in this manner, the affective *a priori* are transcendental factors in Kant's sense of the term. Aesthetic experience "brings veritable *a priori* of affectivity

3. *Bulletin de la Société française de Philosophie* (June–September 1955), p. 119. This dialogue occurred after the reading of Dufrenne's paper, "Signification des *a priori*," which forms an early sketch of *La Notion d'a priori* (see *ibid.*, pp. 99–116).
4. *Ibid.*, p. 98.
5. See *Phénoménologie*, II, sec. 4, 543–613.

into play, in the same way that Kant speaks of the *a priori* of sensibility and understanding." [6] Yet whereas the Kantian *a priori* structure an object that is primarily conceived, the affective *a priori* construct objects or worlds that are *felt;* although the role of perception, imagination, and reflection cannot be overlooked in an analysis of aesthetic experience, it is mainly through feeling that affective qualities are apprehended.

Near the end of his *Phénoménologie*, Dufrenne promises the reader a more detailed study of the *a priori* in terms of a tentative tripartite division.[7] This promise is largely fulfilled in *The Notion of the A Priori;* but instead of classifying all *a priori* as "noetic" or intellectual, "vital" or corporeal, "affective" or aesthetic, Dufrenne is now more concerned with the crucial distinction between "formal" and "material" *a priori.*[8] The formal *a priori* are those objective structures found in all objects and all experience—e.g., space and time, conjunction and disjunction. They are characterized by universality and necessity, but they are not strictly "analytic" because they are forms of the real; for Dufrenne, a putative *a priori* having no relation to reality is no longer *a priori* at all. As he has written recently, "the *a priori* is often situated on the side of the formal and, for logicism, reduced to the analytic. But is the formal here really *a priori*? If the formal is independent of experience, this is because of having been drawn from it by the procedures of formalization which begin with language . . . thus it does not assume the constitutive function of the *a priori*—unless it retains from its origin the privilege of saying something about the real." [9] Yet even if the formal *a priori* is a universal structure, the material *a priori* "bites" more deeply into reality; among the material *a priori* we find those of the body, sociality, imagination, and affectivity. Borrowing the term from Max Scheler, Dufrenne means by "material": having a content that constitutes the *meaning* of an object, not just its *being* (as do the formal *a priori*).

6. *Phénoménologie*, II, 539.

7. *Ibid.*, p. 568n.

8. For a comparison of these two modes of classification, see *Bulletin de la Société française de Philosophie* (June–September 1955), pp. 112–13.

9. Mikel Dufrenne, *Jalons* (The Hague, Nijhoff, 1966), p. 19. For other discussions which bear on this subject, see the first and second chapters of the present book, as well as *Language and Philosophy*, pp. 50–68. In the latter book, Dufrenne indicates his essential agreement with Henry Veatch's conception of "intentional logic," along with its metaphysical commitments (see Henry B. Veatch, *Intentional Logic* [New Haven, Yale University Press, 1952]). The reader might also consult two recent essays: "Wittgenstein et Husserl," in *Jalons*, pp. 18–27; and "Wittgenstein et la Philosophie," in *Les Etudes Philosophiques*, no. 3 (July–September, 1965), pp. 281–306.

Both formal and material *a priori* may be considered as either objective or subjective: one method of classification cuts across the other. Seen objectively, the formal and material *a priori* make experience what it is for the subject who feels, perceives, imagines, reflects, and knows. Seen subjectively, the *a priori* is responsible for the immediate recognition of its objective counterpart in experience; the sum of the subjective *a priori* with which a person confronts experience constitutes his "existential *a priori*"; and the intersubjective structures of society and the body are also composed of subjective *a priori*—or, more precisely, the subjective aspect of the *a priori*. For, in spite of their irrevocably dual aspect, the *a priori* form unities. This is indicated by the fact that, as Dufrenne says repeatedly, man is "capable of the world" because of his virtual knowledge. Similarly, the world seems made for man —for his knowledge, perception, and feeling. Thus, man and world are linked by a primordial "affinity" or "accord" which reveals them as equal partners—equally constitutive and equally meaningful. The description of the manifold relations between man and world is the task of phenomenology. But if we delve beneath the fatal embrace of man and world—a union made possible by consciousness, memory, and time—we uncover an area that can no longer be handled by phenomenology. Here we are at the level of the "*a priori* of the *a priori*" or the common ground from which man and the world surge: Nature. This is the province of ontology, and we seek here the "onto-genesis" of man and the world: the ontology of all essentially "ontic" phenomena.

Even if this language is reminiscent of Heidegger, Dufrenne's own concern with ontology represents no mere aping of the German sage. The following characteristic movement of Dufrenne's thought was announced as early as the *Phénoménologie:* "We shall pass from the phenomenological to the transcendental, and the transcendental will lead to the metaphysical." [10] It is nevertheless true that at this stage he used the language of Being; the *a priori* is even defined as "a determination of Being," [11] and it is declared that "we must succeed in subordinating both the attitudes of the subject and the attributes [*visages*] of the object to a principal Being which contains and produces them." [12] But Dufrenne diverges from Heidegger in three basic ways.[13] First, the

10. *Phénoménologie*, I, 27.
11. *Ibid.*, II, 672.
12. *Ibid.*, p. 568.
13. For further discussion of Heidegger by Dufrenne himself, see *Jalons*, pp. 84–111 and 127–49.

movement to the ontological plane is not made to the detriment of man, who remains unsurpassable in his relation of equality with the world; fundamental ontology "proceeds from a phenomenology of subjectivity: beginning with man, it cannot abandon him on its way." [14] Dufrenne agrees here with Sartre that the *pour-soi* can and does hold its own with the surrounding *en-soi*. Secondly, although Dufrenne confesses his desire to "discover the ground [*fond*] under the fundament [*fondament*]," [15] he believes that it will be found not so much in "the Being of beings"—the Heideggerian formula that tends to emphasize the "ontological difference" between Being and beings—as in "the Being *in* beings." Dufrenne even claims that Being *is* "the very beings that are always already there, with all their density and force, in their totality." [16] Finally, he now prefers to speak of "Nature" rather than "Being"; and he considers his "philosophy of Nature"—a term taken from Schelling—to be opposed both to Heidegger's philosophy of Being and Sartre's philosophy of consciousness.

In fact, Dufrenne is much closer to philosophers of immanence like Aristotle, Spinoza, Hegel, and Merleau-Ponty than to philosophers of transcendence like Plato, Sartre, or the early Heidegger. By his own admission, Dufrenne feels most drawn to Spinoza, from whom he would "request patronage, because in conceiving a *natura naturans* he conceived Being not only as totality, but especially as plenitude." [17] Dufrenne even hazards this rhetorical question: "Might I say that I have tried to follow Spinoza in my own way, by substituting aesthetic experience for knowledge of the third degree?" [18] Dufrenne's debt to, yet divergence from, Spinoza is palpable in his own definition of Nature: "It is Substance, though without attributes; hence it cannot be conceived, but only felt—or imagined as in myths and poems—according to the visages presented by the world." [19] There is, however, one grave flaw in Spinoza; for him, "man, one mode among [all] finite modes, is abolished in Substance." [20] It is difficult to claim that the Spinoza of the *Ethics* was a humanist.

Merleau-Ponty was a humanist, and it is he, among contempo-

---

14. *Ibid.*, p. 21.
15. *Le Poétique* (Paris, Presses Universitaires de France, 1963), p. 144.
16. *Jalons*, p. 13.
17. *Le Poétique*, p. 160. For Dufrenne's recognition of the importance of Schelling, see *ibid.*, p. 149 and p. 161.
18. *Jalons*, p. 26.
19. *Ibid.*, p. 24.
20. *Ibid.*, p. 10.

rary philosophers,[21] to whom Dufrenne is perhaps closest. Both men seek Nature or "l'être sauvage" in "the unconceptualizable and most profound immanence." [22] As meaning for Merleau-Ponty is incarnated in creative speaking [*la parole parlante*] and in the perceiving body, so Dufrenne finds that "sense [*sens*] is always immanent in the sensible" [23]—a formula dating from his first reflections on art, which he considers in turn as "the apotheosis of the sensible." [24] And just as Merleau-Ponty was finally led to an ontology in which the visible and invisible, the "outside" and "inside" form an indivisible if imperfect and dehiscent whole, so Dufrenne has presently come to rest in a monistic philosophy of Nature in which things and men speak to each other through poetry, thereby revealing a common origin in Nature. Dufrenne might well subscribe to Merleau-Ponty's cryptic description of Nature as "the flesh of the world." [25] Yet he is finally critical of the equality Merleau-Ponty maintained between Nature and man; for Dufrenne, Nature (though not the world, which remains co-ordinate with man) takes the initiative: it solicits and creates man. In this sense, Dufrenne is more "naturalistic" than Merleau-Ponty, as he is more "materialistic" than Sartre. At the end of his eloquent eulogy of Merleau-Ponty, Dufrenne asks: "How can we disavow a priority of the perceived [over perception], an anteriority of Nature with respect to man, and above all a reality—an inhuman reality—of time which would guarantee this anteriority?" [26]

Nevertheless, in constructing his philosophy of Nature, Dufrenne follows Merleau-Ponty's lead in two significant ways. First, with respect to the very question of time, he draws on Merleau-Ponty's statement that (in contradistinction to Kant or Husserl) "time cannot be deduced from temporality . . . time is the foundation and measure of our spontaneity." [27] Dufrenne further agrees with Merleau-Ponty that "the entire essence of time, as of light, is to *make visible* [*faire voir*]." [28] But time is not, of itself, creative, as Merleau-Ponty seemed to suggest; only Nature is pro-

21. As somewhat lesser influences, mention should also be made of Max Scheler, Edmund Husserl (especially the Husserl of the *Formale und transzendentale Logik*), and Alain, whom Dufrenne greatly admired as a teacher.

22. *Jalons*, p. 13.

23. *Phénoménologie*, I, 131.

24. *Ibid.*

25. *Le Visible et l'invisible* (Paris, Gallimard, 1964), p. 320.

26. "Maurice Merleau-Ponty," *Les Etudes philosophiques* (January–March 1962), p. 91.

27. Quoted by Dufrenne in *Le Poétique*, p. 157.

28. *Ibid.*

ductive, and hence only Nature is truly temporal: "Nature is what is temporal. If time prefigures the self [as Merleau-Ponty claimed], Nature alone is able to produce man." [29] Secondly, Dufrenne shares Merleau-Ponty's passion for language; but, even though he largely agreed with the latter's views on the expressive and gesticular nature of language at the time of writing the *Phénoménologie*,[30] his more recent treatments of this subject [31] strike out in a divergent direction. For if language renders possible the relation of man and the world (a view that could be attributed as easily to Cassirer as to Merleau-Ponty), it is primarily through *poetic* language that Nature speaks to man: "Poetry is thus the primary language, man's means of responding to the language of Nature, or rather that which makes Nature appear as language." [32] As in the case of time, the impetus is seen as coming from Nature to man, who is regarded as a "witness" of Nature: its correlate and yet also an integral part of it.

Dufrenne's theory of imagination is perhaps the keystone of his "post-critical naturalism," as he sometimes terms his present philosophical position. For him, the most significant imagining has nothing to do with the "unreal," as Sartre had held, or even with Bachelard's notion of the "surreal." [33] Here Dufrenne is directly at odds with the thesis that perception and imagination are absolutely discontinuous or, in Merleau-Ponty's words, that "the imaginary is without depth." [34] According to Dufrenne, this view is true as a description of fatuous fiction, but it does not appreciate the fact that a) the imaginary is situated in the very fringes of perception and that b) it is through a certain kind of image that Nature, having no other language, speaks to man. The "pre-images" [35] of Nature—e.g., morning, the sky, the mountain, the sea—are the forms assumed by Nature to appeal to the poet in man—or more precisely, to "the poetic" in him. For it is at this point that the *a priori* re-enters the discussion. On the one hand, there are various *a priori* of the imagination—for instance, "the elementary," "power," "depth," and "purity" [36]—revealed by the "ontological qualities" inherent in the pre-images Nature exudes;

29. *Le Poétique*, p. 158.
30. See *Phénoménologie*, I, 173–84.
31. See *Language and Philosophy*, pp. 69–101; and *Le Poétique*, pp. 7–49.
32. *Le Poétique*, p. 169.
33. See "Gaston Bachelard et la poésie de l'imagination," reprinted in *Jalons*, pp. 174–87.
34. *Phénoménologie de la perception* (Paris, Gallimard, 1945), p. 374.
35. For a discussion of this term, see *Language and Philosophy*, pp. 92–96.
36. See Dufrenne's essay, "Les *A Priori* de l'imagination" in *Archivio di Filosofia* (1965), pp. 53–63.

on the other hand, "the poetic" is both that which makes the reception of these pre-images possible and "the *a priori* of all aesthetic *a priori*." [37] Here Dufrenne's aesthetics and ontology form a continuity, for it is under the aegis of the poetic, the highest "aesthetic category," that man communicates with Nature and that Nature is completed in man. More generally, art is "the way in which man lets beings [*l'étant*] be, that is, allows Nature to express herself." [38] And Nature, as the "ground" of the "fundament" formed by man and the world, is "the *a priori* of the *a priori* linking man to the world." [39]

In spite of the evident expansion of Dufrenne's philosophical reflection in recent years, I am convinced that the *a priori* remains at the heart of his speculation. The *a priori* not only forms a continuous thread through the maze of his thought—for which *The Notion of the A Priori* is the central and crucial document— but it also points to the sharp edge of Dufrenne's entire enterprise: his humanism. For where there is an *a priori*, there man is as well. Man, along with the *a priori*, has remained of constant concern to Dufrenne throughout his writing career. His characteristic question is, "How can man be recognized for what he is?" [40] In Dufrenne's view, "the philosopher seeks only to become aware of man in the world." [41] One of his first published essays, "God and Man in Spinoza," [42] sought to ascertain the ambiguous position of man in Spinoza's metaphysical system. In this same post-war period Dufrenne found in Karl Jaspers' notion of *Existenz* a more satisfactory theory of man; the result was *Karl Jaspers et la Philosophie de l'existence*,[43] a book he wrote in collaboration with Paul Ricoeur. By 1950, both Ricoeur and Dufrenne had tempered their enthusiasm for existentialism, turning instead to phenomenology. Yet Dufrenne's existential orientation is still evident in his *Phénoménologie de l'expérience esthétique*, submitted as his principal thesis at the Sorbonne for the degree of Docteur ès-lettres; in this two-volume work, truth in art is held to be the expression of a subjectivity, and the authenticity of the artist is given a high value. But Dufrenne's existentialism, as revealed

37. *Le Poétique*, p. 181.
38. *Jalons*, p. 26.
39. *Le Poétique*, p. 181.
40. *Phénoménologie*, II, 676.
41. *Jalons*, p. 5.
42. Reprinted in *Jalons*, pp. 28–69; see also "La Connaissance de Dieu dans la philosophie Spinoziste," *ibid.*, pp. 112–23.
43. *Karl Jaspers et la philosophie de l'existence* (Paris, Editions du Seuil, 1947).

here, is not a humanism in Sartre's sense of the term; for Dufrenne's theory of man diverges expressly from Sartre's. Dufrenne believes that man cannot be defined wholly in terms of his freedom; man also has a destiny indicated by his "humanity" or human nature. Yet "if there is a human nature, it is not an example of *natura naturata*, but a destiny for a freedom." [44] If it is paradoxical thus to combine freedom and destiny—a destiny we glimpse in the irreversible character of time—it is perhaps even more paradoxical to assert that "when we are most profoundly ourselves, we are closest to others." [45] According to Dufrenne, our common humanity—which represents an *a priori* that will be analyzed in chapters 9 and 10 of *The Notion of the A Priori*—appears precisely when we think ourselves most free; from this we may conclude that "freedom itself is like a nature . . . existence is for man an essence." [46] The reader will perceive the gulf existing between this remark and Sartre's credo that "existence precedes essence." It should not be inferred from this comparison that Dufrenne, in contrast with Sartre, is a dreamer in the realm of essences; the *a priori* constituting humanity "is not an invulnerable structure, but rather a possibility and a task." [47] Moreover, Dufrenne underlines the historicity of the *appearance* and recognition of the *a priori*. The reason for this, as there will be occasion to repeat in *The Notion of the A Priori*, is that "the *a priori* is actualized only *on* [*sur*] the *a posteriori*" [48]—that is, it appears within something empirical and contingent.

Dufrenne's other writings witness a similar concern for exploring the nature and destiny of man. His secondary thesis, published as *La Personnalité de base*,[49] is an examination of Abram Kardiner's and Ralph Linton's implicit theory of man in the context of cultural anthropology. *Jalons*, Dufrenne's most recent book, is a collection of studies of other philosophers; as we learn from the Preface, it might as well have been entitled "Hommages"—to various *men* by whom Dufrenne has often been inspired in his thinking. *The Notion of the A Priori*, written during the author's professorship at Poitiers, elucidates the position of man as endowed with "the dignity of the transcendental" and as

44. *Phénoménologie*, II, 595.
45. *Ibid.*, p. 589.
46. *Ibid.*
47. *Ibid.*, p. 590.
48. *Ibid.*, p. 607. Italics mine.—Trans.
49. Full title: *La Personnalité de base—un concept sociologique* (Paris, Presses Universitaires de France, 1953).

co-equal with the world; it ends in an appeal to poetry that is repeated in the last chapter of *Language and Philosophy*.

Le Poétique, written four years later, provides a response to these two appeals. Although it ends in an ontology in which Nature is given primacy, Nature as here discussed is "consubstantial"[50] with man and becomes "world" only through man's agency.[51] Even though he is created by it, man also completes and perfects Nature, which is held to be "anthropocentric"[52] in that it seems to seek man and human language. The last sentence of this remarkable book reveals Dufrenne's enduring humanism in the midst of his most speculative mood: "To specify the poetic as an aesthetic category, we must invoke the humanity of [Nature's] act of appearing: the poetic resides in both the generosity and the benevolence of the sensible."[53] Thus Dufrenne, like Sartre, embraces a humanism; but he is not led to this position by a passion for *praxis;*[54] instead, he arrives by having been there all the time: by scrutinizing man successively in his existential, transcendental, and poetic aspects. In the final analysis these three aspects are attributes of a unity embodied in the notion of an "*a priori* of the *a priori*" that is Nature and man at once; or rather, this supreme *a priori* is found in the category of the poetic, which is the expressivity of Nature as felt and articulated by man. In this vision, man is no mere mode or even a *Dasein*, just as Nature is no longer conceived as power or plenitude, Being or light. Seen through the discriminating lens of the poetic, man is innocence[55] and Nature benevolence, and the two coalesce in a concrete whole.

Consequently, if Mikel Dufrenne, presently professor at the Faculté des Lettres at Nanterre and codirector of *La Revue d' Esthétique*, ends with a monistic philosophy of Nature, he nonetheless begins and remains at the level of man and the world. As he has recently written, "the itinerary of monism . . . leads through dualism."[56] Since philosophy can construct a philosophy of Nature only obliquely by appealing to poetry, its proper task is to

50. *Le Poétique*, p. 185.
51. For Dufrenne's distinction between world, universe, and Nature, see *ibid.*, pp. 139–52.
52. *Ibid.*, p. 158.
53. *Ibid.*, p. 194.
54. See "La Critique de la raison dialectique," in *Jalons*, pp. 150–73.
55. For the concept of innocence, see *Phénoménologie*, II, 426–27 and 675; and *Le Poétique*, pp. 185–92.
56. *Jalons*, p. 6.

explore the dualism of man and world. This is in fact the aim of *The Notion of the A Priori:* to clarify the various *a priori* that link these two primordial beings. In this book Dufrenne studies "the signs of an accord between man and the world; [although] this accord in turn suggests seeking a common origin of man and the world in Nature . . . the *a priori* proposes these signs in so far as it constitutes both subject and object." [57] It is only natural, then, that this essay should begin with a discussion of Kant, who first surveyed the field of the *a priori* in its constitutive role. But it is left to the reader to judge how far Dufrenne succeeds in his desire to improve upon and enlarge Kant's original project. At least we may say that it is this desire which animates and justifies Dufrenne's entire philosophical enterprise. The best introduction to this enterprise, as well as its definitive statement, is found in *The Notion of the A Priori.*

57. *Ibid.,* p. 27.

EDWARD S. CASEY

Paris
December, 1965

THE IMPORTANCE OF Mikel Dufrenne's *Notion of the* A
Priori does not reside in offering solutions to a presumed "problem of the *a priori*," such as is posed in classical as well as modern
epistemology: For example, what do we know in advance of particular experiences? How do we know it? Even if this book bears
on such questions, it does not address them as such. Nor does
Dufrenne attempt to extend Kant's conception of the *a priori*—as
did Edmund Husserl, Max Scheler, and Maurice Merleau-Ponty.
But he does discuss paradigms of the *a priori* to be found in Kant
and the many successors who grappled with the issue of what we
know about the world before we encounter it up close and how it
is ingredient in the world we come to know. At the same time, *The
Notion of the* A Priori provides detailed treatments of basic kinds of
a priori structure that exceed the scope of Kant's original project:
not only formal structures (on which Kant insisted) but also material ones (as was Husserl's and especially Scheler's focus), including their corporeal analogues (as in Merleau-Ponty's early work).
Dufrenne expands the range of previous claims by tracing out the
a priori elements in the perceived world, in social and political dimensions, and in the realm of art.

The ambition of this book goes beyond compiling a *catalogue
raisonné* of kinds of *a priori* knowledge, mediated as well as intuitive.
An entire cosmology based on a novel conception of the *a priori* is
presented within the scope of a single short book. At a moment
when his contemporaries were composing heavy tomes that took
up matters of comparable magnitude—for example, Karl Jaspers
and Paul Ricoeur, to whom he was otherwise close philosophically—Dufrenne decided to put his own thoughts about a fundamental issue into a brief compass in which no word would be wasted.
Hence the elegance and economy of this gem of a book, barely
more than two hundred and fifty pages in length. My translation
attempts to capture in straightforward English the incomparable
virtues of the eloquent French prose.

Let me here underline two of this book's major theses. First, Dufrenne sets forth the view that human beings are in equilibrium with the natural world and exhibit a deep affinity with it. Instead of assuming that there is something exceptional or counternatural about human beings—as occurs when they are regarded as privileged because they are language-speaking animals or because they have special spiritual powers—Dufrenne affirms that humans belong to nature outright and altogether. This means that "the understanding of nature is the understanding of man" (p. 211 below) and thus that "the world is within our reach" (236). As a consequence, we should attribute to nature not just an indifferent energy and force but a generativity that infinitely surpasses, even as it includes, that of humankind. In short, "nature natures" in Spinoza's clarion concept of *natura naturans,* a phrase that resonates throughout Dufrenne's writings. His twist on this famous formula is that the bond between human beings and the natural world is found in the *a priori* in all its manifold forms. In this capacity, the *a priori* is responsible for the fact that as the world exists for humans so humans exist for the natural world. There is an immersion of each in the other taken as coeval elementary presences. As a consequence, "the *a priori* is not the prerogative of a subject, but the expression of a law which integrates the subject into the system of the intelligible world" (225).

A second distinctive claim to be found in *The Notion of the A Priori* is Dufrenne's treatment of feeling (*sentiment*). This concept is pivotal in the plot of this book—just as affect and affective quality had been central in the volume preceding it, *Phénoménologie de l'experience esthétique* (*The Phenomenology of Aesthetic Experience*), published in 1953. Feeling is what holds nature and human beings together at the level of affect: the "truth of nature must first be sought in the feeling of nature" (236). Further, feeling conjoins the two most basic kinds of *a priori,* "subjective" and "objective," acting as their connective tissue. Yet feeling is not something merely subjective or episodic, as we too often assume: although it is uniquely experienced on each occurrence, it is "made singular by the world that it evokes. . . . [It] is no longer an affair of the heart; it is an aspect of the world" (237). This last assertion distinguishes Dufrenne's discussion of feeling from that of R. G. Collingwood and Susanne Langer, both of whom had proposed a major role for feeling in the experience of art but balked at attributing to it any more expansive significance. In contrast, for Dufrenne poetry "makes feeling the principle of a world" (237). Indeed, poetry "says this world," and in so doing it "expresses the accord between man and the world"

(238). Unlike philosophy (undeniably a critical and reflective enterprise), poetry captures this accord nonreflectively in poetic language enlivened by feeling.

Dufrenne's book represents a signal step forward in the history of phenomenology; it is the only full-scale study of the *a priori* since the movement was inaugurated by Husserl in 1900. It alone thematizes what is left implicit and taken for granted by other leading figures in this same movement—from Husserl through Derrida. It spells out the more exact meaning of such recurrent but unclarified phrases as *schon da* ("already there") in Heidegger's early work and *toujours déjà là* ("always already there") in Merleau-Ponty's writing. The existential structures of *Dasein* as set forth in Heidegger's *Being and Time*—for example, Being-in-the-world, Being-with-others, Being-ahead-of-itself—are *a priori* in character, but Heidegger does not treat their *a priority* as such. Similarly, the lived body's tacit ways of being habitual and innovative, relating to other bodies, and sensing the landscape all have *a priori* status in Merleau-Ponty's conception of *le corps connaissant* (the knowing body) in his *Phenomenology of Perception*—yet, as in Heidegger's study, this status is not explored as such. In pursuing the theme of the *a priori* well beyond where his predecessors were willing to venture, Dufrenne makes an essential and incomparable contribution to the phenomenological tradition. This fact alone renders the reprinting of this translation a welcome event.

But *The Notion of the* A Priori is not just of historical import. In addition to its own substantial philosophical merit and descriptive rigor, it has considerable relevance to contemporary philosophy of a continental cast. The rich idea of "world" that is discussed in this book (and elsewhere, notably in *The Phenomenology of Aesthetic Experience*) undergirds the ideas of "smooth space" and the reterritorialization of specific places and regions in Gilles Deleuze and Félix Guattari's *Thousand Plateaus,* while the emphasis on the creative dimension of nature is carried forward in these authors' concepts of "becoming-woman" and "becoming-animal." Jean-Luc Nancy's model of intersubjectivity in his *Being Singular Plural* is also adumbrated by Dufrenne's pioneering descriptions of the social *a priori* along with its historical and political dimensions, which inform as well Michel Foucault's acute analysis of central institutions in Western modernity—not to mention Jürgen Habermas's astute analyses of the human life-world. It is only to be expected that these more recent works, each original in its own right, take the reader to other conceptual spaces than does Dufrenne. But one idea on which Dufrenne placed a great deal of emphasis in *The Notion of*

the A Priori, namely, singularity, has become indispensable in contemporary philosophical parlance, ranging from that of Levinas to
Lyotard, Deleuze to Nancy, and Foucault to Derrida. It serves as a
fil conducteur throughout these otherwise very different authors. Its
first nuanced discussion is to be found in Dufrenne's *Notion of the* A
Priori, a book that is prescient in this as in other telling ways.

Dufrenne's writing after the publication of *La Notion d'a priori*
in 1959 took him in diverse directions—some continuous with the
present volume (e.g., *Le Poétique* [1963], which explored the special relationship between poetry and nature still further), others
undertaking new forays: *Pour l'homme* (1968) is an impassioned
plea for saving the best in humanism rather than jettisoning the
concept altogether; *Art et politique* (1974) and *Subversion- perversion*
(1977) look into political and psychoanalytic aspects of art; *L'oeil
et l'oreille* (1987) carries the spirit of Merleau-Ponty's great essay
"L'oeil et l'espirit" into the domain of hearing. These volumes and
others were framed by three volumes of collected essays in aesthetics, *Esthétique et Philosophie* (1967, 1976, 1981). All of these works
reflect the structuralist and poststructuralist debates of the 1960s
through the 1980s; together they embody a distinctive voice in this
fecund period of continental thought.

Near the end of his career, Dufrenne returned to the question
of the *a priori* in a major work entitled *L'inventaire des a priori: Recher-
che de l'originaire* (1981). This is a comprehensive book that surveys
and describes virtually every significant sort of *a priori* structure, including those at stake in biology and life more generally and those
he explored in depth in his very last essays under the heading of
the "*a priori* of the imagination." These latter have a very particular
cosmic significance, and in this respect they, like the inventory of
the *a priori* itself, represent a return to the earlier project of *The
Notion of the* A Priori—to this book's crisp descriptions of leading
kinds of *a priori* and their wider cosmological ramifications. By the
end of his career (he died in 1995 at age eighty-five), Mikel Dufrenne had come full circle. But the cycle itself would not have
happened without the initial publication of the present volume,
which at once deepens the achievements of the phenomenological
school and breaks new ground of its own. It is as timely today as it
was upon its first appearance five decades ago.

EDWARD S. CASEY

New York City
July 2008

The Notion of the *A Priori*

Author's Introduction

THE NOTION of the *a priori* is one of the principal
themes elaborated in Kant's philosophy, and is the very origin of
his Copernican revolution. For Kant, pure *a priori* knowledge is a
fact, a fact of both theoretical and practical reason. The *quid facti*
precedes the *quid juris;* to speak of a fact of reason is in no way
contradictory, for we are not subordinating reason to the dominion
of fact. Instead, we are affirming the reality of reason. The first
consequence of this discovery of the *a priori* is the assignment of a
positive program to metaphysics: "Metaphysics is the philosophy
which has as its task the statement of [pure *a priori*] knowledge in
[its] systematical unity." [1] But beyond this, the discovery of the *a
priori* requires—as a propaedeutic to metaphysics—a critique
which "investigates the faculty of reason in respect of all pure *a
priori* knowledge" [2] and which establishes the conditions of validity
for all knowledge.

This critique is not, strictly speaking, that transcendental philosophy which Kant distinguishes from natural philosophy and
calls ontology, that is, "the system of concepts and principles
which relate to objects in general but take no account of objects
that may be given." [3] Yet the notion of the transcendental is
introduced early in the *Critique:* "The distinction between the
transcendental and the empirical belongs therefore only to the
critique of knowledge." [4] Here Kant cautions us to distinguish *a*

1. Kant, *Critique of Pure Reason,* trans. Norman Kemp Smith (London,
Macmillan, 1933), p. 661 (A 845–B 873). (Hereafter I shall refer simply to the
"*Critique*."—Trans.)
   2. *Ibid.,* p. 659 (A 841–B 873).
   3. *Ibid.,* p. 662 (A 845–B 873).
   4. *Ibid.,* p. 96 (A 57).

[3]

priori from transcendental: "Not every kind of knowledge *a priori* should be called transcendental, but that only by which we know that—and how—certain representations (intuitions or concepts) can be employed or are possible purely *a priori*." [5] The term "transcendental" does not in any way characterize *a priori* knowledge, but describes instead the knowledge of the *a priori* character of the *a priori:* the reflection on the nature—i.e., the origin—and the function—i.e., the role—of the *a priori.* Thus mathematics involves *a priori* knowledge, and is different from metaphysics in that it constructs its concepts in an *a priori* fashion. But it is not transcendental: "What can alone be entitled transcendental is the knowledge that these representations are not of empirical origin, and the possibility that they can yet relate *a priori* to objects of experience." [6] Only the Aesthetic is transcendental. It is therefore not enough to oppose the transcendental to the empirical. In order fully to grasp the meaning of the transcendental, we must add, in the light of the *Critique,* that whatever is anterior to experience is at the same time a condition of experience. The central problem of the *Critique* is the transcendental deduction, which justifies the *a priori* by showing how it functions, that is, how subsumption is possible.

Kant's successors will be less concerned with exploring the field in which the *a priori* is found or applied. Instead they will reconsider the transcendental as the key to the subject-object relation—to the point of elaborating a monism in which the transcendental is immanent in the object itself and where the transcendental deduction becomes an ontological genesis. We, however, should like to investigate anew the notion of the *a priori* in order to extend its meaning. But first we must return to the transcendental, that is, to the *a priori* considered in its relation to experience.

The *a priori* is defined by this relation, yet is anterior to it. This anteriority is a primary indication of the *a priori*'s transcendental nature. Experience is our relation to phenomena, with sensibility as an intermediary. Its source lies in empirical intuition; for "the only intuition that is given *a priori* is that of the mere form of appearances, space and time. . . . But the matter of appearances, by which things are given us in space and time, can only be represented in perception, and therefore *a posteriori*." [7] Hence experience always involves acknowledging a given which must be

5. *Ibid.,* p. 96 (A 56).
6. *Ibid.,* p. 96 (B 81).
7. *Ibid.,* p. 581 (A 720–B 748).

received by sensibility and which cannot be justified by reason. This given is the material element that Kant opposes to the formal element—the form or rule—by assigning the formal element to the *a priori*. On this basis, he identifies the following two propositions: the material element is given, and the given is the material element. He does this because, as Scheler observes, he substitutes the question: What *can* be given? for the question: What *is* given? And he borrows the theme of his answer from Hume: only a sensible content, an empirical manifold, can be given.[8] The *a priori*, on the other hand, can only be formal and hence cannot be given. It belongs to the constituting [9] activity of the mind, never presenting itself as something constituted. Pure intuition is given *a priori*, but, given as the form of intuition, it proffers nothing material. The objects one can construct in it are only possible objects. Therefore, we do not experience the real *a priori*, for real experience is experience of an empirical given in empirical intuition. Pure intuition involves a given—the mathematical object— only because it is already, if not empirical, at least sensible, and because sensibility is radically distinct from understanding. As a result, the kind of intuition that would furnish the *a priori* in the manner of a Cartesian *intuitis* or a Husserlian *Wesenschau* does not occur in Kant. In this sense, the *a priori* does not present itself as an item of knowledge. We are not forbidden to recognize it, but we recognize it as something proceeding from us which could not be given at the level of intuition. The *a priori* is always anterior to experience.

This anteriority, in which psychologism would attempt to discover a chronological import, has above all a logical meaning. Anterior to experience means independent of experience and consequently not compromised by it. Thus, while empirical propositions concerning the matter of phenomena are particular and con-

8. For Scheler, the given is not an intelligible diversity offered to an intellectual manipulation. When I perceive a die, the die itself is revealed, with its own *Würfelhaftigkeit;* the perception is immediately true. (Cf. Max Scheler, *Der Formalismus in der Ethik und die materiale Wertethik* [Bern, Francke, 1954], pp. 76–77.) Merleau-Ponty will take up this example. But it would also be interesting to confront this critique of Kant's presuppositions with that of Hegel; for Kant, "The manifold of sensibility is not in itself interrelated; the world is a reality which falls into bits, owing its objective connectiveness and stability to the unique gift of the self-consciousness of men endowed with understanding. . . ." (Cf. G. W. F. Hegel, "Glauben und Wissen," in *Sämmtliche Werke*, ed. by Hermann Glockner [Stuttgart, Fromann, 1927], I, 303; French translation by Marcel Méry in *Premières publications* [Paris, Gap, 1964], p. 213. I shall continue to cite both references below.—Trans.)

9. *Constituante* will be translated as "constituting," "constituent," and (for the most part) "constitutive," depending on the context.—Trans.

tingent, propositions concerning their form are necessary and universal. It is contingent that cinnabar is red; but it is necessary that any one thing have a causal relation of existence to some other thing. Necessity has a primarily logical meaning; it is defined as that whose contrary is contradictory: the impossible is the unthinkable. But what about the material necessity of facts? Must it not be founded on the logical necessity of ideas?

For the *a priori* has a transcendental function as well: if it is anterior to experience and if its validity does not depend on experience, it is still not without some relation to it. Above all, it grounds it. What is here "the essence of ground"? [10] To ground is to render possible, not in the order of fact, but in the order of reasons. It is not to cause or provoke, but to justify or authorize. If an object is grounded, the acting subject is too: we say that we have sufficient grounds for believing that. . . . In this sense, a "ground" or "fundament" differs from a merely objective "foundation": it can be employed in reference to a subject. To ground is to make something viable for a subject. Since Kant defines the subject principally in terms of reason, to ground is for him, as Paul Ricoeur says, "to elevate to intellectuality." [11] To render experience possible is to confer meaning on it: the possibility of being meaningful for a subject (in the sense in which Husserl says that the world as correlate is "meaningful" for transcendental subjectivity). Here the presuppositions of Kant's thought come together: this meaning cannot directly belong to experience, which only furnishes a manifold. It must come from the subject who determines objects as phenomena by structuring this manifold: "The intellectualist philosopher could not endure to think of the form as preceding the things themselves and determining their possibility . . . so far is the matter (or the things themselves which appear) from serving as the [ground] . . . that on the contrary its own possibility presupposes a formal intuition (time and space) as antecedently given." [12] But sensibility is not the only source of the *a priori*. The fundament must also be intellectual: for experience to have a meaning it is not enough that a manifold be simply given in accordance with the subjective structure of sensibility. It must also be unified. Included in the principle of meaning—that

10. There is an implicit reference here to Martin Heidegger's essay, *Vom Wesen des Grundes* (Frankfurt, Klostermann, 1955). See also Heidegger's *Satz vom Grund* (Pfullingen, Neske, 1957), pp. 207–29.—Trans.

11. Paul Ricoeur, "Kant et Husserl," in *Kantstudien*, Band 46, I, p. 61.

12. *Critique*, p. 280 (A 267–B 323). I have changed "foundation" to "ground" in keeping with the author's distinction.—Trans.

is, the principle of the objectivity of the object—is the unity required by the "I think": "the necessary unity of consciousness, and therefore also of the synthesis of the manifold." [13] The norms of intellectuality under which the manifold must be subsumed to render experience possible express the modes of unification of the manifold. Moreover, so close is the link between intuition and concept (as Heidegger has insisted) that these modes of articulating the manifold also structure temporality, as indicated by Kant in his chapter on the schematism of the pure concepts of understanding. The form that grounds experience, which Kant sometimes calls "the objective form of experience in general," [14] is therefore both sensible and intellectual as a result of the finitude of a knowledge subjected to sensible intuition. In every case, this form, which is the *a priori*, is transcendental because it is the condition for the possibility of *a posteriori* knowledge.

But does not this possibility of experience presuppose its own reality? The possibility grounded by the *a priori* is an intentional possibility and not a merely logical one; it is a possibility of . . . , or a possibility for. . . . The categories do not possess a purely logical value; they are not limited to expressing the form of thought analytically. They "refer to the possibility, actuality, or necessity of things." [15] In other words, "Only through the fact that these concepts express *a priori* the relations of perceptions in every experience, do we know their objective reality, that is, their transcendental truth." [16] Consequently, if the *a priori* grounds the *a posteriori*, it aims at or intends [*vise*] the latter. The task of the *Critique* is to present the *a priori* in such a role and to delineate its limits. All that the understanding draws from itself without borrowing from experience is useful only when finally employed in experience. One cannot make a transcendent use of the transcendental.

But how is this possible? Does not aiming at experience, even if it be to ground it, presuppose experience? For experience to be referred to, must it not be a source? Must we not admit that the *a priori*, the principle *of* experience, has its principle *in* experience since it is given to it? We shall try to justify this empiricism of the transcendental by our own reassessment of the notion of the *a priori*. Kant would obviously not allow this, though he grants the

13. *Ibid.,* p. 137 (A 109).
14. *Ibid.,* p. 239 (A 220).
15. *Ibid.,* p. 239 (B 267).
16. *Ibid.,* p. 241 (B 269).

premises of empiricism—the idea of a nonlogical organization of the given.[17] Yet we cannot overlook the role he assigns to empiricism in the very construction of the idea of the transcendental.

In fact, one could say of the *a priori* what Kant says of intuition in particular: it is receptive or passive. If it signifies the possibility that something be given, by itself it gives nothing. Experience—inasmuch as it gives itself—cannot be engendered. When the possible is not deduced from the real, it is deduced from the *a priori* only insofar as the *a priori* is taken as the formal and objective condition of experience in general. Experience in general precedes particular experiences, but also presupposes them: experience in general implies the possibility of knowing an object given in empirical intuition—i.e., not through simple concepts. It is therefore quite true that all knowledge, even *a priori* knowledge, "begins with experience."

It may seem, as Jules Vuillemin has observed, that Kant's *Metaphysics of Nature* occupies a more defensible position than the *Critique:* in the former, the principles of understanding no longer bear on the object in general, but on the object as given. It retains therefore something of the sensible given, or rather of that which characterizes the given as such: "how is it possible to know the nature of things and to arrive at a rational physiology according to principles *a priori*? The answer is this: we take nothing more from experience than is required to give us an object of outer or of inner sense." [18] Nevertheless, Kant's transcendental philosophy cannot borrow so directly from experience because, being ontology and not physiology, it claims to concern the object in general, not empirically given objects as such. Yet as Vuillemin comments, "although it does not utilize this given and treats only the transcendental object $= x$ without specifying it as matter—since we become conscious of matter only when it affects our senses as movement—transcendental philosophy can constitute and construct the possibility of this object as existence only in reference to the *tertium* represented by the possibility of experience and thus also the possibility of an empirical affection." [19] To refer to possible experience, as the notion of the transcendental demands, is necessarily to invoke a given: possible experience implies real experience.

Certainly the *a priori* always refers itself to experience in order

17. We shall be tempted on the contrary to admit the conclusions and not the premises.

18. *Critique*, p. 663 (A 848–B 876).

19. Jules Vuillemin, *Physique et métaphysique kantiennes* (Paris, Presses Universitaires de France, 1955), p. 24.

to ground it, without subordinating itself to experience as if it were its product. But the *a priori* has as much need of experience as experience has need of the *a priori*. This is especially apparent in Kant's notion of dynamic principles, through which "the synthesis is applied to the existence of a phenomenon in general," as Kant says. "If the reader will go back to our proof of the principle of causality . . . he will observe that we were able to prove it only of objects of possible experience." [20] Only on this basis does "something happen." The demonstration of principles is therefore not accomplished here on the logical plane alone: "When we are required to cite examples of contingent existence, we invariably have recourse to alterations, and not merely to the possibility of entertaining the opposite in thought." [21] In brief, "in order to understand the possibility of things in conformity with the categories, and thus to demonstrate the objective reality of the latter, we need, not merely intuitions, but intuitions that are in all cases outer intuitions." [22]

And yet the *a priori* is not in itself material: it is essentially a rule or a principle. (This is more clearly manifested in the *Critique of Practical Reason,* where universality is not only the form of the imperative but the imperative itself; the same is true even for the judgment of taste.) But the principles of understanding, for which the categories are the index, only ground in reason what one could call the principles of sensibility—i.e., the formal conditions to which all sensations, and hence all knowledge, are subordinated. They ground in reason what is grounded in nature, and they do this in accordance with the nature "of the subjective constitution of the object." The principle confers on representations the dignity of a relation to an object. In introducing "something necessary," it transforms the given—the *Gegenstand* which is "set over against" [23] knowledge by means of the structure of sensibility—into an *Objekt,* for this *Objekt* is what "can always be found in the connection of perceptions in accordance with a rule." [24] It could be said to convert the *de facto* intentionality expressed by spatiality as the *a priori* form of sensibility—as Ricoeur has indicated[25]—into a *de jure* intentionality. From this point on, the object guarantees the objectivity of knowledge. Or, more exactly, the rule defining objectivity also determines the object.

20. *Critique,* p. 253 (B 289).
21. *Ibid.,* p. 254 (B 290).
22. *Ibid.,* p. 254 (B 291).
23. *Ibid.,* p. 134 (A 104).
24. *Ibid.,* p. 226 (A 200).
25. "Kant et Husserl," p. 50.

Therefore, "the conditions of the possibility of experience in general are likewise conditions of the possibility of the objects of experience." [26] But this rule is meaningful only insofar as it is applicable to experience, just as pure intuition has meaning only in the form of empirical intuition: "The possibility of experience is, then, what gives objective reality to all our *a priori* modes of knowledge." [27] For "if knowledge is to have objective reality . . . the object must be capable of being given in some manner." [28] The *a priori* only gives a rule, but Kant's astuteness lies in defining knowledge in terms of rules and rules in terms of knowledge: objectivity grounds the object, and the object in turn grounds objectivity. Undoubtedly the legitimacy of speaking of grounding in the second proposition may be contested: the object cannot function as a principle, and cannot give objectivity. Yet it does limit the employment of a rule and, in so doing, justifies it. If the categories retain a meaning independent of the schemata—"the sensible concepts of the objects" which represent things in general "as they appear"—this meaning is purely logical, and the real meaning of the categories derives "from sensibility, which realizes the understanding in the very process of restricting it." [29]

In short, transcendental reflection on the employment of the *a priori* makes it appear as the condition for the objectivity of the *a posteriori*, and the *a posteriori* appears as the condition for the legitimacy of the *a priori*. The *a priori* is enacted and realized only by the *a posteriori*. This reciprocity raises the question: can one maintain some sort of equilibrium between rationalism and empiricism? Even if the *a priori* is anterior to experience—since it is only valid in relation to it—may one say that it is discerned in it? We shall see later on that Kant cannot dismiss this question. But it remains the case that for him the *a priori* has a primarily transcendental function, according to which the given is related to the subject. It grounds experience; it is not grounded in it, and it is limited to experience only in its employment. Now, defining the *a priori* in this way creates a cluster of difficulties to which Kant and his successors address themselves. Contemporary thought still feels the weight of these difficulties, in which two related problems may be discerned: that concerning the being of the subject and that concerning the relation of subject and object.

26. *Critique,* p. 194 (A 158).
27. *Ibid.,* p. 193 (A 156).
28. *Ibid.,* p. 192 (A 155).
29. *Ibid.,* p. 187 (B 187).

The Being of the Subject

THE FIRST PROBLEM concerns the nature of the subject as the possessor of the *a priori*. If the *a priori* grounds objectivity, it can only be assigned to a subjectivity to the extent that, being constitutive, it makes experience possible without being discernible in it. Kant establishes this early in the *Critique* by showing that the necessity and universality of *a priori* propositions cannot result from an induction: "Owing, therefore, to the necessity with which [a concept] forces itself upon us, we have no option save to admit that it has its seat in our faculty of *a priori* knowledge." [30] Therefore, the *a priori* refers to the *cogito*—a *cogito* which is perhaps impersonal, and lacking selfhood [*ipséité*]—but this reference to the *cogito* is such that the "I think" becomes an "I can." How do these two terms combine to define subjectivity as capable of knowing the *a priori*?

Perhaps we should first distinguish between the pure knowledge which has been made explicit and proposed as a fact and the pure knowledge which functions as the condition for empirical knowledge. To the degree that it is made explicit, it requires a concrete subject—e.g., a Thales or a Kant—and thus puts a psychological activity in motion. But one really grasps this knowledge in its purity only by considering it in its actual functioning— i.e., as conditioning all experience. If Thales was the first geometer, the intellectual revolution that he effected inaugurated geometry historically, but did not found it. He simply made explicit an implicit geometry already at work in all knowledge; thus Kant as well as Merleau-Ponty could invoke the Malebranchian notion of a natural geometry. All progress in mathematics is made by developing the implicit. This does not in any way mean that mathematics consists in analytic judgments, for the concepts that it constructs are new. In this manner mathematics is capable of progress, though the material used in its construction (pure intuition) remains exactly the same. Similarly, when Kant educes the metaphysical principles of a science of nature, he is not inventing anything; he is merely rendering explicit the propositions underlying all research in physics and even in the most unspecialized knowledge. The same thing holds for the field of ethics, where he attempts to elucidate a natural morality such as we find

30. *Ibid.*, p. 45 (B 6).

presupposed in the *Foundations of the Metaphysics of Morals*. "We are in possession of certain modes of *a priori* knowledge, and even the common understanding is never without them." [31] A *priori* knowledge is expressed by necessary and universal propositions, because it functions necessarily and universally and because it is necessary to empirical knowledge: the *a priori* is pre-eminently transcendental.[32]

But in considering the transcendental in its activity, we cease to isolate it: pure knowledge, which required an empirical subject to elucidate it in the *Critique*, always appears as immanent in empirical consciousness and as bound up with psychological subjectivity. But how then do we distinguish between or unite the transcendental and the psychological? In order to establish simultaneously the nature and function of the *a priori* manifested by synthetic judgments, Kant performs both a reflective analysis which makes the transcendental subject appear and an analysis—termed phenomenological by Ricoeur [33]—which tends to psychologize the transcendental. The reflective analysis, basing itself on synthetic judgments, shows that "the highest principle of all synthetic judgments is therefore this: every object stands under the necessary conditions of the synthetic unity of the manifold of intuition in a possible experience." [34] These conditions make transcendental subjectivity appear. The *medium* of all synthetic judgments is the "whole in which all our representations are contained"—i.e., inner sense, whose *a priori* form is time. And the unity required in judgment "rests on the unity of apperception." This unity, which tends to emphasize the "I" of the "I think," is, at least in the second edition of the *Critique*, the keystone of the Kantian system. But we find it even in the first edition: all empirical consciousness has a necessary relation to transcendental consciousness—"namely, the consciousness of myself as original apperception." [35] For "we are conscious *a priori* of the complete identity of the self in respect of all representations which can ever belong to our knowledge." [36] It is therefore an absolutely primary

31. *Ibid.*, p. 43 (B 3).
32. Thus, purity of knowledge does not signify, as it does for Scheler, the clarity or essentiality of the intentional object: these are accessory criteria concerning the *a priori* inasmuch as it is already made explicit. But that which conditions the *a priori* in its functioning is the activity of the mind: pure knowledge is only a knowledge of the object in general because it expresses the subject without being encumbered by particular objects.
33. "Kant et Husserl," *passim*.
34. *Critique*, p. 194 (A 158).
35. *Ibid.*, p. 142, note a.
36. *Ibid.*, p. 141 (A 116).

principle that the various empirical consciousnesses must be linked to one unique consciousness of self. This consciousness is the simple representation: I. Kant adds: "Whether this representation is clear (empirical consciousness) or obscure, or even whether it ever actually occurs, does not here concern us. But the possibility of the logical form of all knowledge is necessarily conditioned by relation to this apperception as a faculty." [37]

Yet this faculty does further enlighten us concerning the nature of subjectivity. Above all, it permits us to discern in the "I think"—"this spontaneity" by means of which I can "call myself an intelligence" [38]—the act of understanding: "The unity of apperception in relation to the synthesis of imagination is the understanding." [39] From this point on, the understanding will become an element in a system, one faculty among others, and the idea of a structure of subjectivity will thus be introduced. And is this not necessary? For if the "I think," insofar as it is an "I can," is active, its activity must be described; and this activity is precisely the exercise of the *a priori* in its transcendental function. Yet such an enterprise cannot be easily accomplished. For the unity of apperception has been found to be a formal and non-constitutive principle. What right do we have to lend it life and to make it into an active principle? With what right do we identify possibility and capability,[40] formal unity of representations and spontaneity of intelligence, by saying that "the possibility of the logical form of all knowledge is necessarily conditioned by its relation to this apperception as a faculty"? In other words, with what right do we identify the whole (or, more exactly, an indissoluble form: the representation "I") with the part? [41] The difficulty appears to be that apperception is sometimes invoked as an absolutely primary principle and sometimes as one of the "three subjective sources of knowledge" [42]—along with the senses and imagination, the latter being identifiable with the understanding. The same difficulty viewed from another angle culminates in the analysis of the relation of imagination to apperception—an analysis in

37. *Ibid.*, p. 142, note a.
38. *Ibid.*, p. 169, note a. I have changed "entitle" to "call" here.—Trans.
39. *Ibid.*, p. 143 (A 119).
40. The French word for "faculty" is *pouvoir*, which (like its German counterpart, *Vermögen*) implies capacity or capability, as well as power or activity.—Trans.
41. Let us note in passing that the same problem arises with Descartes, where the "I" is discovered as "I think," and where the multiple attributes of thought disclosed in the explicitation of the *cogito* are subordinated to intelligence as the essential attribute.
42. *Critique*, p. 141 (A 115).

which the two editions of the *Critique* disagree as to the exact relation of the productive synthesis of imagination to synthetic unity as such. Heidegger writes that in the first edition "Kant, in characteristic fashion, hesitates to determine with precision the structural relations which link [this] unity to the unifying synthesis. . . . But he confidently asserts that transcendental apperception presupposes the synthesis." [43] By contrast, the second edition, in refusing to dismember the "I think" or to emasculate formal knowledge, reduces imagination to understanding: "The understanding, under the title of a transcendental synthesis of imagination, performs this act upon the passive subject, whose faculty it is, and we are therefore justified in saying that inner sense is affected thereby." [44] At the same time, the second edition subordinates sensibility to understanding—the understanding determining the inner sense which "contains the mere form of intuition, but without combination of the manifold in it." [45] This hesitancy regarding the primacy of the imagination is rich with meaning, as Heidegger has seen. For our present purpose, it signifies that the "I think" appears both as a principle and as an agent.

Such hesitation undoubtedly results from the ambiguity of the transcendental element, for it can be understood both as the result of a formal analysis of the conditions of possibility and as the instrument of a real activity [*pouvoir*]. In the first case, the *cogito* is a supreme requirement; in the second case, it serves as the locus for a constitutive activity. But can it be one without being the other? If the *a priori* is a condition of knowledge, is it not essential to *apply* the condition? Subsumption is inevitably constitution (in the non-ontological sense to which Kant limits himself). This is why Kant must juxtapose the reflective analysis which discovers apperception as an inescapable requirement and the phenomenological—more precisely, noetic—analysis which describes the transcendental activity as putting the *a priori* into operation. The site for this activity, the seat of the "transcendental acts" is *das Gemüt,* that is, the mind insofar as it contains a structure and can operate concretely. Thus knowledge is the product of the mind, the three sources of knowledge are its organs, and the three syntheses by which the objectivity of the object is elabo-

43. *Kant and the Problem of Metaphysics*, trans. James S. Churchill (Bloomington, Indiana University Press, 1962), p. 84. Heidegger makes allusion to the formula of the first edition: "The principle of the necessary unity of pure (productive) synthesis of imagination, prior to apperception, is the ground of the possibility of all knowledge, especially of experience" (*Critique*, p. 143 [A 118]).

44. *Critique*, p. 166 (B 153–54).

45. *Ibid.*, p. 166 (B 154).

rated are its operations. Through these structures, the subject takes on shape. No longer is the opposition only between a form and a matter; it is between the subject and the object. The forms of objectivity—such as "the objective forms of our mode of intuition"—are also the structures of our "subjective constitution." Subjectivity is not only determining, but determined; it is a human subjectivity, or at least assignable to "all finite, thinking beings." [46] The fundamental question becomes: what is man?

Consequently, the *a priori* requires a new meaning: it must designate both a formal condition of experience and a condition issuing from the subjective nature of the mind, a law which the mind imposes on nature because it is assigned to its own nature. It expresses the nature (and even, as we shall say later, the singularity) of the subject. For example, if there is a principle which "holds *a priori* and may be called the transcendental principle of the unity of all that is manifold in our representations," [47] this is because there is "a common function of the mind which combines [the manifold] in one representation." [48] The mind "is conscious of the identity of this function" by which it conceives *a priori* "its identity in the manifoldness of its representations." [49] Therefore, the *a priori* is rooted in a function of the mind. Similarly, time may appear as an *a priori* form of sensibility because "the mind distinguishes . . . time in the sequence of one impression after another" [50] and because the mind has a certain fashion of arranging its representations, being "affected through its own activity (namely, through the positing of its representation) and so is affected by itself." [51] Thus it is as if receptivity were a result of activity, as if time were engendered by consciousness. Similarly, space may be referred to the activity of the mind; as Ricoeur asserts, space is "the very movement of consciousness towards something; it is thus the possibility of displaying, discriminating, pluralizing any impression whatsoever." [52]

Hence the *a priori* is seen by Kant as pure knowledge conditioning empirical knowledge, but it is the knowledge of a rule, and this rule is the expression of a method—i.e., of an activity manifested by the mind through its structure. The *a priori* is the form impressed on what is known by the action of knowledge, the

46. *Ibid.*, p. 90 (B 72).
47. *Ibid.*, p. 142 (A 116).
48. *Ibid.*, p. 137 (A 109).
49. *Ibid.*, p. 137 (A 108).
50. *Ibid.*, p. 131 (A 99). (I have changed "upon" to "after" here.—Trans.)
51. *Ibid.*, p. 87 (B 67).
52. "Kant et Husserl," p. 50.

reflection in the object of the transcendental acts of the subject. Kant is therefore justified in deducing the categories from the logical form of judgments, since judgments are already "acts of the understanding" whose logical functions "yield an exhaustive inventory of its powers." [53] Cohen's and Brunschvicg's objection, taken up later by Vuillemin, is not decisive here. According to Cohen, the movement from the categories to the principles is illusory, because the categories imply a subjective and psychological interpretation of consciousness: "The bearers of the *a priori* in the Kantian system—space, time, and the categories—must be conceived as methods, not as forms of the mind." [54] But must not these methods be practiced? And is not their practice the operation of the subject as *Gemüt*? The *a priori* [55] result from the subject's nature—a nature that is given before experience and that orders experience. In particular, the theory and the deduction of the various *a priori* are dependent upon the human duality of receptivity and spontaneity, the duality of a sensibility and an understanding united by the imagination.

But independently of the orientation it imposes on the notion of the *a priori*, such an implicitly phenomenological analysis of the constitution of objectivity forces Kant into a dilemma that will reappear in post-Kantian thought. This dilemma stems from the necessity of distinguishing the transcendental from the psychological factor in the subject. With Kant, the difficulty assumes a precise form. If the mind whose acts constitute experience as objective represents a subject already concrete in the sense that it already has a structure manifested by the *a priori* it possesses, what will be the status of this subject? Can it be constitutive if it is constituted? Kant has posed the problem in such a way that it ends in an insurmountable impasse (whereas for Hume the subject is constitutive only if already constituted by "the principles of human nature"). The subject of Kant's reflective analysis is in no way constituted: apperception is only a transcendental power [*pouvoir*], capable of exercising the function of unity. The self is only a "simple representation" concerning which "there is not even a question of reality": the "I" of the "I think" is not yet the first person of the verb. One cannot say that the *a priori* related to it furnish it with a nature: rather than being their support, it is their source. A great part of Kant's analysis is conducted as if the "I

53. *Critique*, p. 113 (A 79).
54. Hermann Cohen, *Kants Theorie der Erfahrung*, 2nd ed. (Berlin, Dümmler, 1885), p. 584; cited by Jules Vuillemin, *L'Héritage kantien et la révolution copernicienne* (Paris, Presses Universitaires de France, 1954), p. 146.
55. Here "*a priori*" is plural.—Trans.

think" were only formal and impersonal, and even non-temporal, for "the subject, in which the representation of time has its original ground, cannot thereby determine its own existence in time." [56] In brief, it is as if the *cogito* were a *cogitatum est*. Transcendental consciousness can only be self-consciousness, not self-knowledge, as Kant expressly says. [57] The knower cannot be known because that which is known is immediately reduced to the status of object. But consciousness is at least self-consciousness, that is, consciousness of a *self*. Here lies the obvious origin of the misunderstanding that troubles any rational psychology. If it is necessary to say that "I exist as an intelligence conscious merely of my power of synthesis," at least there is an *I* who *exists*—i.e., possesses something more than the being of a mere logical condition. Existence could not serve here as the model category whose intervention would again submit the "I think" to the rules of objectivity. Kant strives to seize existence in the very act of thought; the "I think" contains within itself the proposition "I exist." Although the self referred to here is still only a purely intellectual representation, "I think" is an empirical proposition because it expresses "an indeterminate empirical intuition," [58] which Kant calls elsewhere the "feeling of an existence"—that is, an intuition occurring before the moment when the categories determine it: "Here existence is not yet a category." [59] Thus nothing can be known in such a manner: the *sum* does not in any way constitute an internal, thematizable experience. The form of apperception inherent in all experience does not by itself constitute an experience. It remains the case, however, that the "I think" is at least assured of its existence, even in the face of other existences. For, in order to apply its activity, the "I think" needs a matter; it is equivalent to "I think something," as the well-known theorem of the refutation of idealism shows. As Ricoeur has observed, this represents a definition of intentionality antedating the more explicit formulations of Brentano and Husserl. [60] Every exercise of apperception, since it is

56. *Critique*, p. 377 (B 422).
57. *Ibid.*, p. 169 (B 158): "The consciousness of self is thus very far from being a knowledge of self."
58. *Ibid.*, p. 378, note a.
59. Does Kant succeed, "between the inaccessible self of apperception and the self known in the internal sense, in justifying the *sum* of the *cogito*"? Jean Nabert does not think so; the idea of an indeterminate intuition appears to him as lame, for "this intuition already involves a determination by apperception," even if the sensation has not yet been converted into an empirical object. ("L'Expérience interne chez Kant," *Revue de métaphysique et de morale* [April 1924], p. 222.)
60. "Kant et Husserl," p. 52.

linked to an external intuition for the sake of determination, is therefore consciousness of my existence as mine; and the "I" of "I exist" acquires its meaning and its existence simultaneously.

Yet Kant refuses to naturalize the subject as energetically as, for example, Sartre, who makes a psychological reality out of self-consciousness.[61] Kant always maintains the distinction of the transcendental from the psychological. Although he does not explicitly situate *Gemüt,* he certainly does not authorize its identification with the objective self of psychology, and the functions or faculties he discerns in it are strictly transcendental. In a certain sense, for Kant the transcendental duplicates the psychological without ever mingling in it. This is the case with imagination: "Insofar as imagination is spontaneity, I sometimes also entitle it the productive imagination, whose synthesis is entirely subject to empirical laws, the laws namely of association." [62] Similarly, there is a pure sensibility whose object is pure intuition, and which is merely sensibility viewed formally; for this formal sensibility, affection is self-affection (intuition being here "nothing but the mode in which the mind is affected through its own activity"). And there is also an empirical sensibility that has "sensation in general [for] its matter." [63] Finally, the same duality is found in the understanding. Thus Kant speaks of a pure understanding: "The unity of apperception in relation to the synthesis of imagination is the understanding; and this same unity, with reference to the transcendental synthesis of the imagination [is] the pure understanding." [64] The categories reside in this pure understanding. If Kant does not explicitly oppose an empirical understanding to it, this is because the understanding as such is always the unity of apperception. But when the understanding is related to the empirical synthesis of the reproductive imagination, and therefore to a sensible matter, it may be termed empirical: "The empirical faculty of knowledge in man must therefore contain an understanding which relates to all objects of the senses." [65] Hence the transcendental element in man acts as a "formal principle," [66] while the psychological element performs, we might say, as a concrete organ.

61. Dufrenne here refers to Sartre's notion of *conscience de soi,* which differs from the pre-reflective *conscience (de) soi* by being more explicit, definite, and hence psychologically "real."—Trans.

62. *Critique,* p. 165 (B 152).

63. *Ibid.,* p. 82 (A 42).

64. *Ibid.,* p. 143 (A 119).

65. *Ibid.*

66. *Ibid.:* "Pure understanding . . . is a formal and synthetic principle of all experiences."

But can a real activity be related to a principle? And up to what point may we distinguish the transcendental from the psychological? We always encounter the same difficulty. The phenomenological analysis, which is juxtaposed with the reflective analysis, describes the operation of subjectivity in its constitutive power, thus accomplishing the Copernican revolution. Yet it tends to psychologize the subject transcendentalized by reflective analysis, which does not consider the transcendental in its actual functioning, but only in its role as a principle. Between these two possibilities offered by Kant, his interpreters have as a whole adopted the second. They have developed the theme of a transcendental philosophy and outdone themselves in trying to purify the transcendental and cleanse it of any taint of psychologism. Hence they have stressed the difficulties of a theory of subjectivity.

Thus Cohen finds and denounces a psychological interpretation in Fichte: "For Fichte, the transcendental signifies self-consciousness in all of its psychological extensibility." [67] The real problem in Cohen's eyes is an epistemological problem, the problem of the constitution of the rules of scientific experience, and metaphysics exists only to serve epistemology. Consciousness, like self-consciousness, derives its meaning from the knowledge it must promote, and its analysis is related to its place in the system of sciences. The supreme principle is always the principle of the possibility of experience; and the unity of apperception, far from being a subjective and personal unity serving as a psychological foundation, signifies the unity of the object—the object of possible experience. This is why the categories, even though deduced from the table of judgments, are understood only in terms of the principles which apply them, thus making the possibility of knowledge explicit. Self-consciousness is understood only through consciousness of the object; consciousness contains the *a priori*— that is, the means to a necessary and universal knowledge—only by virtue of its necessary relation to this knowledge. Consciousness of the object is therefore the "supreme principle," the only one which can be unconditional. "What makes the supreme principle possible? Nothing other than itself. There is no court of appeal above the supreme principle; there exists no necessity above thought." [68]

Does this not imply that consciousness, interpreted as the

67. Cited by J. Vuillemin, *L'Héritage kantien et la révolution copernicienne,* p. 146.
68. *Kants Theorie der Erfahrung,* p. 139.

principle of the possibility of experience, does not have to be real and thus that it is impersonal? It is real as a principle or a systematic method, not as a fact. In this way transcendental philosophy is to be distinguished from positivism. Vuillemin, inspired here by Cohen, insists on this: "The transcendental method does not and cannot presuppose science as a fact since it moves from the question of reality to that of possibility." [69] The transcendental quest is established in the universe of the possible because it returns to the sources of knowledge. But is there not an ambiguity here? Does not the possible derive its meaning from its reference to the real, as Kant himself has shown? The transcendental designates a condition of possibility—a possibility having two interpretations in no way incompatible with each other. Either it is a logical possibility which concerns the real in the form of thoughts already formulated, that is, as a science previously established: this is why Kant starts by accepting the existence of a pure science in his search for its meaning; or the possibility is a power that acts by appealing to a reality which is the very activity of the mind: this is why Kant describes the actions of *Gemüt*. By converting the transcendental into the ontological, Heidegger will identify the possible and its silent force with Being. In either case, the possible evokes the real, the double reality of a thought already thought out and of a thought caught in the act of being thought through. The passage from the real to the possible—from knowledge to the sources of knowledge—does not warrant a denial of the dual reality of constituted knowledge and of a constituting subject.[70]

In other words, may transcendental consciousness, seen as a source of possibilities, be considered as itself a possibility? This is what Cohen suggests in underlining Kant's distinction between apperception and internal sense: the "I think" is the unity of consciousness and not the consciousness of a unity; its being is that of a formal condition, not that of a material reality. It founds the reality of experience, but it is not founded upon the experience of a reality. As a supreme and unconditional principle, it is an absolute possibility related to every reality without being subordinated to any particular one: "Transcendental apperception is apperception considered as a transcendental condition and not as

69. *L'Héritage kantien et la révolution copernicienne*, p. 147.
70. Vuillemin indicates Cohen's hesitation here: if the latter affirms that "the transcendental method does not presuppose science as a fact," he also says that "the double fact of Newtonian science and of the moral demand prevents us from accepting a purely empirical subjectivity because of the ultimate meaning of experience" (*ibid.*, p. 137).

the transcendent state of a personal consciousness whose relation to experience is absolutely immediate." [71] And Vuillemin adds: "The supreme transcendental principle is therefore the absolute equal of consciousness and is identical with it. . . . Far from having to deduce the principle of the possibility of experience from the 'indubitable' fact of self-consciousness (as Descartes and the Fichtean idealists did), transcendental analysis obliges us to reverse the Cartesian position and to base the unity of consciousness on the Copernican correlate of the unity of possible experience." [72] The *cogito* is saved only by becoming lost in its own activity.

After the neo-Kantians, the phenomenologists follow in the same direction—that of a deepening of transcendental purity. For phenomenology encounters the same difficulty: to what degree is the noetic correlate of the noema a pure act? To what extent is phenomenology still psychology? To avoid psychologism, it makes the same effort as Kant did to distinguish the transcendental from the psychological, the self-principle from the self-phenomenon. In fact, the whole phenomenological movement is unanimous in denouncing psychologism. But this condemnation can have two different senses, discernible already in Husserl, but especially evident in his disciples. In the first sense it does not necessarily imply the irreducibility of the transcendental subject that is demanded in the second sense: to condemn psychologism is merely to condemn a psychological doctrine which, in misunderstanding the being of consciousness, reduces its acts to states or facts. Sartre's criticism of the notion of "psyche" [73] is a well-known example. To the ego as a phenomenon he opposes the for-itself [*pour-soi*] as consciousness (of) object and (of) self; he does not oppose the ego to a transcendental consciousness which is anonymous and free of all existential predicates. Between *The Transcendence of the Ego* [74] and *Being and Nothingness* [75] Sartre moved further away from Husserl. The second work, although it claims to confirm the conclusions of the first, refuses to characterize the for-itself as a merely impersonal contemplation. Instead, it assigns to the for-itself "a fundamental selfhood [*ipséité*]" and specifies that consciousness, from the moment that it appears and throughout the pure, nihilating movement of reflection, per-

71. *Ibid.*, p. 142.
72. *Ibid.*, p. 186.
73. By "psyche" Sartre means the self or ego conceived as an object.—Trans.
74. J.-P. Sartre, *The Transcendence of the Ego*, trans. Forrest Williams and Robert Kirkpatrick (New York, Noonday Press, 1957).—Trans.
75. Sartre, *Being and Nothingness*, trans. Hazel E. Barnes (New York, Philosophical Library, 1956).—Trans.

sonalizes itself: "What confers personal existence on a being is not the possession of an ego, which is only the sign of personality, but the fact of existing for oneself [*pour soi*] as presence to oneself [*présence à soi*]." [76] We can see from such a statement that this theory of consciousness does not impugn all psychology: rather than a transcendental philosophy, it initiates the phenomenological psychology exemplified in *The Psychology of Imagination* [77] and in the *Outline of a Theory of the Emotions*. [78] This psychology grants consciousness its role without identifying it with the psyche.

Merleau-Ponty's *Phenomenology of Perception* [79] tends even further to identify phenomenology (at least genetic phenomenology) with a reflection on perception and to pursue this reflection as if it were itself a kind of psychology. Here phenomenology willingly admits to being psychological, though psychologism and the introspective method are disavowed. In his own way, Merleau-Ponty repeats Brentano's distinction between the kind of observation that objectifies psychological realities and the internal perception that, always adequate to its object, seizes the experienced [*le vécu*] in an act of self-coincidence. Far from justifying psychologism, the psychological thus defined includes the transcendental. The psychological and the transcendental are even identified in the notion of existence, since the transcendental for Merleau-Ponty is the body as body-subject and as being-in-the-world [*être au monde*]; and it is the critique of psychologism that allows the delineation of this notion. As a result, phenomenology need not apologize for being psychology: it is both a descriptive and a transcendental psychology, and in this manner it furnishes an answer to the problem of the identity of the empirical and transcendental selves—a problem left unresolved by Kant's *Critique*. Constitutive activity does not consist in imposing a form on matter, in subsuming an intuition under a concept, or in ordering an event according to a rule. The concept here is less a rule than a general idea in Bergson's sense, and constitutive activity consists in grasping a meaning, offered in a concrete form having the status of objectivity only because it also signifies the vital pact linking sub-

76. *Ibid.*, p. 103. (In general, I shall follow Barnes's translation, except for minor changes.—Trans.)

77. Sartre, *The Psychology of Imagination*, trans. Bernard Frechtman (New York, Philosophical Library, 1948).—Trans.

78. Sartre, *Outline of a Theory of the Emotions*, trans. Bernard Frechtman (New York, Philosophical Library, 1948).—Trans.

79. Maurice Merleau-Ponty, *Phenomenology of Perception*, trans. Colin Smith (London, Routledge and Kegan Paul, 1962).—Trans.

ject and object. Hence constitutive activity does not belong to a formal object, but is the expression of this concrete form; it belongs to a being in the world [*un être dans le monde*]. The constitutive is constituting only because it is at the same time constituted. It is not only a movement of transcendence toward the world; it is immanent in the world, intramundane. Its finitude does not reside in its transcendence alone—i.e., in the necessity, assigned to it by receptivity, of being project and expectation; it resides above all in its incarnation and temporality: reflections on the flux of experience are themselves inserted into this flux. If transcendence is temporalization, as Heidegger believes, this temporalization implies temporality, and temporality in turn involves incarnation.

We shall have to return to all of these notions, for we shall consider them on our own. But we must now indicate that the condemnation of psychologism has a second sense: it may also signify a refusal on the part of phenomenology to compromise with any and all psychology in the desire to preserve the purity of the transcendental. With Husserl, this attitude is seen in the logical and epistemological character of his early work: here any reference to the psychological is felt to alter the purity of the essence and obscure the *Wesenschau*. If evidence determines truth by being the basic mode of intentionality—i.e., evidence understood as the presence of an essence—this is because evidence is not a "psychological index"; [80] it is independent of the subjective stream of representations or psychological conditions of its appearance. Thus the notion of evidence as the privileged moment of the constitutive act invites us to reconsider the problem of constitution and the transcendental subject. Now the interpretation of constitution suggested by a phenomenological psychology can be challenged and even abandoned for the more radical interpretation belonging to a transcendental idealism that frees subjectivity from all connection with the empirical ego and reproaches Kant for having located the "I think" at the level of the world.

With Eugen Fink this interpretation finds its most systematic expression. He observes that constitution is often clarified by the notion of intentionality. But one must surpass the psychological conception of intentionality to which Husserl's *Ideas* remains at-

80. Edmund Husserl, *Ideen*, trans. P. Ricoeur (Paris, Gallimard, 1950), p. 484. (English translation by W. Boyce Gibson [New York, Macmillan, 1958], p. 400, §145.) Instead of relying on Gibson, I shall give my own translation of passages from *Ideas*, basing myself upon Ricoeur's admirable effort. Hereafter, references will be given only to the paragraph in which a given passage occurs.— Trans.

tached in defining subjectivity as regional consciousness and its relation to the object as intramundane. In this view, intentionality is only a property of consciousness viewed as given and not as giving.[81] Even when defined by the correlation of noesis and noema, it retains a certain psychological immanence, for the noema can still be conceived psychologically. The noema endows the subject's intentional acts with a meaning—the meaning of the *Erlebnis* (experience), which is "distinct from the being to which it is related" [82]—and announces itself by this meaning as the term of an indefinite approximation, achieved through fulfilling [*remplissantes*] identifications. For Fink, the transcendental noema is "the thing itself" [*l'étant lui-même*] or better, "the meant [*visé*] itself," which is no longer the correlate of a psychological act, but a value for transcendental subjectivity. Fink discusses this difficult theory in a later article.[83] There he again uses the language of intentional analysis in taking over the notion of operative intentionality from Husserl; he opposes this to an intentionality already given, and defines it as "the living function of a consciousness that bestows meaning," or as "the living creation of meaning." This definition precedes that given by Merleau-Ponty, for whom operative intentionality manifests our being in the world [*l'être dans le monde*] by representing "our relation to the world such as it expresses itself indefatigably in us . . . and such as philosophy can only place under our regard." [84] But Fink's definition of 1938 lags behind that proposed in his earlier article of 1933, in which transcendental intentionality appears as "productive and creative." At this point, several questions arise. What does this productivity mean—a productivity which is no longer a creation of meaning, but a fundamental bestowal [*donation*] of it, and even a creation of the world, since the noema is here transcendent (and even identical with the world insofar as the world is the correlate of transcendental subjectivity) and since "the real theme of phenomenology is the becoming of the world through the constitution of transcendental subjectivity"? [85] And how can this latter assertion be true? Does it not provide transcendental subjec-

81. The French word *donnant* (or *donatrice*) is the equivalent of the German *gebend*, which literally means "giving"; for Husserl, giving has the sense of bestowing meaning.—Trans.

82. Eugen Fink, "Die phänomenologische Philosophie E. Husserls in der gegenwärtigen Kritik," *Kantstudien*, XXXVIII (1933), 364.

83. Eugen Fink, "Das Problem der Phänomenologie Edmund Husserls," *Revue internationale de philosophie* (January 1939), pp. 226–70.

84. *Phenomenology of Perception*, p. xviii.

85. Fink, "Die phänomenologische Philosophie E. Husserls," p. 370.

tivity with an *intuitis originarius* in Kant's sense—i.e., with a mode of intuition "such as can itself give us the existence of its object," [86] and not simply the form of objectivity? In any case, this affirmation is legitimate for Fink only in the perspective of the reduction, whose employment definitively separates phenomenology from Kant.

Since the reduction is unknown to Kant, he remains in the natural attitude, posing only the mundane problem of the possibility of knowledge, and maintaining a mundane status for the "I think." The reduction deepens the Kantian question; it represents a movement of transcendence that loses the world, only to recover it later as an absolute. The belief in the world that is the essence and general thesis of the natural attitude finds itself bracketed. Yet to bracket is also to accentuate; the belief does not disappear, but instead reappears in all its purity as an enigma: thus it is unsurpassable. Man himself is surpassed insofar as this belief, experienced unconsciously, defines him and at the same time turns him into a kind of object, since he is himself included in the world he intends. Far from being the suppression of the belief in the world, the reduction brackets it "in the believing human"; as a result, there appears "the true subject of the belief, the transcendental ego for whom the world is a *universum* of transcendental value." [87] The reduction therefore implies an extreme effort on man's part to "conquer himself"—yet an effort that is always unmotivated, because philosophy is gratuitous. This effort leads to the discovery of "the life of transcendental belief," the *strömendes Aktleben* that is transcendental subjectivity.[88] It is this leap to the absolute that radically distinguishes the Kantian quest for the being-for-us of beings [89] from the phenomenological search for the being-for-transcendental subjectivity of the world. In other words, a distinction is drawn between epistemological constitution, which always possesses a moment of receptivity, and ontological constitution, which is total spontaneity. But what is transcendental subjectivity? Is its flux temporal? Is its life pre-reflective [*irréfléchie*]? It can no longer be understood in relation to the human self, which is an ontic phenomenon: "The specific character of the

---

86. *Critique*, p. 90 (B 72).
87. Fink, "Die phänomenologische Philosophie E. Husserls," p. 351.
88. It is this "incessant flow of universal apperception" which requires the intentional analysis discussed above for the infinity of its constitutive acts.
89. *L'être pour nous de l'étant—étant* is the French equivalent of the German *Seiende*, by which Heidegger designates ontic "beings" in contrast with *Sein* or "Being."—Trans.

transcendental ego cannot be understood as being based on the individuality of the human 'I.' " [90] The transcendental ego is no longer the Kantian "I think," which is only "the form of unity of the mundane 'I,' " and which is merely situated in the world instead of at its origin.

Thus the Kantian problem concerning the identity of the known and the knowing selves is complicated, instead of being solved. It is complicated first of all—though we cannot develop this point here—by the dawning awareness of the problem of the other (such as we find in the fifth of Husserl's *Cartesian Meditations*) and by the development of the transcendental egology into a monadology: What does intersubjectivity mean when an ontic meaning is no longer given it—as in sociology, for example? Fink is content merely to affirm that "the transcendental whole of the monads is not the ultimate concept of absolute subjectivity." [91] Then, the problem of self-identity is further complicated by the introduction of a third ego side by side with the human ego and the transcendental ego: the theoretical spectator operating the reduction who, in thematizing the belief which founds the world, prevents himself from participating in it by stationing himself outside the world. But what is the status of this radical reflection? Does the theoretical spectator really cease to be in the world? If he escapes from a belief in the natural world, and by this move breaks free from the truly concrete life of the transcendental subject, his reflections still form part of the flux of life. Though a disinterested spectator, he is not a pure spectator; there is no unimpregnable position where he can avoid the risk of being compromised by the world or of compromising in turn the purity of the transcendental ego. This third ego risks reviving the third man argument: the threat of an infinite regression from subject to object. Thus the problem of the unity of the subject in view of the plurality of the ego remains intact; Fink scarcely resolves it by saying that "the phenomenological reduction . . . transcends the indissoluble unity of the human ego, dividing it and yet reassembling it in a higher unity." [92]

Therefore, it is at the price of encountering the most serious difficulties that phenomenology carries the distinction between the psychological and the transcendental to a point beyond even Kant's demands. Yet this distinction is one of the most characteristic features of recent philosophy—viewed as the enterprise of

90. Fink, "Die phänomenologische Philosophie E. Husserls," p. 367.
91. *Ibid.*, p. 368.
92. *Ibid.*, p. 357.

"returning to the ground," [93] an enterprise which, in doctrines wishing to be transcendental by condemning psychologism, creates still more difficulties. We have just seen one example in Fink, when he criticizes Kant by using the neo-Kantian arguments of Husserl. Heidegger is yet another example: his reflection involves the movement of the transcendental element from the epistemological to the ontological sphere; as a result, we are supposed to speak of "transcendence," but in such a way that it is no longer exactly clear who does the transcending or what constitutive subjectivity means. This movement is initiated by meditating on the ground, where "the transcendental possibility of the intentional relation becomes a problem." [94] It appears that this relation is only possible by means of transcendence, the movement by which *Dasein* projects the bases of a world while feeling itself possessed by this world: *Dasein* is both source and passion.[95] Transcendence is therefore not the attribute of a transcendental subjectivity, and it would seem that Heidegger has not effected the phenomenological reduction. But the problem is not so simple as this. Transcendence is also a kind of motivation. On the one hand, it can be motivation only if it is itself capable of ontological truth—of what Kant called knowledge *a priori*—that is, if Being is revealed to it sufficiently to allow the question "why?"; on the other hand, it can be motivation by virtue of the freedom in which it originates. But transcendence here represents an abyss; the *Grund* is an *Abgrund*. Why is this so? Heidegger's recent writings help us to understand that motivation and freedom both involve a reference to Being; motivation implies an unveiling of Being, and freedom an initiative on Being's part. Freedom is not complete in man, and on this condition it is identified with transcendence, since it is the act of Being in man—the act by which Being calls to man in order to be revealed. There is a hierarchy of concepts here: the transcendental, far from being a storehouse of *a priori* knowledge, and still less a group of psychological faculties, has meaning only through transcendence in the phenomenological sense of the intentionality of meaning-giving [*donatrice*] consciousness. This transcendence, in turn, has meaning only through transcendence in the ontologi-

---

93. For this concept, see Heidegger's 1949 Preface to *Was ist Metaphysik?* translated by Walter Kaufmann as "The Way Back Into the Ground of Metaphysics" in *Existentialism from Dostoevsky to Sartre*, ed. Walter Kaufmann, Meridian Books (Cleveland, World Publishing Co., 1956).—Trans.

94. Martin Heidegger, "L'Essence du fondement" ("Vom Wesen des Grundes") in *Qu'est-ce que la métaphysique?*, trans. Henry Corbin (Paris, Gallimard, 1938), p. 102.

95. "Passion" retains here its root meaning of a certain passivity.—Trans.

cal sense. The relation of man to Being that defines intentionality is the effect in man of the relation of Being to man that defines truth; for man is capable of truth only because Being is light and because it obliges man to remain in this light. For man, freedom is project only insofar as it is at the same time—and here "at the same time" is more than a metaphor—submission: freedom is essentially finite. The finitude of *Dasein,* and therefore of transcendence considered as the essence of *Dasein,* is the counterpart of the infinitude of Being.

We can now see what Heidegger is pleased to find in Kant: a way to render this finitude explicit in terms of the conjunction of receptivity and spontaneity. Moreover, as the criterion of the transcendental and of *a priori* knowledge, the theme of purity in Heidegger (as distinguished from the purity of the abstract that Husserl opposes to the psychological concrete in an ambiguous fashion, even in *Ideas* [96]) allows the *a priori* to be assigned finally to Being. For Heidegger is much less preoccupied than Kant with discovering and tabulating the various *a priori:* to provide a content for pure knowledge is to risk sullying its purity. Thus, though he has shown that man's commerce with beings [*l'étant*] requires a pre-conception of Being, instead of elucidating this pre-conception or showing its historical modalities, he prefers to define it as the truth that is the ground of all truth and to identify it with Being. The *a priori* becomes the manifestation in man of the movement by which Being is revealed and, in being revealed, is constituted as time. It therefore expresses the finitude of man, the central theme of Heidegger's existential analytic. This theme possesses undeniable theological echoes—not because the finitude of the creature is measured by the infinity of the creator, but because a) this finitude is the fact of Being in man, b) Being as transcendence achieves in man the act of transcending, and c) man with his future is only the instrument or the witness of an adventure of Being.

Phenomenology thus ceases to be psychology, but at what price? By eluding the problem of subsumption, Heidegger has extended the limits of the transcendental to the point of identifying it with Being; hence he has excluded the possibility of a transcendental deduction and cannot return from the ontological to the ontic. He can no longer consider the problems posed by the subject-object relation: the subject has somehow evaporated into Being; being-in-the-world [*l'être au monde*] no longer suffices to define *Dasein,* for, by an inflation of meaning, the world has come

96. Fink, "Die phänomenologische Philosophie E. Husserls," p. 362.

to signify Being. And at the same time the object has lost the objectivity which transcendental reflection proposed to found. Objectification can no longer be understood as the activity of a constitutive subject; the relation of truth to truths, of pure knowledge to empirical knowledge, is blurred.

Heidegger is certainly right to underline the theme of finitude in Kant. This is one of the keys to the Kantian system and the only means of avoiding the difficulties in which Husserl is involved— and Hegel too, as we shall see. Yet must we subscribe to Heidegger's interpretation of finitude? Kant at least clarifies the nature of finitude by firmly maintaining the duality of mind and world: he avoids defining in idealistic terms the immanence of mind in the world—i.e., the operation of the *a priori*. Since concepts without intuitions are empty, the *a priori* gains meaning only in the *a posteriori*. Form does not produce content, and synthetic judgment requires the mediation of intuition (even when the given is the pure form of the object). Furthermore, if the mind makes the world appear, the world is precisely that which is not mind and does not proceed from it. The famous distinction of phenomenon from noumenon confirms this: the thing in itself is above all the affirmation of the in-itself [*l'en-soi*], the upholding of dualism, the assurance that the object is exterior and that sensibility is receptive. The thing in itself is therefore the affirmation of finitude, not only because transcendence is privation—as Heidegger says—but also because that towards which it transcends is something definite. The affirmation of the in-itself is both the refusal of idealism (against Husserl) and monism (against Hegel).[97] Moreover, Kant makes the mind finite by giving it a nature, as we have seen. In order to manifest the receptivity of knowledge required by dualism, he combines sensibility and understanding in the mind; as a result, the *a priori* is diversified and expresses the forms of receptivity as well as the rules of intelligibility. In doing this, he refuses to cut up the mind of the concrete subject and tends to confuse the "I think" and *das Gemüt*, which, if untreatable by empirical psychology, cannot be the object of reflective psychology either.

In sum, the theme of finitude is linked to dualism, to the relation of the self as subject with the object—that is, with beings [*l'étant*], not with Being (and the thing in itself is still a being).

97. Furthermore, what distinguishes Kant from someone like Sartre is the fact that the affirmation of the in-itself has a double use: it is also applied to the for-itself and allows us to comprehend it as freedom, not only theoretical but practical—as a first cause. The in-itself guarantees both the material reality of the object, its radical otherness, and at the same time the mental reality of the subject, his freedom.

Heidegger undermines his own thesis when, by an excess of zeal, he ontologizes finitude and attributes it to Being itself. Of course, he does not restore, in order to identify it with subjectivity, a Leibnizian God: Being is not creation; it is light. (Therefore the subject as a natural light, as an opening to presence, is an avatar of Being, a moment of *logos*.) But Heidegger tends to infinitize finitude, and it is for this that Vuillemin criticizes him. Whether through the formal character of Cohen's system of the *a priori* or through the formal character of temporalization found in Heidegger—in either case the subject is endowed with a kind of eternity: "The universal reduction of truths to time and finitude ends by rooting this reduction itself in eternity." [98] For Kant, by contrast, the finitude of the subject is unambiguous, because it signifies above all that intuition is not productive [*originaire*], that seeing is not creating. By relating time to the nature of the subject, Kant prevents himself from referring temporalization to Being, and he no more subordinates Being to the subject than the subject to Being. The only activity expressing the subject's finitude—since this finitude is related to the receptivity of knowledge and regulated by the necessity of realizing the concept in intuition—is the constitutive activity. And this activity implies dualism.

THE RELATION OF THE SUBJECT TO THE OBJECT

THIS BRINGS US to the second problem arising from transcendental philosophy: that of the subject-object relation. There is no way to avoid this problem. It does not suffice to say, as Heidegger does, that this relation is only ontic in order to dismiss it; ontological reflection can be justified only by rediscovering this correlation in an effort to ground it, not by dismissing it. We approached this problem only a moment ago, when we reflected on the being of the subject. But we have just seen how Heidegger in a certain sense devalues the subject to the profit of Being, and especially how Husserlian phenomenology in Fink's interpretation comes to replace Kant's dualism by the idea of a transcendental subjectivity in which constitution becomes creation. It is to Hegel that we now must turn to show how the treatment of the *a priori* can end in a monism by taking another path parallel to that of Husserl and yet equally untenable.

Let us begin again with Kantian dualism. Kant poses the problem of subject and object in terms of a transcendental philosophy.

98. Vuillemin, *L'Héritage kantien et la révolution copernicienne*, p. 295.

For him, it is not crucial to know what produces the Being of beings [*l'être de l'étant*], but what determines the objectivity of the object. The existence of the object is not in question, being implied by the very experience of self-consciousness that refutes material idealism (whether problematic or dogmatic in form). The internal experience by which I determine my own existence in time becomes possible by means of external experience. This internal experience assures me of the existence of exterior objects immediately, making use of a sensible intuition which, according to the Transcendental Aesthetic, "determines [my] existence solely in relation to given objects." [99] By concerning himself with the objectivity of the object—with the intelligibility of the real—Kant escapes the impasses in which Leibniz was caught. Thus Kant circumvents the problematic passage from the possible to the real by claiming that the real is primarily given, along with self-consciousness. Kant also avoids the pitfall of pre-established harmony, which is the consequence of making the universe mental and which reduces the sensible world to being a well-founded appearance; the monad is enclosed in the subjectivity of a psychic development, so that the transition from the monad to the monadology requires a *deus ex machina*—the operation of a divine wisdom willing the maximum of being at each instant and submitting this being to the laws of compossibility. But Kant avoids the return to metaphysical dogmatism only by introducing the idea of subsumption (which others will term constitution), and this raises even more questions.

What does subsumption really mean? How can the *a priori* structure the *a posteriori*? How can the concept rule intuition for the sake of understanding, imposing its law on nature? Can the activity of *Gemüt* be described without on the one hand falling into a mythology of intellectual operations and syntheses, or, on the other, denying the theme of finitude by making the mind the creator of the universe—hence, granting subjectivity the privileges that Leibniz reserved for God? These questions will continue to concern us. Hegel, however, is undeterred by them: he wastes no time in embracing monism. What he denounces in the theory of subsumption is not the risk of excessiveness [*démesure*] that it involves and that will reappear in Husserl; rather, to the extent that this theory implies dualism, he attacks its very excess of measure, its dullness and insipidity. Only the affirmation of the identity of subject and object is to be respected from Hegel's speculative point of view.

99. *Critique*, p. 90 (B 72).

Even in his earliest reflections on Kant, Hegel denounces the psychologism menacing the Copernican revolution: "The absolute identity of subject and object has become a formal relation (though manifested as a causal relation), and transcendental idealism has become a formal, or more accurately, a psychological idealism." [100] The constitutive subject exercising this mental causality is opposed, inasmuch as subjective, to the object: "The entire system of principles is subjective. . . . The objectivity of categories in experience and the necessity of relations derive from the contingent and the subjective. This understanding is a human understanding. . . ." [101] And yet, in Hegel's eyes, the reduction of the transcendental to the anthropological may open the way to the speculative: [102] "Already from the simple fact that the understanding is posited as subjective, it is recognized as something non-absolute, and it should be indifferent to formal idealism whether the understanding—which is necessary and known according to the dimensions of its form—is posited subjectively or objectively." [103] If so, the understanding is already viewed by Kant through the lens of reason—i.e., the sort of thought that considers itself identical with its object and that assumes and surmounts contradiction: in short, the dialectical identity of the concept as thing and of the thing as concept. Nevertheless, observes Hegel, the treatment of reason in the Transcendental Dialectic of the *Critique* belies these promises. Reason for Kant "makes no claim to autonomous dignity or to auto-generation; it remains a prisoner of its own sterility and of its unworthy resignation to the dualism of a pure unity appearing to reason and a multiplicity pertaining to understanding, and it does not realize the necessity of a middle term or of an immanent knowledge." [104] This middle term can be found through another interpretation of the notion of the understanding, by conceiving of an understanding whose content would be immanent in its form and with which "nature is in harmony, and not by chance," as Kant writes in the *Critique of Judgment*. Such is the idea of an archetypal "intuitive understanding," an "absolute intermediary," as Hegel says; we can add: an interme-

100. Hegel, "Glauben und Wissen," *Sämmtliche Werke*, I, 304; *Premières publications*, p. 212.
101. *Ibid.*, *Sämmtliche Werke*, I, 306; *Premières publications*, p. 213.
102. Hegel terms "speculative" the thought concerning the identity—the dialectical identity, as he will later say—of subject and object; this is the form that absolute knowledge assumes in philosophy.
103. *Ibid.*, *Sämmtliche Werke*, I, 308; *Premières publications*, pp. 214–15.
104. *Ibid.*, *Sämmtliche Werke*, I, 311; *Premières publications*, p. 217.

diary between nature and mind, between object and subject. This is an understanding which ceases to be human in order to be both human and natural, or rather, if we are to surpass this opposition, to be *logos*.[105]

Hegel finds in Kant's ethical writings another forerunner of this speculative reflection. The notion of autonomy signifies for Hegel both the abolition of the duality of nature and reason and the final identification of self-consciousness with object-consciousness. "The pure volition that wills itself is being in general or all being," comments Jean Hyppolite.[106] This is why Hegel denounces the postulates of practical reason as a vice of the Kantian system: postulating, instead of affirming, a synthesis of nature and morality implies a step backwards, a return to the separation of form and content. Yet this is a retreat only in Hegel's eyes. Kant never thought that nature and morality, object and subject, could be identified at the outset; he never said that the pure will is all being. Certainly one wonders whether the postulates are necessary —that is, whether we must interpret the finitude of knowledge as a limitation imposed by faith, or whether the totality of being must be conceived as God. But the contradiction to which the postulates offer a solution (granted, a debatable one) is not a contradiction "in thought"; it is the contradiction inherent in morality itself. The moral consciousness, Hegel says, "produces its object consciously and by itself, and we do not see it encounter its object as an alien thing. . . . It knows essence to be itself, for it knows itself as producing essence." [107] But what the moral consciousness thus knows immediately as its essence is duty: the object that it creates here is not God, and it cannot be reproached for positing duty as both beyond the self and produced by means of the self. The contradiction found at the core of the moral problem resides rather in the fact that duty is at once real and unreal. It is real inasmuch as it is an expression of pure will; and its manifestation as an imperative means that dualism cannot be surpassed, because the moral consciousness encounters the resistance of a nature found both inside the subject—where reason is opposed to

---

105. This idea is taken up again in the *Logik*, ed. Georg Lasson (Hamburg, Felix Meiner, 1934), II, 232. [English translation by W. H. Johnston and L. G. Struthers, *Science of Logic* (New York, Macmillan, 1929), II, 227.]

106. Jean Hyppolite, *Genèse et structure de la phénoménologie de Hegel* (Paris, Aubier, 1946), II, 454.

107. Hegel, *La Phénoménologie de l'esprit*, trans. Jean Hyppolite (Paris, Aubier, 1939–41), II, 156. [English translation by J. B. Baillie (London, George Allen and Unwin, 1964), p. 629.]

sensibility, just as the transcendental is opposed to the psychological—and outside the subject in an in-itself opposed to the for-itself. Yet the imperative is unreal insofar as it must be realized in the nature that it negates; form must be given an adequate content, but the matter of this content does not arise from form. The dissimulations (*Verstellungen*) of moral consciousness denounced by Hegel spring then from the necessity of reconciling purity and efficacity by surmounting a difference that is not merely verbal as Hegel claims, since it expresses the condition of man as an incarnate Word.[108] And noetic consciousness is subjected to a similar necessity: it must employ intuition to realize the concept, to think the object in general on the basis of the empirical object, and thus to find for form a content without which it is empty but which it does not engender.[109]

At this point the imagination intervenes. The second guarantee that Hegel finds in Kant for speculative identity lies in the experience of beauty, where "the form of the opposition between intuition and concept disappears." [110] The aesthetic idea is, as Kant says, "an intuition of the imagination," and the imagination is the privileged place where the mediation required by speculative thought can occur. The idea of an intuitive understanding is clarified by the notion of imagination: such an understanding is "nothing other than the idea of the transcendental imagination," [111] and in turn, "this imagination is nothing more than reason itself." [112] Kant's great merit is to have discovered the imagination. "One cannot understand anything about the unity of the

108. The French is *verbe incarné*, in which expression the "verb" is understood as the "word" in a quasi-Biblical sense. Present also are overtones of Merleau-Ponty's notion of language as incarnation.—Trans.

109. The moral world must be constituted by morality, as the physical world by subsumption, without form being able to acquire its content immediately. This is not without consequence for the *a priori*: it always appears as a rule to be applied, whether in conceiving the world, or in realizing morality. Therefore, in Kant, it implies the duality of subject and object so that this application may have a meaning; perhaps it also implies the concrete character of an acting subject so that this application may be realizable; for the subject capable of the *a priori* must and can oppose himself to nature only if he is himself nature in some sense, just as he can conceive the world only if he is in the world [*au monde*]. The dualism of subject and object can thus be understood only if it is prolonged and perhaps even surmounted by a dualism within the subject. But it remains to be seen what this transcendence of dualism in the subject means—a transcendence which does not allow the dualism of subject and object to be overcome.

110. "Glauben und Wissen," *Sämmtliche Werke*, I, 317; *Premières publications*, p. 220.

111. *Ibid.*, *Sämmtliche Werke*, I, 318; *Premières publications*, p. 221.

112. *Ibid.*, *Sämmtliche Werke;* I, 301; *Premières publications*, p. 210.

transcendental deduction . . . without distinguishing what Kant calls the faculty of the original synthetic unity of apperception from the self, which, for him, is restricted to accompanying all representations, or without recognizing this imagination as the unique in-itself—an imagination conceived not as an intermediary between an absolute, existing subject and an absolute, existing world, but as that which is primary and productive [*originaire*] [113] and as that from which both the subjective self and the objective world are derived, giving rise to an appearance and a product that are necessarily counterparts." [114] Thus the imagination is at the origin of the originally synthetic unity. As such, it is the source of the transcendental deduction, grounding the synthetic judgments that express the identity of subject and predicate —the identity of the particular posited as object and the universal posited as thought—because it may be said to be the original [*originaire*] identity of subject and thought. Hence it is distinguished from the abstract self: it no longer belongs to subjectivity, but is situated instead at its origin as well as at the origin of the object: it is the in-itself. What does this mean? Some light may be thrown on the ontology of the transcendental imagination by the psychology of the empirical imagination: the imagination is that which is least human in man. As in a Pythic delirium, it wrenches man away from himself and plunges him into ecstasy; it puts him into secret communion with the powers of nature: "Who speaks to me, with my own voice?" [115] The genius yielding to inspiration no longer belongs to himself; he is a force of nature; his "I" is an other.[116] Thus the imagination is an origin [*est originaire*] because it alienates man to join him to that which he is not. But the imagination conceived ontologically is not this faculty of losing oneself in a strange speech [*parole*] that may end in madness; it is this speech itself, the truth of being anterior to (though expressed by) the distinction between the subjective self and the objective world. Or else, as the *Logic* will say, it is "the truth such as, unveiled, it is in itself and for itself . . . [the truth] whose con-

113. *Originaire* means both productive ("originating") and first ("original"). —Trans.

114. "Glauben und Wissen," *Sämmtliche Werke*, I, 300–301; *Premières publications*, pp. 209–10.

115. Dufrenne alludes here to a line from Paul Valéry's "La Pythie": "Qui me parle, à ma place même?" (*Oeuvres*, Edition de la Pléiade [Paris, Gallimard, 1957], I, 131).—Trans.

116. An adaptation of Arthur Rimbaud's declaration "Car *je* suis un autre" (from "Lettre du voyant," *Oeuvres complètes*, Edition de la Pléiade [Paris, Gallimard, 1963], p. 270).—Trans.

tent is the representation of God as He exists in His eternal essence before the creation of the world and any finite mind." [117] The imagination is the *logos* itself whose dialectical movement engenders nature and mind.

It is worth noting that all the doctrines which attempt to save the transcendental from the psychological by directing it towards the metaphysical stress the role of the imagination. This is undoubtedly because the imagination, representing the inhuman in man, best undermines psychological interpretations, best manifests that man is not the measure of all things, and, by a curious paradox, gives truth the greatest authority by liberating it from subjectivity. [118] We know how much Heidegger has insisted on the imagination; yet he does not give it a central role in the analysis of *Dasein,* since he interprets the latter as temporality. But long before Heidegger, Schelling had tried to reconstruct Spinoza with the help of Schiller. For Schelling, the philosophy of the imagination guarantees a philosophy of substance; *natura naturans* cannot be grasped by empirical or transcendental reflection, but only by penetrating into, and as it were losing oneself in, the object of knowledge; this is why the imagination is a privileged term, as well as a method, in Schelling's philosophy of the Absolute.

As Hyppolite observes, [119] Hegel, in the article to which we have just referred, adopts Schelling's perspective. He demands that speculative philosophy surpass dualism by conceiving "the absolute identity of thought and being . . . an idea absolutely identical with that recognized by the ontological argument and all phi-

117. Heidegger cites this Hegelian formula at the end of his book on Kant (*Kant and the Problem of Metaphysics,* p. 253) in order to show that Hegel is unfaithful to Kant, or at least too faithful to the movement by which Kant, between the first and the second editions of the *Critique,* comes to retreat from his discovery of the primacy of the imagination and to restore the traditional privileges of logic. Hegel thus forgets "what Kant had established, to wit, that the intrinsic possibility and necessity of metaphysics must be borne and maintained by the original [*originaire*] development and deepening of the problem of finitude" (*ibid.,* pp. 252–53). But Heidegger in turn forgets that Hegel has acclaimed and adopted the Kantian theory of imagination, and that he would not disavow the interpretation of imagination in terms of time inasmuch as he invents dialectic; and if Hegel combats the thing in itself, it is not because he neglects the theme of finitude.

118. But then it is no longer merely a question of paying homage to the role of the imagination in constitutive activity; Cohen, for example, relates the productive imagination interpreted as the power of schemata to the understanding, and links the imagination as the faculty [*pouvoir*] of images to sensibility. (Cf. Vuillemin, *L'Héritage kantien et la révolution copernicienne,* p. 190.) For imagination to keep its metaphysical meaning, it must be incommensurate with sensibility and understanding, or it must at least be their common root, as Heidegger holds.

119. *Genèse et structure de la phénoménologie de Hegel,* p. 11.

losophy as the first and unique idea, the only one that is true and philosophical." [120] Hegel presents this idea in many ways, but he tends simply to assert the principle of identity rather than to justify the various expressions he gives to it: e.g., the identity of empirical multiplicity and absolute unity, the identity of the particular which is given and of the universal which is thought, the identity of subject and predicate in the absolute judgment of which the synthetic *a priori* judgment is a first expression (for example, when I say that all perceived alteration has a cause in thought). The identity may also exist between the finite and infinite, either of the terms of an infinite opposition being finite or infinite according to whether it affirms or denies the opposition (for example, the "I think" as "an absolute intellectual point . . . is both conditioned by infinite opposition and absolute in this finitude" [121]). When later, in the *Phenomenology,* Hegel renders justice to Fichte's subjectivism, the identity characterizing the Absolute is the identity of certitude and truth—i.e., the equality for consciousness of knowledge and truth. Yet this identity is not only produced within consciousness by a mere deepening of knowledge; what consciousness must discover in coming to truth is its own identity with the object. When it knows the object, the object knows itself. In other words, in its own act of knowing, the Absolute reflects upon itself and constitutes itself as self-consciousness, that is, as subject; hence consciousness is only the instrument of the Absolute. More exactly, it is the instrument of the advent of the Absolute: for the identity in which the Absolute becomes conscious of itself appears only at the end of the development of consciousness. And this is why such an identity is dialectical.

Undoubtedly, the notion of dialectic was already implicit in Hegel's first works. But it is debatable whether the explicit introduction of this notion into his later writings facilitates the understanding of speculative thought. The problem is to know if Hegel here is not perhaps the sorcerer's apprentice, who, in thinking he has tamed contradiction and inserted it into his system, has actually been overcome by it. The word "tamed" may be unfair: Hegel has sufficiently insisted on the seriousness of the negative, on death, and on war. Nevertheless, it remains the case that for him everything has a meaning and even, if we may say so, that everything turns out right: the finite is a moment of the infinite, the sin

120. "Glauben und Wissen," *Sämmtliche Werke,* I, 324; *Premières publications,* p. 225.
121. *Ibid., Sämmtliche Werke,* I, 312; *Premières publications,* p. 217.

of particularity is pardoned in the universal,[122] and negation is negated. The scandal of finitude or separation, like the terror of the slave, is whisked away in the movement of history. The term "dialectic" signifies that movement is more real than what is moved, and that mediation is more real than the terms it opposes and unites. The Absolute triumphs, but only as Idea, as Marx will declare. For history is not the last word, and Hegel becomes the prey of the very forces of contradiction he has awakened, because dialectic means both the advent of history and its absolutization. The *Phenomenology* leads to the *Logic:* mediation—the moment of rupture and opposition—is meaningful only if it ends in a new immediate. If history has an end [*fin*], this means that there *is* no history, since the end for Hegel is found in the beginning: the next immediate is already present in the immediate now being set in motion by mediation. Time is once again the moving image of eternity, and any progress in thought since Spinoza appears to be illusory. The logicality of being and history is only a reflection of the being of logic, and the movement of *logos* is a logical move-ment. Vuillemin's objection to Heidegger could also be addressed to Hegel: temporality is eternal precisely because it is the act of *logos,* the absolute subject. Everything returns to *logos,* including the nature and history in which *logos* becomes alienated. Thus dialectic negates itself once more; it makes itself absolute instead of dialectical. Contradiction lies at the heart of being, but it is being which contradicts itself; opposition, in the multiple forms revealed by the *Logic,* is always transcended, and truth is found only in this transcendence. Realizing this is important for our own project. For, though one might think that dialectic would restore dualism, this is not at all the case. If there is a last word to be said, it definitely belongs to identity. Of course, identity is not pure and simple equality, and on this point Hegel transforms Spinoza: identity is mediation, but the mediation that negates immediate terms is itself an immediate. For it is finally the manifestation of the Absolute, and the Absolute is precisely its own manifestation, the non-temporal becoming of *logos.*[123]

122. We have seen Hegel accuse Kant's morality of hypocrisy because it plays on the opposition of the self of moral consciousness and what is beyond it, since the opposition of purity and efficacity is presumed to be unsurmountable in this world: but Hegel reconciles them in a self which is a first form of the Absolute. (See *The Phenomenology of Mind,* pp. 687 ff.)

123. "As this movement of becoming explicit which relates itself to itself and then is an absolute identity with itself, the Absolute is manifestation not of something interior, not of something other, but absolute manifestation, manifesta-tion in itself and for itself; thus it is the actual reality." (See *Science of Logic,* II, 167.)

Thus, whether he starts from Schelling or from Fichte, Hegel invites us, unlike Kant, to think the unthinkable, the identity of subject and object. At the core of this identity, subject and object possess only the evanescent existence of dialectical moments, as products of an alienation that must itself be surpassed. This is seen clearly in the fact that absolute reflection, the mediation in which being reflects upon itself, does not originate with man; it is accomplished *through* man—through the subjective reflection of consciousness as such.[124] To proclaim the identity of subject and object is therefore to slight the subject if by "subject" is meant the concrete human being. Hegel does say that the Absolute is subject; but this elevation of subjectivity to the Absolute involves neither empirical nor transcendental subjectivity. It signifies first of all that the Absolute is a relation of itself to itself and that it negates itself by positing itself and then negates its own negation: thus it is both for-itself and in-itself. It also means that thought remains a privileged element; this is seen in the term "reflection," which is employed by Hegel to designate the dialectical movement of being. This thought must be understood somewhat like thought in the Aristotelian sense: it is universal in itself. But what does "universal" mean?

We see now the implication of this doctrine for the notion of the *a priori*: the *a priori* loses its meaning. Hegel says this explicitly in his essay on "Faith and Knowledge": the idea of an intuitive understanding, which would be both the understanding of consciousness and the understanding of nature, is "the purest idea of an understanding that would also be *a posteriori*." [125] The reasoning is clear: the *a priori* is conceived by Kant as a function of dualism; it belongs to a subjectivity which imposes it on the object. The determinations of understanding and sensibility are realized and isolated, acquiring from this fact a formal validity. Kant, says Hegel, "thinks of the *a priori* in terms of the formal concept of universality and necessity"; at the same time, "he considers it as a pure unity that is not originally synthetic." [126] To be truly synthetic, the synthesis would have to be not only a formal rule for empirical knowledge, but also the absolute identity

---

124. Hyppolite has quite forcefully described this speculative reflection, which is opposed to transcendental reflection as absolute knowledge is to critical knowledge. Its movement is exposed by the *Logic* after the *Phenomenology* led to the threshold of the *Logic*. (See his *Logique et existence* [Paris, Presses Universitaires de France, 1953], p. 122.)

125. "Glauben und Wissen," *Sämmtliche Werke*, I, 309; *Premières publications*, p. 215.

126. *Ibid., Sämmtliche Werke*, I, 302; *Premières publications*, p. 210.

of predicate and subject—i.e., the identity of the universal as given *a priori* and of the particular as given *a posteriori*. Form would have to engender content in order to be identified with it—in other words, the content must appear as a determination of form, as posited and then negated by form in order to actualize itself. Finally, the *a priori* would have to exist as the spontaneity of *logos* in its movement of identification with the *a posteriori*. While for Kant the *a priori* is a form which determines content without being compromised by it and which makes experience possible without being experience itself, for Hegel there is no need to ground experience in something non-experiential, because experience grounds itself: the *a posteriori* is in turn *a priori*. Experience is absolute because it is the experience of the Absolute—that is, the experience enjoyed by the Absolute in manifesting itself as the identity of subject and object.

In this way Hegel eliminates the transcendental; or rather he allows transcendental reflection, but only on the condition that it be finally interpreted as absolute reflection. Thus the Transcendental Analytic, instead of setting forth the conditions for the possibility of experience, would show how the understanding discovers itself in experience and recognizes itself as the understanding of nature; as a result, Kant's transcendental logic is, properly interpreted, an ontology. For the life of *logos* is nothing more than a knowledge of self *in* the content, a reciprocity of subjectivity and objectivity. Thus conceived, the transcendental retains a position because, as Hyppolite says, "it expresses the logicality of being; it goes beyond notions of subject and object, by stating their *original identity* as it appears in the judgment of existence." [127] In other words, the transcendental is kept on the condition of being a form of the Absolute, of participating in the dialectal dance which is the Absolute itself. The *a priori* is the *logos* in relation to which the *a posteriori* is experience, and this is why Logic—pure knowledge or pure truth—is the kingdom of the *a priori*. What Hegel does eliminate is the theory of subsumption or constitution, which presupposes that the transcendental is found outside experience; this theory tempts us to attribute constitution to subjectivity and to grant subjectivity the status of an autonomous, concrete being or of a creative power in Fink's view.

Now, if we wish to avoid the problem of constitution, must we adopt Hegel's solution? In so doing, do we not fall from Scylla into Charybdis? For, if form is no longer imposed on content, what does the immanence of content in form—or better, the identity of

127. *Logique et existence*, p. 101.

form and content—mean? Can one really conceive the identity of experience and the possibility of experience, of nature and mind? Can one really surpass the duality that alone preserves the purity of the *a priori*? And do we comprehend the relation of the *a priori* to the *a posteriori* by identifying them, with the sole gain of eliminating the theory of constitution? Yet, if we refuse the Hegelian ontology, are we not left with the idea of constitution, and thus led to Husserlian phenomenology? We know that the latter involves us in the idea of a radical subordination of the object to the subject conceived as a constitutive subjectivity. Instead of Hegel's formula: the Absolute is subject, we are now exhorted to endorse the formula: the subject is absolute, since it expresses the ontological function of intentionality, the identity of seeing and creating. This is another means of absolutizing the transcendental, this time by making it produce the empirical. For Hegel, reason asserts itself as "the auto-generation of progeny": form posits content, but only in order to identify itself with this content, thus negating it in the very act of positing it. Hence, the notion of determination as negation is denied, and dualism is obliterated. By contrast, for Husserl—the Husserl of Fink—form posits content outside itself, ensuring dualism. In both instances, the absolutization of the transcendental leads to the "unthinkable." For Kantian notions are in fact at stake here—notions that are both refined and justified. In one case, Kant is retained at the price of becoming a Hegelian; in the other, he is kept by becoming a Husserlian. In both instances, the character of transcendental reflection is in question, because it poses the double problem of the nature of the subject and of the relation of the subject to the object.

Should we then interpret Kant differently, refuse to "return to the ground," and renounce the effort to purify the transcendental—an effort ending in its absolutization and in the disqualification of the human subject? How can the notion of the *a priori* be developed in another direction? Our problem is the following: can we comprehend the notion of the *a priori* in its transcendental function—that is, in its relation with the *a posteriori*—without assigning it exclusively to subjectivity (and thus avoid the pitfalls of constitution), yet without radically identifying *a priori* and *a posteriori* (and thus escape the snares of dialectical identity)? And if we can clear a path for ourselves between these two traps, what role should we assign the human subject in relation to the *a priori*? How will the transcendental and psychological elements be related in this subject? Shall we be forced to accept for the subject a monism that we refuse outside him, and will there be some way to understand the psychological as determined by the transcendental, instead of as producing and reducing it? In other words, will it be possible to interpret the psychological as itself *a priori*—as an existential *a priori*—and as psychologically, not biologically, constitutive, so that constitution can acquire a new meaning, or rediscover its original one?

Part I
The Objective *A Priori*

1 / Why the "*A Priori*"?

BEFORE RESUMING our analysis of the *a priori*, perhaps we should pose a more basic question: why should we continue to use the term "*a priori*"? Why maintain this notion in a context different from that in which it has traditionally been elaborated? It is easy to see that in defining the *a priori* as the mediating factor in the fundamental and prerequisite accord of man and the world we risk alienating ourselves from Kant on at least two points. In the first place, we shall speak more readily of man than of the subject, since we will be trying to give a concrete nature to the subject instead of considering him as the impersonal correlate of pure knowledge, or as the abstract unity of a system of syntheses; at the same time, we shall refuse to grant this subject the power to constitute the object in the fashion of a transcendental demiurge. We shall diverge from Kant in a second way because, instead of conceiving the *a priori* as a universal condition of objectivity imposed by an objectifying subject on a sensible manifold, we shall consider it as a structure immanent in the object and apprehended during the very act of perception, although known implicitly or virtually before perception occurs. We shall distinguish between a subjective and an objective aspect within the same *a priori*. In our opinion, the main reason for retaining the notion of the *a priori* is found in the fact that there is an accord of man and the world which is realized in knowledge (and in work, though work is founded on knowledge); this accord manifests itself less as a power of man over the world—or, from a naturalistic perspective, as a power of the world over man—than as familiarity, the consubstantiality of man and world. For knowledge is possible only if the world is open to man and vice versa: the *a priori* expresses this reciprocal openness. The *a priori* is the

[45]

meaning present and given in both object and subject, and it assures their communication while maintaining their difference. Yet is it unique in assuming this role? Might not knowledge dispense with it?

Here lies the heart of the difficulty. As a result of protesting against the idealistic interpretations of Kant, we risk falling back into a pre-Kantian position: empiricism. For we are obliged to say that the *a priori* is given in experience, rather than imposed by the mind on experience. The mind's activity is limited to recognizing the *a priori*, to assuming and enlarging this meaning to which the mind is attuned before all experience; yet the mind does not know that it is linked with this meaning until experience presents it. It is already apparent that such a proximity of the *a priori* and *a posteriori* in experience is going to make precise discernment of the *a priori* quite difficult. The following questions are always conjoined: why the *a priori*? and what is its exact scope? Our means of arriving at an answer to the second question will not be perfectly clear and decisive. For if the *a priori* is itself material and can be isolated only in experience, unlike Kant we shall not be able to invoke formal criteria to define it. And it will be difficult to distinguish it not only from the *a posteriori*, but also from the general idea, to the extent that the general idea is rooted in perception and results—at least in its elementary form—from an immediate essentialization. Insofar as this conception of the *a priori* invites us to extend its domain—i.e., if the *a priori* is indeed a meaningful objective structure given in perception—we are not constrained to restrict it to the formal conditions of objectivity. As a presupposition from now on, we shall say that values, affective qualities, and mythical meanings—understood as categories of feeling and imagination—are just as much *a priori* as forms of sensibility or categories of the understanding (including in these latter the *a priori* belonging to what Husserl calls material regions, e.g., the *a priori* of life or intersubjectivity). But if we may postpone our full answer to the second question, we must immediately begin to respond to the first: why the *a priori*? To answer this requires a defense of our recourse to the *a priori* against empiricism, not by condemning empiricism but by expanding it into an empiricism of the transcendental.

Why not simply cast in one's lot with empiricism? This doctrine proposes a very simple solution to our problems by rejecting the notion of the *a priori* altogether. According to empiricism, experience provides objects for knowledge—thereby instructing us—and it lets us learn and increase our knowledge: to experience something is to be continually learning about it. Thus, all knowledge that we consider *a priori* is in fact a posteriori. Moreover, knowledge can itself be an object of experience: theoretically at least, one could write a history of its progress and assign empirical, psychological, or cultural conditions to its development. At this point empiricism can easily turn into positivism, psychologism, or sociologism. Consequently, the *a priori* is in a certain sense rejected twice: the empiricist theory of knowledge makes experience the sole authentic source of knowledge; and the psychology and sociology of experience, representing the experience of experience—i.e., an experimental study of experience as receptivity and as a learning process—reveal the mechanisms of formalizing thought and denounce the *a priori* as an illusion. Experience is twice invoked, both to replace and to deny the *a priori*.

It is true that empiricism and positivism are not necessarily related. It is also true that their respective conceptions of experience are not necessarily linked—empiricism defining experience as receptive, positivism considering it as determined and possessing a determinate history. But the combination of these two conceptions is noteworthy because it signifies that experience is self-sufficient. One could guess that the second conception will give rise to our main doubts. Yet we can and must grant to empiricism all the considerable truth it possesses.

Thus we have to admit, as Kant did, that all knowledge begins with experience. In doing this we stress the fact that perception teaches us something and that it is irreplaceable in this function: the person born blind will never know what a color is; he is able to know many things about color—for example, optical theory—but he will never experience color, and the word "color" will never have the same connotation for him as for those who have sight. Even if he cannot become a painter, he may become a physicist; this possibility raises the question as to how necessary perception is for science: is the immediate grasp of the sensible really knowledge? We shall return to this problem; it is significant that empiricism asks itself such a question. For the present, let us recognize that sensible intuition is irreplaceable: through it, the first contact is established between subject and object, even if this relation does not yet involve truth; nothing can replace the plenitude of sensible evidence in the here and now—however precarious or ephemeral it may be in Hegel's opinion. But we must go further, perhaps even further than empiricism itself: experience is not only the beginning of knowledge, but also its end [*fin*], and the *a posteriori* is the terminus [*fin*] for the *a priori*.[1] As we shall contend, the *a priori* is not only the formal condition of experience, or the structure of objectivity; it is a meaning given by experience. Therefore, it is not merely *for* experience, it is *in* experience, always mixed in with the *a posteriori;* for it is presented by experience, which awakens in us what we shall call subjective *a priori* knowledge—a knowledge that is independent of experience.

Yet we must concede this much to empiricism: although subjective *a priori* knowledge is independent of experience in principle, it is not wholly so in fact. Not only does the *a priori* appear in [*sur*] [2] the *a posteriori*, but our awareness of its appearance and our very clarification of it also depend on empirical circumstances. Thales and Greece were both required for the emergence of geometry. Several distinctions must be drawn at this point— and first of all within the *a priori* itself, according to whether it is conceived in its native state as the immediate but confused knowledge of a meaning, or in its explicit state, elaborated by reflection and sometimes developed into a pure science. Spatiality, for example, may be considered from the viewpoint of a natural or of a Euclidean geometry.[3] Further distinctions occur between the *a priori* themselves, for some *a priori* are more universal than others. Everyone possesses a certain natural geometry, but not everyone is capable of grasping the sense of the tragic, a mythical form, or a moral value; that is, not everyone can recognize the presence of certain *a priori*, and correlate the objective and subjective aspects of a given *a priori*. It is true that the recognition of the objective *a priori* [4] must always depend on a condition which is itself transcendental: the presence of the subjective *a priori* in the subject—i.e., the transcendental nature of the subject (which we shall term the subject's existential *a priori*). Yet it is necessary to say that even the transcendental depends on the empirical and especially on the psychological, at least to be put into practice. For

1. The French word *fin* can mean either end or aim—a dual meaning possessed to a lesser extent by the English word "terminus."—Trans.

2. Literally, *sur* means "on," but I shall usually translate it by "in" as this sounds less barbaric in English and yet retains the author's basic view of the relation between *a priori* and *a posteriori*.—Trans.

3. Dufrenne refers here to Malebranche's notion of a "natural geometry."— Trans.

4. The terms "objective *a priori*" and "subjective *a priori*" are abbreviations for objective and subjective *aspects* of the particular *a priori* under discussion. These shortened expressions will be retained throughout the book.—Trans.

there are negative conditions determining the apprehension of the *a priori:* faulty perception, inattention, and non-sense tend to conceal the *a priori* from me. Of course positive conditions also exist; education, habits, and environment can improve my perception, as well as my reflection on what I have perceived, that is, my clarification of the *a priori:* Greece formed Thales.

Nevertheless, we say "conditions" and not "causes"; empiricism can explain the action or development of the transcendental when the transcendental is presupposed. Yet is it necessary to go further and admit that empiricism can explain even the acquisition of the transcendental? We might be tempted to grant this when we attempt to understand the possibility of radical changes in someone's pattern of life—i.e., the possibility of abrupt mutations in his existential *a priori;* but if such changes do occur, perhaps we should attribute them to freedom and cease trying to explain them entirely in terms of empirical causes. In this way, freedom preserves the purity of the transcendental. For by granting that the genesis of the subjective *a priori* is explicable by an empirical causality, we reduce it to illusion: here we must maintain our position against psychological or sociological positivism. And this is not easy because, just as the *a priori* and *a posteriori* are closely connected objectively, so the transcendental and the psychological are bound together subjectively. We shall even insist on this proximity, for the concrete subject is given proper justice on this basis. Yet this justice will be accorded by raising the psychological to the transcendental, not by reducing the transcendental to the psychological.

Meanwhile, we must maintain the distinctions drawn above and thus keep our distance from empiricism and positivism. This will be done first by affirming that perception has a meaning and then by contending that this meaning requires an *a priori.* Let us examine the first point. If sensible content is completely separated from meaning, and if this content is interpreted as a pure given, how can we look for the truth of such a content or make it the criterion of truth? We do not ask that thought be its own content —as it is in the Hegelian logic, where "the formal possesses a content conforming to its form" [5]—because even this content would be formal. But should we not recognize that we are "in" the truth and that form must be given as immanent in content? It is significant that empiricism, insisting on the autonomy of content,

5. Cited by Jean Hyppolite in his *Logique et existence* (Paris, Presses Universitaires de France, 1953), p. 212.

is always tempted by phenomenalism—as Hume, for example, is by atomism—and that, starting from the idea that the norm for knowledge is experience, it concludes by denying that experience is knowledge. The irreplaceable given here is meaningless, and it is difficult to see how it can either suggest or verify meaning. Carnap's notion of experiences that are immediately given without a subject and Schlick's "confirmations" (*Konstatierungen*) are close cousins of Hume's "impressions." For Schlick, confirmations are "absolutely valid," and just as valid as tautologies, but they have the advantage that "while an analytic, tautological statement is empty of content, an observation statement supplies us with the satisfaction of genuine knowledge of reality." [6] Schlick recognizes, however, that any confirmations in the form of "red patch here now" must be expressed by a designative gesture, for the "here now" loses its meaning as soon as pronounced or written. The content here is radically alienated from the form which would give it a meaning, and this is why empiricism, dialectically identifying contraries without meaning to do so, is tempted toward the other extreme of a pure formalism. To avoid the metaphysical problem created by an adequation of knowledge and the object of knowledge, Neurath affirms against Schlick that even direct statements of observations cannot be compared with the objects they describe and that their truth depends not on their agreement with objects observed, but on their accord with the truth of all observation statements accepted at a given moment. "The effort to attain a knowledge of fact is reduced to the effort to put scientific statements in accord with the greatest possible number of protocol statements" [7]—i.e., observation statements that cannot be dismissed, even if a privileged status is given to their syntactical character. Yet in the end Neurath, like Hume, is forced to have recourse to "common life" in order to distinguish fairy tales from knowledge of the real: the wager represented by formalism cannot be maintained indefinitely.

As against these desperate solutions, it seems to us imperative to realize that perception has the character of synthetic thought—i.e., of knowledge [*connaissance*]. What kind of knowledge? Schlick, in modifying Russell's distinction between knowledge by

6. Moritz Schlick, "Uber das Fundament der Erkenntnis," *Erkenntnis*, IV (1934), 97. [English translation by David Rynin, "The Foundation of Knowledge," in *Logical Positivism*, ed. A. J. Ayer (Glencoe, The Free Press, 1960), p. 225. For Carnap's point of view, see the article, "Psychology in Physical Language," *ibid.*, pp. 165–98.—Trans.]

7. Otto Neurath, "Radikaler Physikalismus und 'Wirkliche Welt,'" *Erkenntnis*, IV (1934), 356.

acquaintance and knowledge by description, terms it acquaintance as opposed to knowledge or *Erlebnis* in contrast to *Erkenntnis* [8]—a distinction that Hospers uses to pit science against art.[9] In accordance with this distinction, authentic knowledge is always knowledge *about,* and the knowledge *of* X is always a knowledge *that* X is Y; whereas perception is consciousness or immediate awareness, not knowledge. It seems to us, however, that Gestalt psychology corrects this phenomenalism by showing that perception is already knowledge—not knowledge *about* but knowledge *in:* the object presents itself to me as meaningful. It offers itself as an object detached from me and open to others; as objective, singular, and identifiable, it contains a certain structure (a universal, as Hegel would say) permitting us to know, recognize, and name it. Certainly my perception is not naive and passive; it awakens images or even previous knowledge, bringing judgments into play as well as a spontaneous essentialization which is as much the act of the body as of thought. Phenomenology is concerned with the elucidation of this imbroglio. It could always be said that the meaning thus elaborated, though discerned *in* the object, is still *about* the object. But it seems to us that the synthesis of intuition and concept is not simply the effect of a conceptualizing activity; in fact, we are authorized to speak of an *a priori* by the immediate presence of a meaning. However difficult it is to distinguish it from merely empirical meaning—and this is made all the more difficult since the *a priori* itself appears as multiple as soon as it is isolated—the *a priori* is the structure constituting the object as object: its unity, its spatiality, its temporality, its inert or animated character, and, in certain cases, its expression, affective quality, or imaginary aura. Perception is immediately meaningful because the *a priori* is given in it, as Gestalt psychology suggests. Empiricism would be true if it were an empiricism of the transcendental.

From this emerges our second point of disagreement with empiricism. In order to create knowledge from impressions which are not themselves knowledge, one is obliged to invoke an intellectual activity immanent in all perception: empiricism is more intellectualistic than intellectualism. Schlick, for example, shows that the proposition "this is blue" implies an intellectual act of comparison

8. Is it not contradictory, after speaking of observation as "substantiation," to say that "*Erlebnis* is neither the highest nor the lowest degree of knowledge, but the undescribable given preceding all the rest"? (Schlick, *Gesammelte Aufsätze* [Vienna, Gerold, 1938], p. 193.)

9. John Hospers, *Meaning and Truth in the Arts* (Chapel Hill, University of North Carolina Press, 1946), p. 233.

or association. We should also recall here the role Locke [10] gives to the human understanding, or Hume gives to the imagination.[11] Now it is precisely this activity which we must limit: it is not the only agency responsible for the meaning that perception garners. The subject is not a *tabula rasa* onto which sensible qualities come to imprint themselves or (as Hume thought) in which impressions encounter one another and execute the laws of association and feeling. We shall merely say that the subject sees because he possesses his own eyes. Perception is oriented not only by man's corporeal organization, but also—to the extent that the body orients him toward the world—by his opening onto the world, and by his aptitude for apprehending meaning. Thus perception implies an *a priori* definable, insofar as existential, in terms of the ability of the subject to apprehend meaning and hence to attain accord with the world: this *a priori* designates the structure of an incarnated consciousness, a body which is not only thing, but consciousness.

As we have suggested above, this means that though experience always teaches us something, knowledge is not entirely a matter of learning: something is always previously known or presupposed. There is no total genesis of meaning, and the *a priori* is precisely that which has no genesis. Perhaps it is not necessary to operate the Husserlian reduction in order to pass from the empirical to the transcendental, for although the reduction neutralizes the empirical by suspending the natural attitude, it does not uncover a new domain. This return to the origin is a return to the transcendental: we are here present at the upsurge of a meaning contemporaneous with the advent of consciousness. We shall not contend however, as Husserl does, that transcendental subjectivity is the constitutive *a priori* itself; instead, we prefer to say that the subject possesses various *a priori*. For Husserl every

10. It is true that Locke imputes error—i.e., confusion—to words more than to the understanding: "I charge this rather upon our words than understandings" (*An Essay Concerning Human Understanding*, ed. Fraser [Oxford, Clarendon Press, 1894], II, 118). But words are *institutio hominis*, as the nominalists said, and nominal essences are—the phrase is repeated many times—"the workmanship of the understanding." The same initiative of the understanding forms ideas and forges words, as when Adam called Zahab a gold ingot; for "between the nominal essence (which is nothing more than the abstract essence) and the name there is a narrow and constitutive connection" (*ibid.*, p. 27).

11. Of course one must not understand the imagination here in the sense that Hegel gave to it in commenting on Kant; rather, it is the instrument of an unconscious and passive activity, since the principles of human nature operate before the subject is constituted—in this, Hume is even more profoundly empiricistic. The activity of the understanding is the natural prolongation and correction of this subliminal activity.

intentional act (and every essence, as we shall see) risks becoming *a priori* because the *a priori* resides principally in the operation of consciousness: the whole psychological realm is transcendentalized. Yet a more distinct line can be traced between the *a priori* and *a posteriori,* and the idealism involved in the notion of constitution can be avoided by defining the *a priori* as the immediate for which there is no empirical genesis or learning process; here the *a priori* is the pre-predicative evidence presupposed by all other evidence. Even when it appears after an act of perception has taken place, the *a priori* appears to me in its immediacy: in the same way that something assumes form in Gestaltist experiments. The immediacy of the *a priori* is as inexhaustible as the object for which it is the meaning, but it always presents itself— every time it is given to me in a new perception—as immediate. This immediacy is not that belonging to perception—i.e., the immediacy of the ever new, ever refreshing contact that I enjoy with the sensible, even when this contact is mediated by habit and knowledge. It is rather the immediacy of a meaning, of an evidence and not of a contact, because the *a priori* is revealed as a necessary structure of the object perceived: an immediacy already logical, not psychological. And this immediacy implies that I previously possess an immediate comprehension of the *a priori.* The actualization and elucidation of the *a priori* are linked to empirical conditions, but its virtual presence in the subject is not confined in this way. The immediacy of knowledge—or rather, the immediacy of our recognition of the *a priori*—implies this virtuality. The immediacy of the experience of the *a priori* in its objective aspect means that in its subjective aspect it is independent of experience, and consequently immediate also: we shall be obliged to connect the immediacy of meaning with the immediacy of the aptitude for comprehending meaning.

In other words, just as there is no total genesis of the apprehension of the objective *a priori,* so there is no total genesis of the subject as possessor of the subjective *a priori.* We must refuse the reduction of logic to chronology. Empiricism seeks to explain what is pre-historical by an historical account; it does not allow an absolute beginning, either in perception or in the subject, in the order of knowledge or in the order of being; therefore, it is doomed to recounting a history with no real beginning. Evidently—and this is the same problem that we encounter in the case of freedom —this beginning is situated in history; but in order to comprehend it, history must be left behind. Of course we cannot escape time, but the *a priori* is temporal like something not explicable in terms of time. Consciousness is thoroughly temporal, yet in such a way that time also dwells within it. Consciousness is consciousness *of* time, not just consciousness *in* time.

Does this aid us in understanding that the subject, being the possessor of the *a priori*, may be seen as an absolute beginning? Can we now envisage each act of the subject, each actualization of the *a priori* in a perception, and consequently each perception insofar as it is an apprehension of a meaning, as a starting point *for* knowledge and *of* knowledge? Yes, for meaning escapes time, as Spinoza profoundly understood: one cannot speak of meaning in terms of time. Even if the apprehension of meaning takes place in time, it cannot be explained as a temporal process. The possibility of immediately grasping a meaning in experience invites us to understand the subject as immediately constituted, as transcendentally contemporaneous with the world because in accord with the world. The subject possesses a transcendental nature. Empiricism is correct in affirming that only the individual exists, but it risks finally dissolving individuality into empirical determinations. Yet can the transcendental be made into an individuating principle? Perhaps—if we conceive of individuality as singularity, the unity of universal and particular. The universal involved here is not an abstract universal or a system of logical conditions; and it is not easier to distinguish it from the individual than it is to disentangle the *a priori* from the *a posteriori*. Even in its logical form, the *a priori* does not belong to a separate understanding which puts it into action; the *a priori* constitutes the very nature of the subject. If this is indeed the case, we shall be obliged to make a dangerous *rapprochement* between the psychological and transcendental realms which we have just attempted to disjoin; but we shall have to interpret the psychological as transcendental without neutralizing the transcendental in the psychological. Just as there is an immediacy of comprehension, there is an immediacy of the subject; the subject is himself a beginning insofar as he is capable of a knowledge which is a starting point and insofar as he can comprehend the meaning which springs up before him. This human beginning, however, is also situated in history: birth is a bivalent event which confers a nature on the subject, yet also invests him with the dignity of the transcendental. For this event is an advent: to come into the world is to be capable of the world. Genetic theories cannot affect this absolute genesis: one can write a history of consciousness or life, but it is always consciousness which explores and examines animal and vegetable behavior.

Consciousness writes its own history, though it considers itself the product of this history.

What consciousness, if not that of the conscious subject? Empiricists (with the possible exception of Hume) cannot explain the subject's genesis except by transcendentalizing the psychological. This is why they usually end by recourse to something unengenderable, borrowing from idealism the notion of a transcendental consciousness under the guise of "understanding," "imagination," or "principle of human nature." Thus they can invoke a formalizing activity and, like logical positivists, justify a formal logic. But the thought which says "I" is a self too. It is a thinking nature; the transcendental subject is a subject only when it is concrete. There is no incarnation as such; there are only incarnated subjects: you and me, "O flesh!" as Descartes said to Gassendi. Yet Descartes would also suggest that the body of man is not comparable to that of an animal: this is another way of saying that in the complete singular substance, in a person, nature and mind are one. And the person is the truly unengenderable being.

Therefore, it is clear that if we maintain the notion of the *a priori*, we do not do so in order to denounce empiricism, but to respect more than it does the privileged aspects of experience: to account for the fact that experience presents meanings immediately and that these meanings are accessible to a concrete subject. Moreover, empiricism does not exclude the notion of the *a priori*; we only dispute the conception of it proposed by empiricism and by a certain kind of idealism. This is why our first task will be to delogicize the *a priori*, putting its feet back on the earth; we shall discover that it is immanent in experience when objective, and borne by the concrete subject when subjective.

2 / The *A Priori* as Formal

THE OBJECTIVE *a priori* is the meaning which exists in the object and with which the subject is in primordial accord: it is formative without being formal and without being impressed from the outside on a content as if it were the seal of logic being put onto an empirical matter. A certain amount of time was needed, however, for the idea of a material *a priori* to dawn on phenomenology—an idea which is not, as we shall see, without ambiguity and which may well seem startling. For the idea of a formal *a priori* recommends itself by the priority it grants to logic, and above all by the logical character it confers on the *a priori* itself. This is clearly seen in the writings of Husserl, where a proliferation of the *a priori* corresponds to the desire to discover the path of an authentic science. But the same thing is evident even in Kant, for whom the *a priori* is defined by strictly logical criteria.

These criteria are the necessity and universality which may characterize a proposition. When he introduces these factors, Kant relates them to judgment: "If we have a proposition which in being thought is thought as necessary, it is an *a priori* judgment." [1] It is true that later on he speaks of the universality and necessity of the concept (when dealing with the concept of cause) as well as "other pure *a priori* representations—for instance, space and time." [2] But the pure concepts of understanding or the pure forms of sensibility must be made explicit in propositions— i.e., in principles of the pure understanding or in mathematical theorems. These propositions may be necessary and universal: as

1. Kant, *Critique of Pure Reason*, trans. Norman Kemp Smith (London, Macmillan, 1933), p. 43 (B 3).
2. *Ibid.*, p. 223 (A 196).

are synthetic *a priori* judgments, which attest to "a special source of knowledge, namely, a faculty of *a priori* knowledge." [3] Even when the field of the *a priori* is extended to ethics or aesthetics, it will always be expressed in *a priori* judgments and referred to logical criteria. This is not without consequences. First, one comes to recognize only formal *a priori*—the only *a priori* meeting the Kantian criteria—and as a result undue limits are placed upon the field of the *a priori*. Then, having assigned these *a priori* to a constituting subject, itself formal, one is led to the idea of constitution. Therefore, if we seek to establish on the one hand that the *a priori* is not always formal and on the other hand that the formal is not always *a priori*, we must consider these criteria carefully and question their exclusively logical signification.

Kant himself can aid us in this task, first of all by suggesting how the province of the *a priori* may be extended beyond the formal domain. It is undeniable, however, that he never conceived of a material *a priori*. Scheler reproaches him for this: "The identification of the *a priori* with the formal is the fundamental error of Kant." [4] Similarly, Husserl regrets that "Kant lacked a phenomenologically correct conception of the *a priori*." [5] In order to justify the idea of a material *a priori*, we must first establish the diversity of the *a priori*; we shall try to show that the *a priori*'s variety forces us to relax Kant's criteria. Yet we shall remain faithful to the Introduction of the *Critique of Pure Reason* by defining the *a priori* as knowledge [*connaissance*] (thus giving it a positive content) and as rule or principle (hence restricting it to a formal being without presupposing as Hegel did that form can engender content). Moreover, Kant provides us with a first example of the possible diversity of the *a priori*. In assigning several sources to it, especially that of sensibility, he prevents himself from totally logicizing it. When the formal *a priori* designates the forms of sensibility, a logical formalism is no longer implied. Furthermore, one could show with respect to these forms—more easily than in the case of categories of the understanding (although this would not be impossible)—that though they are *a priori* they do not proceed from the subjective nature of the subject. Spatialization and temporalization, which are certainly acts of the subject, are only a response to a space and a time originally and previously

3. *Ibid.*, p. 44 (B 4).
4. Max Scheler, *Der Formalismus in der Ethik und die materiale Wertethik* (Bern, Francke, 1954), p. 74. (Hereafter I shall refer to this work as *Der Formalismus.*—Trans.)
5. Husserl, *Logische Untersuchungen* (Halle, Niemeyer, 1913), II, 203.

given; they are constitutive with respect to phenomena. Yet because "the understanding determines the sensibility," [6] Kant contrasts the form of intuition which "gives only a manifold" with the formal intuition which "gives unity of representation." Here the formalist signification of the formal is restored at the expense of the irreducible originality of intuition. As Tran Duc Tao says, the result is "to suppress the autonomy of the Aesthetic and to absorb all objective meaning into the logical conditions for knowledge." [7] In any case, the *a priori* character of the original [*originaire*] space and time given in intuition is compromised by measuring this character in terms of the logical quality of the propositions delineating space and time—not in terms of the original [*originaire*] quality of the objects of these propositions. At the same time, a privileged position is given to the *a priori* of the understanding for which this delineation is a matter of course.[8]

6. *Critique*, pp. 170–71, note a. The same reference is the source of the other two quotations in this sentence.—Trans.

7. Tran Duc Tao, *Phénoménologie et matérialisme dialectique* (Paris, Editions Minh-Tan, 1951), p. 110.

8. At one point in his career Heidegger wanted to resuscitate the transcendental Aesthetic. But in this effort he compromised the *a priori* rather than restoring its diversity. Instead of favoring the understanding, he affirmed the essential unity of intuition and concept which characterizes finite knowledge and is manifested in the truth-giving synthesis. Yet he finally assigned to the understanding what really belongs to sensibility: "The fundamental act of the understanding . . . is the *Gegenstehenlassen*" ("objectification"); (see *Kant and the Problem of Metaphysics*, trans. James S. Churchill [Bloomington, Indiana University Press, 1962], p. 78). Now, *Gegenstehenlassen* is the act of turning oneself "towards" in order to encounter something. It is true that that "towards which (*Woraufzu*) we turn . . . can no longer be intuited by us in the form of empirical intuition" (*ibid.*, p. 126); the *Woraufzu* is the transcendental object = x, which must be distinguished from the thing in itself as the horizon of transcendence. But this consciousness of horizon does not bring the understanding into play to a greater extent: the concepts of understanding have a more specific meaning; instead of representing totality, they determine it. Moreover, Heidegger attributed the opening of this horizon to the transcendental imagination. By this move, however, we are unable to discover the specific *a priori* of the imagination, and we lose sight of the *a priori* of the understanding as well. The subordination of concept to intuition in the phenomenology of the *Gegenstehenlassen* ends by discovering nothingness [*le néant*] as the foil for Being: "It is only when the *Gegenstehenlassen* . . . consists in holding oneself in nothingness, that an act of representation occurring within this nothingness can encounter, instead of nothingness itself, something that is not nothing—that is, something like a being" (*ibid.*, p. 76). This is not without importance: Heidegger was so intent upon maintaining the finitude of a knowledge [*connaissance*] subordinated to the receptivity of intuition that the only initiative on the part of subjectivity appeared to him to be the act of holding oneself in nothingness as in a clearing where something (whether Being or a being) can appear. This Heideggerian humility is, however, as fatal to the *a priori* as is Hegelian presumptuousness. For the *a priori* itself, inasmuch as it is part of man, is nothing but nothingness; or, if you like, the empty horizon of objectivity is nothing but the expectation of the object, not a

A second means of delogicizing the *a priori* consists in discussing each of the criteria Kant gives for it individually. Perhaps these criteria would lose their authority if one ceased to consider the *a priori* in its elaborated state, set forth as an element of pure knowledge. In fact, the *a priori* is termed formal not only because it is limited to expressing the form of discourse—a purely logical demand—but also because we are aware of the form in which it is expressed, considering it as the source of universally valid propositions. Thus, Scheler makes the *a priori* the object of an immediate intuition which guarantees its validity. We must, however, resist this temptation to locate the *a priori* in its form—a temptation which leads to defining it *as* a form. In this fashion, the *a priori* is made into a logical character of propositions—and finally, as with Schlick, of analytic propositions alone. This is because it is first logicized in order to be made explicit, and because what is said becomes less important than the way in which it is said. Once again, content is neglected in favor of form, and the form is made the only criterion of the *a priori*. If this criterion is contested, however, our attention will be led back to the content.

The first precaution to be taken against the formalizing tendency should be to consider the *a priori* in its native state: not as it appears when elaborated by reflection—this only renders it explicit and exploits it—but as it appears immediately in perception, forming in us a primordial knowledge [*savoir*] which organizes perception without stemming from it (though the *a priori* is reactivated by perception). As examples, we might invoke here the experience of spatiality which we have before we learn geometry, or of plurality before knowing the theory of number, or of the tragic before developing a pure aesthetics as a theory of affective qualities, or of domination before having a pure sociology of intersubjectivity, or of myth before elaborating a theory of archetypes. The *a priori* would then be seen as the immediate meaning grasped in experience and instantly recognized. Its criteria will be developed throughout this book: the *a priori* constitutes the object as meaningful, and it lies in our pre-given comprehension of the meaning given in the object; it assures both the objectivity of the object and the objectivity of knowledge. Yet this knowledge [*connaissance*] is above all a recognition [*reconnaissance*], similar to the feeling of familiarity; it need not be universal and necessary.

---

rule for the object, or even an anticipated structure of the object. The *a priori* designates the way in which finite being encounters the real, which cannot be met with empty hands. Yet, in seeking to return to the ground of the transcendental, the transcendental itself has been lost.

Or rather, universality and necessity undergo a change in meaning, designating the objectivity of an object, not the absolute validity of a proposition. According to the latter meaning, $7 + 5 = 12$ can be considered an analytical judgment—as logical positivism holds—and mathematics can be reduced to logic. But here the *a priori* loses both its meaning and its content; it possesses only the quality of a tautology. In fact, if $7 + 5 = 12$ is a synthetic *a priori* judgment, it is because 12 is a new personage in the series of numbers; the proposition tells me something about the world as spatial and peopled with objects. It tells me this because I am supported by a primordial, pre-empirical experience of space and quantity, thanks to which I can "construct" in space and "manipulate" numbers.

In any case, coming back to the Kantian criteria, it is important to distinguish between the logical necessity and universality of propositions—e.g., of a sequence of mathematical concepts constructed on the basis of pure intuition—and the necessity and universality of the *a priori* itself. But we must first of all distinguish the physical necessity found in nature from the intellectual necessity residing in *logos*—that is, distinguish the avalanche which crushes me from the idea which imposes itself on me, or (in other terms) constraint from obligation. Necessity can be the material constraint imposed on an object by another object (e.g., the necessity that water boil when sufficiently heated) or by its own nature, more or less in concurrence with the action of exterior causes (e.g., the necessity for a certain kind of bud to become the same kind of flower)—a constraint which can also be exercised on myself insofar as I am a thing among things. Or it can be the obligation in which I, as a subject, must subscribe to certain kinds of evidence: be it the evidence for a principle such that in adhering to this principle my intelligence is properly autonomous —since my intelligence ratifies a law which is its own law and thus is in harmony with itself—or be it the evidence for an idea which itself expresses or explicates physical necessity. In any event, the necessity of evidence must be distinguished from the necessity of constraint.

These notions must be refined in order to introduce a new distinction: that between physical necessity and the thought of this necessity. This thought can consider the necessity of fact in two ways. First, when it is situated in the order of modality and when the "not-being of something can be thought," [9] the necessity

---

9. *Critique*, p. 254 (B 290). I have changed the word order here.—Trans.

of fact appears as contingent and consequently unjustified. This kind of factual necessity is always opposed to the logical necessity which regulates the connection of ideas and which is justified and rendered justifying by its own rationality, since it is by virtue of logical necessity that reasoning is correct. But, secondly, when the thought of physical necessity conceives contingency by "recourse to alterations, and not merely to the possibility of entertaining the opposite in thought," it defines contingency in terms of "the fact that something can exist only as the effect of a cause," [10] and thus as identical with the necessity affirmed by determinism. This thought introduces an order into succession; it converts brute necessity into intelligible necessity. Or rather, it permits us to grasp and to comprehend brute necessity by expressing it in an empirical law, without justifying it and converting it into logical necessity, and without producing it by creating the event. In brief, the fact that an avalanche is descending upon me is contingent only when seen as unjustifiable—therefore, as a fact opposed to law. Yet it is explicable by causality, just as a fact may be understood by an idea, though remaining distinct from this idea.

We are thus led to discern two aspects of intellectual necessity, according to whether it reflects upon itself or thinks about factual necessity. When I form an idea of an avalanche, including its causes and effects, it is no longer a question of logical or formal necessity (as when I term necessary that whose contrary implies contradiction, and when I am compelled to be faithful to principles imposed upon me or to the definitions which I posit concerning the formal reality of the idea). Rather, it is a question of the very form or essence of things and their relations, beyond the brute and still contingent necessity of fact. I must be faithful to the objective reality of the idea insofar as the idea is true—i.e., insofar as it says that which is. Truth constrains me, but in such a manner that I can evade it because the evidence does not proceed from myself. Necessity here no longer expresses a demand of logical rigor; it expresses the being of the universe: a necessity of essence which grounds in reason the existence of the thing or the upsurge of the event. This necessity can be called "material"—as opposed to purely formal necessity—although material necessity is not a mere recording of physical necessity. It appears when I say: this is the essence of . . . (e.g., of space: to be three-dimensional; of body: to be extended; of man: to think). In the case of logical necessity, universality follows from necessity—because thought must be faithful to itself and because the denial of a

10. *Ibid.*

necessary proposition is self-contradictory. Material necessity, however, follows from universality, insofar as universality is understood as a structure of the universe and insofar as it is the universe which constrains thought.

Now, it seems to me that the *a priori* possesses material necessity. When I speak of the necessity of space and time, for example, I refer to the necessity of something present and irrecusably given. Space and time impose themselves as features of the universe, just as the moral law according to Kant imposes itself not only as a formal demand of reason, but also as the cement of a universe of consciousnesses; and the affective *a priori* or the *a priori* of imagination impose themselves in much the same way as possible structures of a world. The *a priori* possesses a material necessity by which the universe is revealed and through which physical necessity is perceived. Formal necessity, on the contrary, belongs to synthetic *a priori* judgments insofar as they are judgments, but not insofar as they are *a priori;* it characterizes their form and not their content. The *a priori* itself, if it is a form, is a form of the universe and not of thought; it is not a rule *of* thought, but a rule *for* thought because it is imposed by the universe. Yet are we not saying then that the *a priori* is transcendental only if it is also transcendent, in the phenomenological sense of this word? [11] We should not be too hasty here, however: if the *a priori* is given as transcendent to consciousness, it is given as an essence, not as a thing, and the necessity it manifests is a necessity of essence.

But again, to justify the refusal of formalism we must consider the other aspect of the criteria of the *a priori;* this is the extension of the necessity and universality with which the *a priori* is imposed upon me. These two criteria have an anthropological meaning; and we have the right to confront this meaning with their logical signification, for the idea of the universe is meaningful only when a human community is realized in which theory and practice are united.[12] What is imposed on the mind—on every human mind—is the necessary; the universal is that which is so universally admitted that we cannot think otherwise: logical criteria must be corroborated by cultural reality. But purely logical necessity does not need this confirmation because it presupposes it. The mind whose assent it solicits is an impersonal mind, a

11. This is the sense in which objects intended by consciousness transcend the intentional act.—Trans.

12. See Lucien Goldmann, *La Communauté humaine et l'univers chez Kant* (Paris, Presses Universitaires de France, 1948), p. 130.

general thinking nature which, like the Cartesian *cogito,* is taken to be identical in all minds. As a result, whatever is true for one is immediately true for all, without the historical test of a consensus being required. Similarly, universality has two immediate meanings: it excludes both exception and opposition; both the contrary example and the denial of a universal proposition are dismissed. This is not, however, true for empirical necessity: just as it includes contingency, this kind of necessity allows for failure of recognition. More exactly, since it must be recognized by subjects capable of testing it, it must prove its truth by appealing to such subjects. Only in this way can an empirical law be admitted into the scientific community, and even then it is never assured of remaining uncontested.

Now, it is quite possible that certain *a priori* are imposed only with reservations and sometimes without gaining unanimity. For example, if one admits that aesthetic values or categories are *a priori,* one must also admit that these *a priori* are not universally recognized and that their appearance is historically bound. This will oblige us to say that these *a priori* are structures of a world— not the universe or regions of the universe—and at the same time to acknowledge an irreducible diversity of concrete subjects insofar as they are open only to certain *a priori.* Yet does common assent to the rules of formal logic suffice for recognizing these subjects as subjects? Perhaps they must also agree on certain *a priori* that could be characterized as formal inasmuch as they define the form of the universe—that is, the form of a common object in which subjectivities meet and recognize each other. Space and time are universals for two reasons: they constitute the form of the universe as an object of possible experience, and they define a mode of intuition common to every man—or even, as Kant says, to "all finite, thinking beings," that is, to every "dependent being, dependent in its existence as well as in its intuition." [13] What is historical or contingent here is only the making explicit and, as it were, the exploiting of these *a priori* to the point to which mathematics has developed. With respect to the *a priori* of the understanding, one wonders if they have the same universality: for example, does the category of causality belong to the thinking subject in general, to the impersonal or pre-personal "I think," or only to a certain mentality termed "logical"? Can one conceive of a humanity for whom the principle of causality has no function, or a function such that the principle loses the major part

13. *Critique,* p. 90 (B 72).

of its meaning—a meaning defining an objective succession in which "the appearances of past time determine all existences in the succeeding time"? [14] In other words, does the principle of causality define a necessary form of the universe?

It may seem strange to appeal to sociology here. Is this not just another return to psychologism? Are we not falling back into the empirical sense of universality that Kant proscribed for the *Critique*—a sense which measures universality by the number of observable cases? Yes—yet one wonders if the reference to the empirical might not be implicit even with the person who disavows it. The universality founded on logical necessity is different from generality, though it cannot disregard it entirely. This universality is not only the abstract universality of possible consciousnesses; it aims at realization in the world of men and culture, just as moral universality for Kant aims at being realized in the "kingdom of ends" understood as a concrete community. Undoubtedly, although a universal may judge history and even inspire it at times, it cannot be identified with the historical; unless one identifies fact with reason as Hegel does, one cannot find the universal in the substance of the State. Yet the universal not only tries to be realized in the human world; it is also rooted in it: its very possibility stems from the intersubjectivity experienced in the life-world. But, in speaking of the possibility of an *a priori* which is itself a condition of possibility, are we not looking for an empirical genesis of the transcendental? Yes, in the sense that there can be empirical conditions for the appearance, if not for the being, of the transcendental. Therefore, the *a priori* cannot escape the test of history by denying its own historicity. We shall encounter this idea again, since the *a priori* is a meaning given in perception, and since it defines a concrete human nature, not a "consciousness in general." [15] At present we are led to this point by the examination of the Kantian criteria for the *a priori,* and we may conclude that the universality of the *a priori* does not exclude all reference to empirical generality.

Moreover, this universality retains something of the empirical itself: just because the category of causality is universal in that it is a form of the universe does not imply that it is universal in the sense that it is universally recognized and acted upon. It may not appear to some minds—minds which are different, but not radi-

14. *Ibid.*, p. 225 (A 199).
15. This is Karl Jaspers' term for the Kantian view of consciousness as a "merely" universal structure, possessing no concreteness or *Existenz*, and typified by the notion of a transcendental unity of apperception.—Trans.

cally foreign, just as certain values or forms of the imagination do not appear to other minds (in which case we would still have to say that these minds live in the same universe as ours—if certain forms of the universe are given both to them and to us—though they exist in a different world). In other words, the necessity of the *a priori* is not necessarily experienced. It does not derive from a consciousness in general which is capable of realizing a purely logical necessity. Thus we should not identify *a priori* and formal, even if the formal is assigned to this consciousness.

We must now show conversely that the formal is not always *a priori.* Above, we have maintained that the *a priori* is not always formal out of respect for its transcendental character; in other words, we have considered the *a priori* in its constitutive role (although without appealing to a constitutive activity of the mind). In brief, we have seen that the *a priori* is not necessarily a form guaranteeing the objectivity of the object. The same transcendental character authorizes us to deny that the formal enjoys a monopoly over all other kinds of *a priori.* In this we remain in accord with Kant, who distinguished formal from transcendental logic. It is transcendental logic which discloses the *a priori* by specifying its role: the *a priori* exists *for* an *a posteriori;* here form is for a content, and such form is not merely formal. Although logical necessity is originally distinct from material necessity, they tend to merge when the former founds the latter—and to such a point that Hegel sees in this fusion a first form of the speculative identification of *logos* and nature. The same holds for morality, which is too often defined, even by Hegel, as some kind of formalism. For the form of the intention—i.e., the rational universality of the maxim—not only requires practical action (*act in such a way that . . .*), but also determines and even provides a content. The object of the moral law is the person capable of self-legislation—the person considered as an end, as the second formulation of the categorical imperative teaches; this object becomes the kingdom of ends in the third formulation. Moreover, the fate of the *a priori* is linked not to analytic, but to synthetic judgments, therefore to judgments which say something about experience. Thus, in affirming the idea of a material *a priori,* we are not necessarily pitting ourselves against Kant. We are, however, opposing ourselves to empiricism, which finds the affirmation of a content not empirically given scandalous. If it admits the idea of an *a priori,* empiricism conceives it as rigorously formal: as the character of tautological propositions, not of objective knowledge.

To deformalize the *a priori* is thus to renounce formalism, that is, the idea of a purely logical *a priori* belonging to a logic of form rather than to a logic of truth. Such a purely logical *a priori* only defines the formal conditions of validity for logical discourse, not the objective structures of reality for an object. This sheer formalism is expressible only in analytic judgments, while the *a priori* is made explicit in synthetic judgments. This can be shown in two ways. First, one can emphasize that formal logic (or symbolic logic) does not involve any *a priori*, even though logical positivism considers the analytic *a priori* compatible with an empiricist theory of knowledge. The purpose of formal logic is to clarify the logical structure of a statement and the logical consequences of the designation of certain propositions as true; but here the values of truth and falsity are defined independently of all adequation to experience, and are meaningful only in their mutual opposition. The formal structure of logical discourse has nothing to do with the structure of experience; the *logos* of this logic is certainly not Hegelian. The propositions it formulates are analytic, constituting norms for logical discourse, not for experience. Because of this, their necessity acquires a mechanical character—which in no way detracts from the merit of logicians who formulate them by means of a sometimes difficult act of formalization. This mechanical character explains, however, why such propositions can be in their turn the instrument of a mechanization; thus symbolic logic allows the designing of the theoretical structure of computers. Such machines are made to perform calculations conforming to certain stipulations analogous to the rules of a game of chess. They operate analytically; their additions are not syntheses, and $7 + 5 = 12$ does not have the same meaning for them as for Kant. They do not do mathematics even when they perform mathematical operations. From them, we cannot expect synthetic judgments bearing on experience; their activity is limited to the analytical manipulation of the symbols with which we later try to grasp experience. However ingenious we can imagine a robot to be, it will never act except by virtue of analytic judgments, and it will never do anything other than develop or put into practice certain necessary implications. It will *be* an experience, but it will have no relations *with* experience. It will never attain the true or the false, and truth will exist only for the person using it. The necessity of its "conduct" will illustrate the analytic necessity of logical formalism. This formalism cannot involve any real *a priori*: a robot is predetermined by the rules which assign it a structure; it is not predetermining; it cannot pass judgment on the significance of experiences, comprehend a meaning given by an object, or recognize a meaning which is known implicitly before experience. It is, in brief, only a logically valid discourse. Formal logic does not claim to state truths; it formulates rules bearing on logical discourse—rules which are neither descriptions *of* experience, nor ultimate guidelines *for* experience.[16] Thus, insofar as one remains within the formal realm, the *a priori* cannot be found.

Secondly, one can show that the formal is the result of formalization. Both Husserl and the logical positivists were susceptible to the lure of formalization. Furthermore, it is evident that much of the development of logic and mathematics has arisen from the temptation to formalize. Formalization makes the formal appear: in this respect, we must distinguish it from generalization.[17] Formalization does not differ from generalization in that it includes no relation of the particular with the general: Euclid is a particular case of Riemann. But the subordination of the material to the formal realm is not reducible to a subsumption of the less general under the more general: the formal orders the material logically. What specifically characterizes formalization is that it does not result from a simple abstraction stemming from the material; the formal is constructed systematically. Formalization implies a reflective operation. When practiced by science, it reflects on its own results and refines its own conceptual apparatus: in this way a purer geometry or physics emerges. Yet the formal element achieved in this way is not an *a priori;* it is a new object of scientific thought, elaborated by reflection and hence appearing as a *result.* It is not something *immediate* that is discovered. The form is not given as immanent in the content; it is produced with the aim of eventual application to the content.

What happens when formalization is practiced by philosophy? Husserl, who distinguished between formalization and generalization, can instruct us here. His "formal analytic" constructs a logic located entirely within the kingdom of the *a priori.* But does "formal" mean transcendental here? It is worth noting that formal logic for Husserl has two parts: an apophantics concerning judgment, the elementary forms of connection (disjunction, conjunc-

---

16. This leaves open the problem of mathematics, which often has some bearing on experience or at least on physics; but this is because it is more than a language, more than the result of nominalization, that is, more than an expression of formal logic.

17. If the *a priori* does not belong to the formal, we shall have to say that it also does not belong to the general, as if it were identifiable with an essence conceived as a general idea.

tion, subject, predicate, plural, etc.), and the articulations of reasoning; and, secondly, a formal ontology relating to the formal categories of the object (state of affairs, unity, relations, plurality, etc.). The same duality in formal logic, first seen in the *Prolegomena*,[18] is found again in *Ideas*,[19] where Husserl links the categories of signification "belonging to the essence of apophantic propositions"—i.e., the objects of a pure grammar or a pure morphology of meanings—with the "formal objective categories," which he also calls "logical categories or categories of the logical region constituted by the object in general." Formal ontology is in fact formal mathematics. Now this joining of apophantics, understood as the logic of noncontradiction, to mathematics, understood as the logic of truth or as the determination of the object in general, might seem surprising. Husserl insists both on the fact that pure mathematics is animated by an interest in logic—"There can be no other concern for it . . . than that which treats noncontradiction"—as well as on the fact that mathematics implies "a relation to possible objectivity in general." For mathematics is ultimately destined for physics, as logic is destined for science: "In the sciences, orientation towards judgments is only a means of serving the primary interest attaching to the things themselves, and the same is true for the logic which does not lose sight of its epistemological orientation." It is by means of this latter orientation that mathematics is ontology. Yet is there, as the notion of the *a priori* understood as transcendental requires, a real transition from logic to ontology? If it is a logic, can formal ontology really be ontology in the final analysis? Does the being *of* the formal authorize us to speak of being *as* formal? A similar uncertainty appears in Suzanne Bachelard's commentary on Husserl's logic: "When the *mathesis universalis* acquires the specifically logical function of knowledge, there is a conversion of the pure analytic into a real doctrine of science; but one must not forget that the logic of truth remains a formal logic."[20] In any case, Husserl himself seems to authorize the identification of the logical with the ontological.

In fact, formal ontology, as an *a priori* theory of the object in general, is joined to pure logic (of which formal logic is a part) understood as the *a priori* theory of the possibility of a pure

18. *Logische Untersuchungen*, I, §§6–7, 243.

19. *Ideas*, §10. The following quotations are from this paragraph. As before, I have followed Ricoeur's translation more closely than Gibson's.—Trans.

20. Suzanne Bachelard, *La Logique de Husserl* (Paris, Presses Universitaires de France, 1957), p. 197.

connection: "Even when it bears exclusively on significations, apophantic logic thus belongs in the fullest sense to formal ontology." [21] Conversely, the formal categories of the object are logical categories "by means of which the logical essence of the object in general is determined within the total system of axioms; these categories express the unconditionally necessary and constitutive determinations of an object as such, that is, of a something [*etwas*]." [22] Therefore, the formal would be objective, since formal ontology not only comprises the laws of the object in general, but also is an *a priori* theory of the object as such. This object is inseparable from objectivity; as primitive concepts, formal essences properly define the categories of the object, and they always intend [*visent*] the object in order to determine it. But do they really reach the object?

Must we say that the formal is transcendental and that the formal essence is thus *a priori*? It is *a priori* apparently because of its universality, since it constitutes the being of a "something," and also because of its necessity, since "formal ontology prescribes to material ontologies a common formal legislation." [23] Moreover, the movement joining objectivity to the object seems quite analogous to the movement which for Kant proceeds from the conditions of objectivity to the object. Yet Kant and Husserl differ on this very point. It is significant that Husserl includes formal logic in formal ontology: the formal for him is less profoundly engaged in the object than for Kant. Objectivity for Kant is *Objektivität*: the relation with the object as capable of being given in an empirical intuition; and the *a priori* is the rule for the structure of the empirical object. For Husserl, objectivity is *Gegenständlichkeit*: the status of the something in general, the object insofar as it is the subject of a true proposition. But this something in general is not the Kantian "something in general = x" [24] which compels us to add an ontological meaning to the logical or epistemological meaning of objectivity. Although this x is "nothing to us—being, as it is, something that has to be distinct from all our representations," [25] it is at least the index of the radical exteriority of the in-itself, the *Gegenstand was dawider ist* (the object standing over against us). For Husserl, by contrast, the something in general has only the logical exteriority of the noema, the intentional

21. *Ideas,* §10.
22. *Ibid.*
23. *Ibid.*
24. *Critique,* p. 134 (A 104).
25. *Ibid.,* p. 135 (A 105).

correlate of the noesis. One might say that at the level of formal ontology the notion of intentionality finds more significant employment with Kant than with Husserl. This is perhaps because Husserl is not attentive to the meaning of spatiality (though he certainly does not ignore temporality), nor is he especially concerned with the *a priori* character of space. For he does not classify geometry or rational mechanics with arithmetic, which he places among the disciplines of the *mathesis universalis.* In other words, for Husserl the *a priori* is not necessarily the source of synthetic *a priori* judgments. Formal ontology is concerned with the *a priori,* but it expresses itself in analytic judgments. (The distinction between analytic and synthetic comes later, in order to authorize the transition from formal ontology to the material ontologies, when it is necessary to specify the type of dependence belonging to "dependent" objects and not indicated in the general and purely formal law of dependence—e.g., the dependence of an idea upon consciousness or the dependence of color upon extension.) Therefore, the formal for Husserl defines pure logic, not transcendental logic understood as the logic of experience.

Thus the object in general, the theme of formal mathematics, risks remaining a purely formal object insofar as the passage from the formal to the transcendental is not effected. The derivation of this object incurs the same objection that Cohen made to Kant's deduction of the categories from the logical function of judgments. Although Kant may be able to answer this objection, as Vuillemin suggests—if the categories are understood as based on the principles and if the principles themselves, at least in the *Metaphysics of Nature,* presuppose a reference to experience—it is not so evident that Husserl has such a defense. Yet he does effect the transition to the transcendental, though very differently from Kant. Husserl's transcendental logic is not another logic, in addition to pure logic; it is a reflection on formal logic, a reflection which is genetic and no longer formalizing. Access to the transcendental implies for Husserl a critique of knowledge, accomplished through a return to the subjective motivations which are at the source of the evidence for logical principles. For Husserl, logic is founded subjectively on a transcendental phenomenology which indicates how evidence is constituted. The transcendental is the genetic. We shall return to this insight, for it justifies the important role Husserl gives to the material *a priori.* We can affirm now, however, that the formal is not primary, since it is the result of formalization and consequently cannot always be invoked as truly *a priori.*

Are we saying then that the formal can never be considered as *a priori?* No. It may be *a priori* if, as a result of maintaining a distinction between ontology and apophantics, the formal is conceived in terms of the form of the object, not the form of discourse. In deformalizing the *a priori,* we are not renouncing the formal *a priori* as opposed to the material *a priori;* we are not denying that there is an *a priori* which is less related to the content of the given than to its given character, to the objectivity of the object. For objectivity is in fact a feature of the object, even if it is also a condition for the object's apprehension. We would like to show that this condition, imposed on us by the object, derives its necessary and universal character from the object itself —not from a further condition imposed by the mind on the object. Basically, the *a priori* is formal in that it is the most general form of the object (without being the result of a generalization), since it determines the object in general and not a certain region of objects. It determines the object in general because it is proposed by all objects, and it is itself known *a priori* as a fundamental meaning of these objects: in this it is already material. Conversely, every *a priori* may be said to be formal if it is understood by this that the *a priori* constitutes the form which gives meaning to the sensible. We might even say that the more material the *a priori*—the more profoundly it is engaged in the matter of the object—the more formal it is: this is certainly the case with respect to the *a priori* immanent in aesthetic objects. Yet usage requires us to reserve the term "formal" for the *a priori* expressing objectivity in general—that is, the most exterior and general form of the object. This form itself, however, is given: at least it expresses the given character of the given. This given is not empirical; it is meaning and not matter: essence, if you like. The material *a priori* is not matter either, but it structures matter more intimately and specifically than does the formal *a priori.*

3 / The *A Priori* as Material

WE MUST NOW CONSIDER the material *a priori*, that is, those *a priori* involving a determinate content that is not logically justifiable: such are the Kantian *a priori* of sensibility, which concern intuition, not concepts. A material *a priori* designates, then, a structure of the object or a feature of the world which may appear in a particular experience, not in experience in general, as a necessary form. Yet it is immediately recognized because the subject already has a virtual knowledge of it. Furthermore, a material *a priori* may be identified with an essence: not any kind of essence, as we shall see, but one which can be given in eidetic intuition.

The crucial transition from formalism to essentialism is proposed by Max Scheler, who in fact refuses all formalism. The logical signification of the criteria of the *a priori* is dismissed by Scheler in favor of an interpretation that could be termed ontological—though in a Platonic rather than an Hegelian sense. According to this view, the *a priori* cannot be subjected to the norms of judgment, or itself be judged according to the standards of the judgments setting it forth, because it is the truth of judgment itself. Necessity and universality are here only exterior and equivocal signs whose employment as criteria runs the risk of subjectivism; for necessity is always in danger of being interpreted as intellectual constraint, and universality is sometimes viewed as a consensus. Yet, "There may perfectly well exist an *a priori* which *only one* person apprehends (and which he alone can apprehend)." [1] The historicity of the apprehension of the *a priori*—insisted upon by Scheler in several ways—does not affect its being.

1. Scheler, *Der Formalismus in der Ethik und die materiale Wertethik* (Bern, Francke, 1954), p. 96.

Its particular character is to be true and to appear as such to the person who grasps it intuitively. Once this is realized, we can see that, instead of the *a priori* having been deduced from the logical form of judgments, the truth of the propositions rendering the *a priori* explicit is subordinated to the truth of the *a priori* itself. Thus content is not judged according to form, nor even less deduced from it, as formalism requires: "Propositions are true *a priori* because the facts by which they are satisfied [*remplis*] are given *a priori*." [2] Kant was wrong not in starting from pure knowledge viewed as a fact, but in considering this fact as a formal condition attributable to subjectivity instead of as a given.[3] The *a priori* is a fact given *a priori,* an essential and not a formal fact; for here the fact, or the phenomenon, is the essence.[4] The *a priori* is not distinguished from the *a posteriori* by virtue of being the presupposition of every possible experience—i.e., by virtue of its transcendental function—but because it has its own mode of being grasped: it is the object of "a pure and immediate experience," while the *a posteriori* is the object of a mediated experience and is conditioned by the peculiarities of the person investigating it. The *a priori* is thus the essence insofar as the essence is fully given and is irrecusably present.[5]

Scheler was inspired by Husserl, and it is Husserl who offers the best support for the idea of a material *a priori.* This conception of the *a priori* occurs when he proceeds from a formal to a material doctrine of knowledge. This transition is inevitable because for Husserl a formal analytic—i.e., formal ontology—does not determine what there is of the general in the object, but rather specifies the object in general, which is not in any way an object: a strictly formal analysis yields an empty form. It is true that this

2. *Ibid.,* p. 70n. (The verb *remplir* will be translated by "satisfy," "realize," or "fulfill" depending on the context. It is the French equivalent of the German *erfüllen,* a key term in Husserl's intuitive theory of knowledge.—Trans.)

3. In a sense, for Scheler Kantian formalism is the dupe of traditional empiricism, which turns it away from real experience by inducing it to pose the question: what *can* be given? instead of: what *is* given? The truth of empiricism, the return to things themselves, is found in phenomenology, which is alone capable of *Wesenschau* (intuition of essences) because it is liberated from all prejudice concerning the nature of the given and because it is not in search of presuppositions. And this is why "one can call empiricism the philosophy which rests on phenomenology" (*ibid.,* p. 72).

4. "We shall consider as *a priori* all those truths of signification and all those ideal principles which achieve self-givenness thanks to the constituents of an immediate intuition" (*ibid.,* p. 68).

5. Thus the criterion of the *a priori,* residing in the quality of the experience which furnishes it—i.e., in the eidetic character of intuition—is phenomenological and no longer logical, and we move from Kant to phenomenology.

void can be filled, since there is always categorical intuition for Husserl, but it is filled by still another void. As Suzanne Bachelard says, "Form is considered as an empty framework which *must* be filled in order to achieve knowledge" [6]—considered, that is, on the plane of formal logic, before transcendental logic reveals that this form originally implies a material nucleus. Husserl does not develop this theme in his *Formal and Transcendental Logic,* where he returns to the formal in order to make it explicit as transcendental and where he ends by suggesting that the formal is already material. In *Ideas,* however, we find a fuller treatment of the theme.

In the hierarchy that *Ideas* institutes among essences, material essences are distinguished from formal essences. The material essence is in its ultimate form the essence of the individual object: "Each sound possesses in itself and for itself an essence, and at the summit there is the general essence of sound in general." [7] From this there results the idea of material, regional ontologies as distinct from formal ontology. The relation of the material to the formal is not exactly that of subordination: "One must not confuse the subordination of an essence under the formal generality of a *purely logical* essence with the subordination of an essence under its eidetic *genera* of higher degrees. For example, the essence of a triangle is subordinated to the supreme genus of spatial form, as is the essence of a red color to the supreme genus of sensible quality. On the other hand, red, triangle, and all essences (whether heterogeneous or homogeneous) are placed under one and the same category—that of 'essence,' a category which does not represent an eidetic genus for all of them, or even for any one of them." [8] Formalization ("when one passes from lived space to Euclidean multiplicity") and generalization ("when one passes from triangles to the supreme genus of spatial form") differ. We must not, however, believe on the basis of this example that the relation of species to genus is found only in material ontology; it occurs also in formal ontology—in which, for example, number in general is a supreme genus with respect to particular numbers, as is color in general with respect to the diverse colors which are the ultimate species of this genus. Formal ontology and material ontology are both presupposed by the empirical sciences, and thus co-operate in the determination of scien-

6. Bachelard, *La Logique de Husserl* (Paris, Presses Universitaires de France, 1957), p. 157.
7. *Ideas*, §2.
8. *Ibid.*, §13.

tific objects. But one cannot say either that formal ontology defines a genus whose species would be the material ontologies, or that it should simply be juxtaposed with them: "That which is termed 'formal region' is therefore not something co-ordinated with material regions; it is not, properly speaking, a region, but the empty form of region in general. Formal ontology contains simultaneously within itself the forms of all possible ontologies, and it prescribes for material ontologies a formal and common legislation." [9] But this legislation is not, strictly speaking, constitutive: one proceeds from the material to the formal level by formalization, but one does not go from the formal to the material by a process of in-forming or structuring. The material is not a substratum for the formal since it contains a substratum in itself formal: the pure something in general.

Thus the formal, as we were saying, determines only formally: its determinations are analytic. This is why the material ontologies retain a certain autonomy with respect to it: in these ontologies, eidetic truths "are not merely particular forms of truths borrowed from formal ontology"; [10] they are synthetic, as are all propositions of the material order, and *a priori* since they are the objects of eidetic intuition. Consequently material essences are "in a certain sense the authentic essences"; [11] they are not pure forms that are completely empty. Regional concepts (e.g., thing, quality, extension) are not purely logical categories; they express what must supervene *a priori* and synthetically onto an individual object of a region—i.e., the material eidetic ground [*fond*] whose law rules empirically given instances. As a result, each empirical science has its foundation both in the pure logic common to all science and in the eidetic science of its material region. It seems that we have at last discovered the real *a priori,* which are not only anterior to experience, but found it, and do so more solidly than the formal *a priori.* Is not the elucidation of the material essences belonging to the various regional ontologies in fact the transcendental logic whose relation to formal logic would be that of material to formal?

But two difficulties present themselves at this point. The first of these will not detain us for long now because we shall encounter it later: how should we divide up the material regions so as to accommodate the various *a priori?* According to Husserl, this division obeys a necessity which is itself eidetic and thus cannot

9. *Ibid.,* §10.
10. *Ibid.,* §16.
11. *Ibid.,* §10.

be suggested by experience. Nor can the division be effected by formal ontology, which contains only the notion of region in general, that is, the empty form fitting all regions. It appears that pure logic is here without further resources and that Husserl abandons us in midstream. Kant could derive the *a priori* of understanding from the logical forms of judgment. But, as soon as the realm of the *a priori* is extended beyond the limits observed by Kant (by being made coextensive with the province of essences), must we not have recourse to an extra-logical principle of discrimination, one invoked by Kant himself: the structure of subjectivity (including all its diverse acts) or, in Husserlian language, the diversity of the modes of eidetic intuition?

The other difficulty stems precisely from our extension of the notion of the *a priori*. Where will it come to a stop? Must we admit that every material essence is an *a priori*? Even the essence of a dog or a cigarette? "And concerning objects such as these, Socrates, which might seem ridiculous—hair, mud, dirt, or any other lowly object—do you think we must posit for each a separate form, distinct from the object our hands touch?" [12] Now Husserl does not distinguish as does Kant between a pure and an empirical concept. Every fact, every individual object, has an essence, a permanent cluster of essential predicates by virtue of which it is what it is and is able to receive accessory and contingent determinations: a *quid* may always be converted into an idea, and eidetic intuition is always possible. But how does one pass from the essence to the individual? Husserl makes this transition by means of the notion of eidetic singularity. This notion presupposes that the eidetic individual is not the empirical individual existing here and now: essence, even if singular, is not existence, although both are irreducible substrata for every new syntactical form. Yet there is an essence of the existing particular, under which the particular is immediately subsumed—subsumption being understood as the transition from the eidetic to the empirical plane rather than as the subsumption, within the eidetic realm, of the species under the genus. For us to apprehend this essence, "concrete eidetic singularity must be distinguished from abstract eidetic singularity: the abstract is the object related to a whole as a dependent part." [13] Species and genus are necessarily dependent, hence abstract; but the concrete is the independent essence which, without being contained in a whole, contains dependent essences within

12. Plato, *Parmenides*, 130 c.
13. Husserl, *Logische Untersuchungen* (Halle, Niemeyer, 1913), II, 267.

itself: the phenomenal thing, which is a concrete essence, contains the abstract essences of extension and quality. The individual is thus "the this-here whose material essence (or whose eidetic singularity) is a concrete," [14] and which hence merits being termed "individual," that is, indivisible. One might well wonder here if granting such an extension to essences—if not to the *a priori*—allows Husserl to do full justice to existence as such. He certainly does not deduce existence from essence, and it is worth noting that the notion of dependence is interpreted in such a fashion that the general depends on the singular, just as the formal depends on the material: "The purely logical form, for example the categorical form of 'object,' is dependent with respect to all that is the matter of objects." [15] The individual is therefore the primordial individual, the *Urgegenstand*. But Husserl adds: "The *Urgegenstand* is what pure logic requires, the logical absolute to which all logical derivatives are related." [16]

Existence as such is thus independent logically, but not with respect to logic itself; existence is not the radical other of essence, nor is the *a priori* the other of the *a posteriori*. The theory of essence is the expression of a formalism which would allow all essences to be termed "*a priori*." If the Husserlian conception of the *a priori* has not appeared to us to be as rigorously constitutive in the relation of formal to material as Kant's conception, perhaps this is because it is *too* constitutive; or, if one prefers, because it does not encounter outside of it a matter to be constituted. In this perspective all essences are nominal; they are not instituted by language—"*institutio hominis*," said Abelard, and Ockham after him—but by transcendental subjectivity. Thus Husserl would end in a rationalistic empiricism which does not retain from nominalistic empiricism the strong sense of the irreducible character of existence, founded for the Medievals on a theology of the Omnipotent; the return to the things themselves would be a return of the *cogito* to itself, a return to the *a priori* of subjectivity. For Husserl, essence is more than a word since it is the object of an intuition which is fulfilled [*remplie*]; yet intuition is not filled by the individual in its irreducible aseity, but by the individual as example and as *infima species*. If essence for Husserl is not completely nominal, existence on the other hand is somewhat so; the object is only an example, that is, a specimen.

Yet are we not forgetting that perception is the privileged

14. *Ideas*, §15.
15. *Ibid.*
16. *Ibid.*

example for Husserl, the "simple act" on which all other acts are founded? [17] Nor should we overlook another aspect of the reciprocity of the eidetic and the empirical: the possibility of intuiting the essence *in* the individual—a possibility which is already a necessity in the *Logical Investigations,* where eidetic intuition as a categorical act is a founded act, not a simple one like sensory perception. This is why we could not conclude that Husserl makes all essences *a priori.* In any case, we shall return to his contentions; for the logicism which one is tempted to attribute to him and which proceeds from the theory of eidetic intuition (itself derived from the notion of intentionality) may be contested in terms of another role given to intentionality within his philosophy: the grounding of all truth in perception. From now on, however, we must be both more and less Husserlian than Husserl himself: less Husserlian—though continuing to refer to him—by bringing the *a priori* and perception closer together, as we shall do in the next chapter; more Husserlian, by more rigorously defining the *a priori* so as to avoid making all essences *a priori,* as a result of reserving the term for the truly constitutive essences—thus somehow preserving the Kantian idea that the *a priori* gives rise to synthetic determinations. Just as we limited the field of the *a priori* on the formal side above, we must now limit it on the material side, and first of all by distinguishing between empirical and *a priori* essences.

Not every essence is *a priori,* and we must find a cutting-off point for our list of the various kinds of *a priori.* Now, what the theory of eidetic intuition means by "essence" is in no way the general idea taken as the posterior, thus *a posteriori,* result of abstraction. This is amply indicated by the eidetic process of imaginary variation, which is not a matter of achieving a generalization, but of arriving at an intuition in its purity. Every nominal essence in Locke's sense (with the exception of those which make the *a priori* explicit), that is, every essence elaborated by the understanding, is *a posteriori:* thus all essences posited and continually redefined by natural science—not only by classifying substances (e.g., the table of elements), but also by defining structures (valences, for example). All that proceeds from observation and intuition in this fashion is *a posteriori.* But there is also a pure science mixed in with and presupposed by empirical science. Shall we situate the *a priori* here? Yes, partially. On one condition,

---

17. For this notion see especially the Fifth *Logische Untersuchungen,* Second Section, §§47 and 48.—Trans.

however: that there be no confusion between the authentic *a priori* which structures experience and the hypothesis which only anticipates it; for the hypothesis precedes experience only in appearance and is in fact always subordinated to it. And with one reservation too: which is that we risk returning to the idea of a form exterior to its content. In this case our provisional identification of the *a priori* with essence would lose its significance, for this identification not only guarantees that the *a priori* is given in eidetic intuition, but also expresses its immanence in the given: an essence is the essence *of* something, and the *a priori* is given only if it is immanent in the given. We should not regress from essentialism to formalism, but we are in danger of doing just this if we define the *a priori* essence only in terms of the purity of the intuition in which it is given.

Let us say then that the pure sciences are *a priori* in that they render an *a priori* explicit and formulate synthetic *a priori* judgments. There are two reasons for doubting that the essences which they elaborate—e.g., the essence of triangle, of number, or of speed—by starting from a given *a priori* are truly transcendental.[18] First, such essences are elaborated by an activity analogous to that found in the inductive sciences: spatiality is given *a priori,* but not the triangle; temporality, but not speed. Secondly, since they are thus constructed, they are too pure: they are essences only of themselves and not of a matter. They are both nominal and real, as Locke would say, but their reality itself is nominal; they are pure because they are only meanings and not the meanings *of* certain objects, and because their matter is only form and their form is not the form *of* something. The essence is here constructed on the basis of an *a priori* and refers to an *a priori;* but the very fact that the essence is constructed independently of any object negates its status as *a priori.*

We deny this status for a reason quite different from that involved in a denial of the notion of an empirical essence: the latter retains from experience only the *a posteriori.* Even if the empirical essence is distantly related to an *a priori* meaning, instead of making the most of this relation, it tends to eliminate it by substituting empirical determinations for the *a priori* meaning. But both empirical and *a priori* essences have in common the fact of being results of a process of amplification, whether by generalization or by construction and formalization. This is why they tend

18. Kant says, "Neither space nor any *a priori* geometrical determination of it is a transcendental representation" (*Critique of Pure Reason,* trans. Norman Kemp Smith [London, Macmillan, 1933], p. 96 [B 81]).

to overlap, to such a point that it becomes difficult to distinguish between them: is the atom a mathematical or a physical essence? Perhaps the best means of discerning the real *a priori* is to seize it in its primary state [*à l'état premier*], before it has been made explicit and when it manifests itself as the essence *of* something: as neither general, nor formal. Then the essence identifiable with the *a priori* is the idea immanent in the thing, the *eidos:* that which can be seen since there is an intuition of essences, but also that which gives us insight into something, that by means of which something is visible.[19] For a theory of essence must connect essence not only with existence, but also, as Hegel does, with appearance; appearance denies essence, but there is appearance only by means of essence. The essence is the truth of something because through its agency the thing can be apprehended and then treated as true or false. This is possible, however, only if the essence is somehow constitutive of the thing and hence can claim a transcendental function; and we then see that the essence is not separate and abstract, but discernible in the thing itself, as the soul is revealed in the body.

Once again, however, we must emphasize that not every essence is *a priori*. Even if the essence is always that which gives us insight into something, and even if the idea is always immanent in the thing, this essence or idea may nevertheless have been formed only with respect to a particular thing and consequently not be truly *a priori*. The *a priori* is logically independent of all experience, yet not anterior to experience. If formal essences constitute analytic determinations, we can also say that certain material essences constitute synthetic *a posteriori* determinations. Only the supreme genera of the material sphere are *a priori*—Husserl's examples being "the thing in general, sensible quality, spatial form, the experienced (*Erlebnis*) in general" [20]—and more precisely the essences constituting the genera proper to each material region which inspire, explicitly or not, the empirical sciences corresponding to each of these regions—e.g., the biological and natural sciences, anthropology, and even history. These essences are situated at a certain ontological distance from the individual and from empirical intuition, yet found the knowledge of the individual. They are not too different from the essences of objectivity in general (i.e., of formal ontology) whose *a priori* character we have already pointed out. Moreover, we may still call

19. *Eidos* ("form") has etymological connotations of vision and sight.—Trans.
20. *Ideas*, §12.

them formal in the sense in which a form exists "for" a matter. In this sense they are also general, and Husserl is justified in distinguishing between the generality resulting from generalization and the generality derived from formalization; but the supreme concepts presiding over the ontology of each region are general precisely because they are formal with respect to concepts and empirical laws, not because they are genera with respect to species.

But can we not go further and speak of *a priori* which are more material, yet are not singular essences? For this we must reconsider the generality and materiality of the *a priori,* and thus the distinction between *a priori* and empirical essences. The generality of the *a priori* is not that of the essence obtained by a generalization and tested by eidetic variation. This generalization implies an intentional act—an arbitrary decision, as the nominalists would say. Whether it is a matter of practical or intellectual activity—i.e., whether the extraction of resemblances is automatic or reflective—generality is here the product of the subject and not of the object. It may be that such generality is guaranteed by the object—i.e., that nature repeats itself or that life operates according to general ideas—so that as a result there are more resemblances between Socrates and Plato than between Socrates and a donkey. Nevertheless, this kind of general is not an *aliquod commune;* [21] it has only nominal being. This is even more true for abstract essences, the general ideas that man fabricates only because he has a general idea of what a general idea is. We must therefore look elsewhere for the generality of the *a priori* and ask ourselves if it does not reside in a meaning immanent in the object, when the essence appears as apprehensible in the object. Stoneness in a stone? No, for stoneness is the meaning of the stone only for the understanding, and with respect to this meaning (once defined) a particular stone appears as an example. Such a stone is invoked to illustrate the essence of stones, not to present it; or rather, it is invoked to represent this essence when reflection returns to the concrete; the example fills out [*remplit*] the essence, but only after the essence has already been defined. It clarifies the essence without presenting it. To apprehend the essence, we must have recourse to experience, that is, to objects considered not as examples, but as problems: what are the specific characteristics of a certain stone? Yet when I discern something savory in the taste of fruit, grace in a dancer's movement, or

21. Literally, "something common"; the general in question is not this kind of ontological identity or shared being.—Trans.

youth in a child's countenance, I immediately discover the essence of the savory, of the gracious, or of youth. These essences do not serve as examples, but as notions by which my implicit knowledge is awakened or reanimated. Such essences are *a priori* because they are immediately given *by* experience and not learned more or less laboriously *from* experience; I already possess them in a certain sense.

But is it a question of essences here? And what exactly does generality consist in? In this: general meaning is given both as the meaning of the object and as vastly surpassing the object— i.e., as true of other very different objects. Yet this generality is not obtained at the price of an abstraction forcefully separating it from these objects. Thus a playing child expresses youth, but youth is also expressed by one of Mozart's melodies or by spring, the "astonishing springtime, lawless, laughing—which arrives unexplained and unannounced." [22] Generality is not manifested here by the number of individuals expressing the essence in question, but by the possibility of correspondences (in Baudelaire's sense of the term) or by the possibility of those metaphors which serve as the very substance of language.[23] The different expressions of the essence are united not by an *aliquod commune*, but by the fact that one and the same meaning is found in them, *seipsis conveniunt:* [24] this is why there can sometimes be a more striking resemblance between objects of different species—e.g., Ravel's music and Mallarmé's poetry—than between objects of the same species —e.g., the music of Ravel and Franck. Hume would say that the similarity of meaning is still the effect of a generalization and that the images of a child, springtime, and a bud must be associated in some fashion, at least through the impressions produced by these three objects. But then the meaning expressed by such objects would not really be a meaning; at least it would not be equally

22. ". . . étonnant printemps qui rit, viole. . . . On ne sait d'où venu?" This is from Paul Valéry's "La Jeune Parque," *Oeuvres,* Edition de la Pléiade (Paris, Gallimard, 1957), I, 103.—Trans.

23. We must not confuse these metaphors with the play on words to which the associations explored by psychoanalysis are sometimes reduced. Similarly, the symbols uncovered by psychoanalysis do not always indicate an essence; there is an obvious difference between the association of a penis and a baton, sword, or key and the association of mountainous heights with rigor or purity (such as we find in Nietzsche). The meaning made explicit by metaphors is an essential meaning, the very soul of objects, not an imaginary equivalent; and the language of metaphors is in no way a coded language with which the mind tries to deceive itself.

24. Literally, "they agree among themselves." This phrase traditionally indicates similarity rather than identity.—Trans.

constitutive for each of them, and would remain exterior to them, as mobile and arbitrary as impressions themselves. For, depending on my mood, the same springtime may seem pleasant or distressing, exultant or anemic; nevertheless, it retains the countenance of youth, innocence, and zest, and I am perfectly capable of distinguishing the objectivity of this meaning from the subjectivity of my reactions. Moreover, this meaning is not constituted by comparing objects with one another; such a comparison only demonstrates the generality of a meaning which in fact adheres closely to each object—to the point of being grasped directly in it. Thus the object is universalized without losing any of its singularity, and the material essence it presents is in it as an *a priori* which constitutes it.

Is this to say that youth or nobility or the savory are *a priori*? Yes, to the extent that they are meanings which are unattainable through generalization or rational definition and which must be experienced in certain privileged objects according to the evidence proper to feeling and imagination. Since this characterization of the *a priori* stands in contrast with the one we have given for the formal *a priori*, we must speak, as Scheler does, of the material *a priori*: "material" in that its content is immediately given in experience as the meaning of the object.

We can now distinguish clearly between the formal and material *a priori*. The formal *a priori* furnishes a meaning for a content, and this meaning is itself formal; it is only the possibility of a sensible and intelligible appearance: from this standpoint a certain horse, for example, may be regarded as one substance among others, linked with them as real and not possible. The material *a priori* on the other hand is the meaning spontaneously expressed by the appearance of a horse and not the empirical meaning derived from observations of its physiology. But we must not separate the formal and the material *a priori* by too neat an incision. We have seen that for Husserl there is not an unbridgeable gulf between the *a priori* of formal ontology (at least of objectivity in general) and the *a priori* which are the supreme genera of material ontologies. If the formal essence is truly *a priori*, it is not simply a rule for rational discourse, but a meaning located in the given and biting into this given. Moreover, if the formal essence is itself given, it is not only an exterior condition for objectivity: it is itself objective. It does not confer meaning on an object externally by making the object an object of possible experience; it is the very object which presents itself as the object of experience: the content manifesting its form. Thus the *a priori* is an essence because it is essential, but essential to the object and not to experience—or, if you will, essential to experience because essential to the object. In this sense the formal *a priori* is already material. Conversely, the material *a priori* is still formal since there is a certain formality in the material essence, as well as a certain logical independence with respect to a particular content. The difference between the formal and material *a priori* is one of degree: the material is a more concrete meaning; it is more closely attached to particular objects, and hence is infinitely more diversified. It determines the object not as an object of experience in general but as already the object of a particular experience. And the general is the preliminary condition for the particular: the object must be an object before being an animate or inanimate thing; it must have a visage before acquiring a *certain* appearance, and it must be spatial before being immense, or multiple before being harmonious. There is not, however, an ontological difference here between the general and the particular.

Yet if the material and even the formal *a priori* are presented as meanings immanent in the given, must not these meanings finally be perceived? Up to this point, we have followed Scheler's lead by identifying *a priori* with essence—with a certain type of essence—in an effort to do justice to the givenness of the *a priori*: the essence is given in an eidetic intuition and the purity of this intuition seems to guarantee that its object is an *a priori*. But this recourse to eidetic intuition to characterize the *a priori* is equivocal: the *a priori* is indeed an essence, but not every essence is *a priori*. Moreover, by rendering the *a priori* explicit, the eidetic reduction presents us with the essence of the *a priori*, but not with the *a priori* as essence: to essentialize the *a priori* is not to found it as *a priori*. Hence the possibility of eidetic intuition is not a sufficient criterion for the *a priori*. We must have some further assurance that the *a priori* is constitutive. For it is not necessarily given in an eidetic intuition, nor need it serve as the basis of necessary and universal propositions. We must refuse this new temptation of logicism. When it has been made explicit, the *a priori* is given in eidetic intuition, but previous to this it is given in another way: in empirical intuition, since the *a priori* is immanent in the *a posteriori*, though distinct from it. In other words, is not the *a priori* also perceived? We must examine this question next if we are to follow an empiricism of the transcendental through to its completion.

4 / The *A Priori* as Perceived

WE MUST BE CAUTIOUS in dealing with the idea that the *a priori* is perceived. An empiricism of the *a priori* may in fact seem incoherent. Kant would consider it scandalous because for him the condition for perception—at least insofar as perception is already intellectualized and passes from apprehension to comprehension, from the judgment of perception to the judgment of experience—cannot itself be given in perception. Such an objection proceeds from a conception of the *a priori* as the subjective condition for objectivity: it is thought in the object and applied in empirical intuition, but not found in the object itself. Yet if we do not assign the *a priori* to subjectivity (even if we hold that the former is known by the latter), the objection falls: then the *a priori* is a privileged structure of the object and can be revealed in perception.

To hold this view of the *a priori*, we need only stop presupposing a Kantian divorce between intuition and concept, and stop considering the concept as exterior (though necessary) to perception, as if introduced into perception by the transcendental activity of the subject at the point of the subject's origin. Moreover, as Jean Nabert observed, we have no consciousness of this activity or of the presence in us of an incoherent manifold it would order. Yet, in affirming that the *a priori* is perceived in the object or the event, we are not returning to Hume. For one can, and must, grant the *a priori* the privilege of always being already known —thus the privilege of always being related to subjectivity and of appearing as an immediately comprehensible meaning. Hence the proposition that every "alteration" has a cause is synthetic *a priori* because it makes knowledge explicit—that is, knowledge which I already possessed; but this knowledge must be awakened and revived by the causality I experience when I perceive a succession. Now, perception does not present me with an incoherent series of appearances. Hume, whose associationism presupposes an atomism, thought it did. So did Kant, who simply substituted the synthesis effected by the transcendental imagination for the principle of association ruling the empirical imagination: when "I perceive that appearances follow one another . . . I am conscious only that my imagination sets the one state before and the other after, not that the one state precedes the other in the object. In other words, the objective relation of appearances that follow upon one another is not to be determined through mere perception." [1] Furthermore, if causality (as a condition of objectivity) does not introduce an order into the course of time as subjectively apprehended, there is, strictly speaking, no object for me: "Appearances, as objects of experience, are themselves possible only in conformity with the law of causality." [2] Does this, however, prevent our perception of causality in a succession? Why should one say that a concept implying a necessity "is not in perception"? This grants too much to Hume, and it presupposes that cosmological necessity (i.e., factual necessity) can only be apprehended as logical necessity. Actually, Kant's examples suggest that the idea of a necessary relation need not be introduced by the understanding and can in fact be given in the apprehension of a phenomenon: if I do not objectify the arbitrary succession of my views of a house I apprehend, while I do objectify my successive apprehensions of a boat floating past me on a river, is it not perception which determines my thinking in causal terms in the latter case and in noncausal terms in the former case? Is it not perception that always tells me under which concept I must subsume an intuition—or more exactly, is it not perception that exempts me from the necessity of subsumption, precisely because it gives me the concept *in* the intuition? As an *a priori* of the event, causality is perceived in the event; the boat is not perceived as being now nearby and later far away, but as simply floating down the river. Similarly, I can judge that a stone is warmed by the sun because I perceive the sun as capable of radiation and as generating heat and life. The myths which celebrate the sun (and the solar myth can itself be considered as an *a priori,* as we shall see) recognize in it the causality of the cause, the dignity of the substance which, as Kant says, is manifested "wherever there is

1. Kant, *Critique of Pure Reason,* trans. Norman Kemp Smith (London, Macmillan, 1933), pp. 218–19 (B 233).
2. *Ibid.,* p. 219 (B 234).

action—and therefore activity and force." [3] Kant adds, "When we seek to explain what is to be understood by substance, and in so doing are careful to avoid the fallacy of reasoning in a circle, the discovery of an answer is no easy task." [4] But is it not perception which breaks the circle and shows us the object as the subject of causality, producing the effect by itself, just as it presents an event as an oriented and meaningful totality?

Scheler remarks that "one criterion for concepts which are *a priori* in that they are satisfied by the intuition of essences is precisely the fact that we inevitably fall back into a circle with every attempt to define them." [5] He concludes from this that *a priori* contents can only be shown, or "made manifest." But it is in perception that they are manifest, and eidetic intuition does not render empirical intuition useless. When considering the various *a priori* which he calls material, Scheler does not deny that meaning is offered in appearance: "The *a priori* given is an intuitive content"; he accepts the term "empiricism" on the single condition that "the pure or absolute facts of intuition be rigorously distinguished from the facts whose knowledge must ineluctably be constituted by a series of observations." [6] This reservation, however, seems to maintain the distinction between eidetic and empirical intuition. Perhaps there is, in fact, an ambiguity in Scheler's analysis of values as material *a priori*. On the one hand, in order to guarantee their *a priori* character, he affirms their autonomy with respect to empirical objects: "The hierarchy of values is completely independent of the existence of the world of goods in which they appear . . . and of the experience for which it is *a priori*." [7] On the other hand, if a value appears, it appears in the object which it inhabits and which is thus a good: the value precedes the object by being the first "messenger" of its particular nature, yet in its being the value is independent of its bearers, since it could just as well be apprehended (as is beauty in a work of art or grace in a movement) without our being able to account for it through an analysis of the objects which bear it, although it

3. *Ibid.*, p. 229 (B 250). Precisely because causality is given in perception, it appears empirically universal; thus it is difficult to conceive of an individual or a culture not recognizing it. We may do this, however, if we observe that what is perceived can only be understood if we possess a disposition to perceive it and consequently to render it explicit; and some may lack this disposition.

4. *Ibid.*, p. 229 (B 250).

5. Scheler, *Der Formalismus in der Ethik und die materiale Wertethik* (Bern, Francke, 1954), p. 70.

6. *Ibid.*, p. 72.

7. *Ibid.*, p. 46.

cannot be known independently of them. And the reverse also holds: a good is not a thing to which a value is added like an accessory predicate; it is rather the exteriorization of the value, because "in it the value is both objective (which it always is) and real." [8] In brief, a value is announced in a good because the good is constituted by the value. Therefore, if values are given *a priori*—*a priori* for the objects that they constitute, this sufficing for the moment to guarantee their *a priori* character—they are given in these objects. The material *a priori* is material not only because of its content, but also according to its mode of presence; it is on this condition that Scheler can claim to escape Kantian formalism completely, denouncing the ruinous opposition of intuition and concept. There is thus no reason to introduce a radical difference between eidetic and empirical intuition,[9] although the *a priori* can in fact be made explicit for itself (as space is by geometry, and values are by an axiology) and then become the object of an eidetic science. But even so, is not pure knowledge elaborated in reference to the intuition of the object for which this *a priori* is *a priori?*

Here again we must refer to Husserl, for he provides a definite support for the idea that the *a priori* is perceived. At first glance, this seems surprising, since Husserl is often seen as such a champion of logicism that for him the material *a priori* would risk being compromised by the formal *a priori*. But Husserl wanted to pass from a formal logic to a transcendental logic in order to found the first on the second. In doing this, did he not invite the enemy into his own camp? Did he not restore a certain kind of empiricism? Did he not contribute in his own way to deformalizing the formal?

What in fact does "transcendental" mean? The term implies a Copernican return of subjectivity to itself, but this time with the intention of observing its life and not of discovering in it a logical apparatus: transcendental logic is a genetic logic which strives to divulge the secret of the constitutive power residing in the life of consciousness. But perhaps this quest ends by dismissing the idea itself of constitution, and by making appear at the origin a given

8. *Ibid.*, p. 43.

9. There is, however, another reason to which we shall do justice later: this is that the *a priori*, even if it is revealed in experience, must be somehow known *a priori*. Scheler satisfied this demand by distinguishing between the ordinary experience which transcends intuitive content (i.e., which aims beyond the given) and the experience of the *a priori*, which he called phenomenological rather than eidetic; in the latter, what is intended and what is given coincide exactly; this is another way of saying that the given does not surpass the intended, and that the intended is equal to the given.

which is not a product, an act of seeing which is not an act of creating. We know where the return to the pre-predicative ends: in establishing that "the nuclei [*Kerne*] are relevant"; that is, in establishing the solidarity of eidetic intuition—which discloses the *a priori*—and empirical intuition. These two kinds of intuition are first presented as analogous. The sixth *Logical Investigation* introduces the idea of essence by affirming the possibility of satisfying logical significations, which concern the form of the proposition, in the same way that perception satisfies the significations concerning things. The two kinds of intuition are original [*originaire*]; each furnishes its object "in person" and independently of the other. But they are also bound together: the empirical intuition of the individual can be converted into an intuition of its essence, and conversely "there is no intuition of an essence if we do not have the free possibility of turning toward a corresponding individual, and if we cannot become conscious of an example to illustrate this essence." [10] It is this reciprocity of empirical and eidetic intuition that Husserl invokes in order to dismiss the Platonic realism of essences.

Yet, when he affirms that what is given in eidetic intuition is a "*pure* essence," [11] Husserl does not add that this essence is given in the object taken as an example. There may be cases where an essence cannot be manifested in an example: when it is a question of the primitive concepts belonging to a pure grammar and defining the form of a proposition—what the Prolegomena to the *Logical Investigations* call the elementary forms of liaison (conjunction, disjunction, subject, predicate, etc.)—in this case, it may be that the categorial intuition apprehending them is independent of all sensory intuition. However, the fourth *Logical Investigation,* which examines these formal significations and their modes of dependence, gives many examples of such concepts. Still, these examples do not contain an obvious reference to perception; the concept seems to be able to dispense with intuition, and the meaning is fulfilled by a simple modification of intention, as in attention. Yet one wonders if these formal significations merit being termed *a priori*: their inability to be incarnated in what is perceived perhaps attests that they do not bite into the real, that they are only formally and not materially constitutive. One also wonders if the intuition which apprehends them really merits the name of intuition. Is not intuition primordial only

10. *Ideas,* §3.
11. *Ibid.*

when it discovers meaning at its origin in an object that is present to us? In other words, is presence not something more than the modification of meaning? Does not presence reveal the radical exteriority of the transcendent object—an exteriority belonging to the perceived object?

In any case, when it is a question of material essences, Husserl might grant that eidetic intuition must be founded on sensory intuition. Is this not the meaning of "the characterization of categorial acts as founded acts" as stated in the sixth *Logical Investigation*? Founded on what, if not on sensory perception, which is precisely a "simple act"? We know to what extent Merleau-Ponty has developed this aspect of Husserl's thought. Actually, Husserl hesitates to admit that perception fills [*comble*] intuition and fulfills [*remplit*] intention. His transcendental idealism tends to deny what is suggested by the theory of intentionality,[12] and an interpretation of Husserl could be proposed in which the transcendental founds the formal without disavowing it or the primacy of logic: the accent would then fall on the immanence of the essence in the individual, so as to deprive existence of its unintelligible facticity. The *a posteriori* would thus be reabsorbed into the *a priori,* and would then be coextensive with it. All material essences would be *a priori,* and there would be no need to distinguish them from the general ideas derived from empirical intuition. Here Husserl would reject Plato only because he would be more Platonic than Plato himself: through the intermediary of essences, the world itself would be immanent in transcendental subjectivity.

The fact that Husserl's logic of truth remains formal means two things: first of all that the consciousness in which logic must be founded is a purely transcendental consciousness. Descartes, says Husserl, lacked the transcendental meaning of the ego—an ego that Descartes discovered by a certain kind of "realist aberration" presenting a temptation to be avoided at all times. Guarding against "psychological falsification," one sees that the ego which "can make itself explicit ad infinitum and systematically"[13] is itself formal: in place of the real ego, Husserl substitutes the *eidos* ego (the formal ego). Yet this essentialism, under the pretext of

12. These are, in fact, the two general directions of Husserl's thought. See L. Landgrebe, "Husserls Phänomenologie und die Motive zu ihrer Umbildung," *Revue internationale de philosophie* (January 1939), p. 316.

13. Edmund Husserl, *Cartesian Meditations,* trans. Dorion Cairns (The Hague, Nijhoff, 1960), p. 31. I have made a substitution for Cairns's "explicitate."— Trans.

denouncing Cartesian realism, emaciates the ego to such an extent that it loses its concrete being. If the ego, as the *Krisis* says, "is not a residue of the world," [14] how can we speak of its being in the world [*être au monde*]? Certainly Husserl is right in refusing to make the ego a phenomenon of the world or an event in the world: we shall oppose a genetic theory of the ego by defending the idea of a fundamental equality of the person and the world. Nevertheless, it remains the case that the person is also in the world and that the transcendental ego does live in a concrete subject. How can we discover this subject if we begin from the formal ego? Between the two, there is the "difference" resulting from the reduction. Does this difference finally have a meaning? Yes, if the reduction signifies a leap to the level of *sub specie aeterni,* a leap to the ontological dimension. But what if it only signifies an option chosen by the constituting subject? What if it is only a means of imposing idealism? In any case Husserl does not directly resolve the problem of the unity of the transcendental with the psycho-physical self; he confronts it only indirectly by forcing it onto the problem of other selves, for according to Husserl the constitution of others is effected through the subject's psycho-physical being.

Husserl's logicism has still another consequence: the world itself, insofar as it is immanent to transcendental subjectivity, risks losing its transcendence. The assimilation of formal ontology to formal logic is established to the benefit of the latter. It is true that Husserl strives to show that transcendence is constituted in immanence. Transcendence first of all signifies objectivity, and objectivity implies intersubjectivity: the world for me is a world for all, but it is for *me* that it is for all. This assumption does not guarantee the radical exteriority of the world to consciousness, nor does it justify defining truth as adequation rather than by formal criteria. To assure these things, we must return to the intentionality of consciousness as revealed in the privileged and incomparable experience of perception. Is this not what Husserl does in returning to the pre-predicative? Moreover, it is not only a realist presupposition that requires this recourse to experience, but also the decision to proceed to a genealogy of logic. And certainly for Husserl "the return to the origin is not animated by a nostalgia for sources or a slipshod primitivism." [15] The origin is not the immediate, for what we are tempted to consider as immedi-

14. *Etudes philosophiques* (July 1949), p. 279.

15. Suzanne Bachelard, *La Logique de Husserl* (Paris, Presses Universitaires de France, 1957), p. 218.

ate is the result of laborious mediations, and our perception is very often a science unaware of itself. But it is true conversely that logic can be perception lacking self-awareness (in the same way that science is a technique which has had little awareness of itself until recently [16]).

If, from the static point of view, the formal must be understood only in terms of formalization and without recourse to concrete examples, from the genetic standpoint the meaning of the formal is rooted in the material. One could say that the ultimate meaning is to have meaning and that experience is always the possibility of meaning. In other words, phenomenology can be interpreted as a sort of archaeology; if it pays homage to the idealizing activity of science, it also renders apparent the primordial character of perception and the irreducibility of sensory to logical evidence: however great its dignity, the formal is not self-sufficient. This is indicated by the transition from the formal to the transcendental; the latter does not make a new form of the formal appear, but proposes a return of the formal toward the material. If full account were taken of *Erfahrung und Urteil*, a work which rethinks the world of experience and experience itself as the experience of the world, it would be seen that transcendental phenomenology is not a philosophy of consciousness to which a philosophy of the concept might be opposed; it is a philosophy of consciousness in its relation to the world. The authority recognized by this consciousness is not the authority of an "absolute logic ruling subjective activity"; [17] rather, consciousness is founded on the authority of the real at the very moment that it seems in turn to found this authority.

This interpretation of Husserl is supported by the theme he often reiterates: the necessary recourse to the example. Claiming that there is no intuition of essence if an example cannot be found to illustrate it is to claim that the essence must be apprehended *in* the object. If eidetic intuition is given the initiative in setting forth the example and occasionally in alerting the imagination (which provokes unlimited variations), it is because the essence is taken to be already known. But if the example has an illustrating function, is it not because the object has a giving [*donnante*] function? Is not the example the recall, either mnemonic or imaginary, of a

16. The reader might consult here Heidegger's essay, "Die Frage nach der Technik," in *Vorträge und Aufsätze* (Pfullingen, Neske, 1954), pp. 13–45.—Trans.

17. Jean Cavaillès, *Sur la logique et la théorie de la science* (Paris, Presses Universitaires de France, 1947), p. 55.

real experience? Does it not reawaken the experience in which the eidetic is given by the empirical element? The individual corresponding to the essence is the object constituted by this essence. The relation between object and concept—between a piece of fruit and the savory, between a choreographic movement and grace, or between an event and causality—is not one of resemblance; the example is not something *like* the concept without *being* the concept itself because supplementary predicates have been added to it, conferring reality on it. (This resemblance may exist between a general idea and a particular object, but the essence here identified with the *a priori* must not be conceived as a general idea.) The example is what actually satisfies [*remplit*] an intuition; it is the essence as present because of its presence in the object. We also speak of "providing an example," of being exemplary: to serve as a good example is to exemplify an act well done—i.e., to reveal excellence in an act expressing this excellence. Now, if exemplariness signifies the provocativeness and inspiration of an example offered to others, it is because the example, in furnishing the essence, confers on it the character of presence. Similarly, "making an example" of something is to present it as immediately perceivable, not to give an idea of it: to show crime as punished, not as punishable. And in like manner, to "take an example" is not to look for an approximate expression of an essence, but to turn toward the object embodying the essence.

In principle the example leaves us a choice, and this possibility of choice implies that the essence has a greater extension than the example. Yet the generality of the *a priori* must not be confused with the abstract generality of the general idea; the *a priori* possesses the generality of a meaning which may belong to very dissimilar objects and which introduces a special relationship between them: a correspondence or analogy more powerful than resemblance. The diversity of examples available for illustrating concepts like causality, the savory, or grace attests that these examples are not the species of a genus or the members of a species—i.e., objects subsumable under one and the same definition. They are rather objects animated by the same meaning. And although this meaning is more or less strictly determinative (depending on whether it is a formal or material *a priori*), it is always present in both kinds of *a priori* as a structure. This structure, however, does not result from an empirical induction based on the number of individuals; it is a structure immediately apprehensible and given in intuition: a condition of knowledge because it is given in an immediate fashion.

Intuition retains something here of its Bergsonian meaning; it indicates, as does intentionality if transposed into psychological terms, a fundamental openness to the object. Yet if we follow Bergson, we must say that the general idea is rooted in an "interested" perception oriented (when not impeded) by an action and concerning itself above all with resemblances. By contrast, the *a priori* essence is apprehended in the object by a disinterested and exemplary perception: an example suffices for this kind of perception to seize the essence, and this act of apprehension is founded neither on the repetition of the identical nor on the vital creation of similarities, but on the presence of meaning in the object. Perception is exemplary because the object is exemplary. Perhaps not *every* object is exemplary: certain objects are meaningless and provoke only the practical perception which is the beginning of an induction—whether these objects have in fact no meaning or whether we do not know how to recognize it. These are ordinary objects that no perception can ennoble.[18] In any case, it is because not every object is equally exemplary that there are good and bad examples and that the imaginary variation which uses fictive examples is needed. Must we say, however, that the choice of the example and the test which the imagination forces it to undergo presuppose a knowledge of the essence? Yes, and by this knowledge the essence is recognized as an *a priori*: the example is judged in terms of the essence and actualizes in us a virtual knowledge of the essence—i.e., the true idea of it that we already possess. But it can only do this by giving us the object of this knowledge, thereby presenting us with the essence directly.

Thus, in returning to the pre-predicative, in regaining contact like Antaeus [19] with the earth, we shall discover that the *a priori* is given in perception. At least the *a priori* in its original state is thus given, before reflection makes it explicit. And it is undoubtedly in this state that the *a priori* justifies its name by performing its function and by being essential to the object and necessarily attached to it. A question is raised here: can we disclose in perception all of the various *a priori* in their primary state? May we say in Kantian terms that they are all in some way the *a priori* of sensibility? If we are led to classifying them according to the

18. Yet the formal *a priori* must be perceived even in these objects, which have at least the meaning of being temporal, substantial, etc. They are only objects on the condition of being invested with these structures, and perception always apprehends them in this way.

19. Antaeus was the mythical monster with whom Hercules struggled and who regained strength each time he could touch the ground.—Trans.

different operations of consciousness—as when we speak like Kant of the *a priori* of understanding and reason, or of affectivity and imagination—should we still look for their root in perception?

To answer this question affirmatively, it does not suffice to show that a more or less marginal perception always accompanies the operations of consciousness. We must be assured that these operations draw their ultimate meaning from perception and that the *a priori* they utilize are already given in perception, at least in their brute state. This assurance is, in fact, gained if the *a priori* are not seen as bringing into play a constitutive activity or as foreshadowing the conditions under which this activity could be exercised. If they are really given to the subject and not introduced by and for his activity, they must be given in perception. When we speak of the various *a priori* of the understanding, this signifies only that the understanding is solicited by these *a priori*, which it exploits, and not that it manifests itself in producing them. Far from producing them, it is provoked by them, and it becomes what it is upon *their* proposal. The world solicits science; although it does elaborate the scientific representation of the world, science does not constitute the world, as we have already indicated above in the case of causality. Therefore, the understanding is not a faculty originating independently of sensibility and then joined to it; there is no strict dualism of intuition and concept. This does not mean, however, that there is no intellectual activity beyond perception: understanding is precisely the activity which builds upon perception as a basis; and it follows a path indicated by perception itself: it is a self-reflective, self-questioning perception which surpasses itself. The whole of consciousness is nothing more than this power of reflection and self-transcendence. There is no more need to assign to it a differentiated structure than to attribute to it a constitutive activity.

Can we extend this conception to the *a priori* of affectivity and of imagination? Definitely to the former. For affectivity, as language attests, is a modality of sensibility. And if affective quality belongs most explicitly to feeling, feeling in turn prolongs and deepens perception, and is not in principle exterior to it. Feeling is more than perceiving; it is a continuation of perception.[20] What about imagination? One recalls here Husserl's analyses, pursued further and even more rigorously by Sartre: is not imagination

---

20. See here the author's *Phénoménologie de l'expérience esthétique* (Paris, Presses Universitaires de France, 1953), II, 462–81.—Trans.

(as these two conceive of it), as well as memory, a specific function of consciousness, distinct from perception? Assuredly, but two points should nevertheless be made here: first of all, imagination is immanent in perception and the imaginary is ingredient in the real—if by imagination is understood what one imagines or can imagine and not what one fancies in abandoning oneself to imagination. No perception exhausts the real; the perceived object is given only in profile and always with a horizon of potentialities. The perceived is both the real and the imaginable, and imagination considered as the power of associating and thus of anticipating or completing the given—of realizing the unreal—accompanies all perception. Secondly, it might be shown that, since we perceive more than the given, imagination is provoked by perception; this occurs when there is a meaning immanent in perception which is later discovered to be imaginary, but which beforehand enraptures perception instead of merely accompanying it. Perception becomes swollen with imagination and invites us to dream. But we must not think that we are necessarily deceived; for, in the first place, when we deliberately abandon ourselves to imagination, or to the evocation of memories, we are aware of it and would be acting in bad faith if we pretended to be duped. In the second place, the images, *a priori* or not, which animate perception and invite us to live in the realm of the imaginary, are imaginary only because they solicit the imagination that will make them proliferate. They are not false in themselves; they appear false only when denounced by the understanding which opposes the objectively real to the subjectively imaginary. Certainly Hume, and Bergson after him, by invoking the extraordinary diversity of unfounded belief, are perfectly justified in denouncing the perils of an exasperated imagination tending toward delirium and refusing all control. But the fundamental themes of the imagination—i.e., the *a priori* of the imagination—reveal a meaning which is not false: the splendor of the sun is only an image in relation to the positive determinations of astronomy, and does not justify the fabrication displayed in solar myths; but in itself it provides a meaning for the sun, as well as for all that warms and revives, all that is truly solar—a meaning which, at the level of perception (that is, of our original pact with the world), is not false and continues to present itself to us.

Thus we must consider perception as the source of all the adventures of the mind, all the discoveries of thought, as well as all the attitudes or operations of consciousness. It is more than a particular mode of intentionality; it contains potentially all intentional modes. We shall return to this point at the end of the present book. For now we must assure ourselves that eidetic intuition, if it does furnish certain *a priori* as essences, presupposes empirical intuition, in which these *a priori* are first given as essences—insofar as they are essential to the object, but not insofar as they give rise to a process of ideation. If these *a priori* can be classified afterwards according to the different attitudes of consciousness, these attitudes are potential in perception, and the *a priori* which correspond to them are already given in it. In brief, eidetic intuition cannot be a criterion for the *a priori;* their evidence is not primarily logical, but sensory.

Husserl's hesitation on this point stems undoubtedly from the fact that phenomenology assumes two very different, though equally urgent, tasks. As intentional analysis, it strives to discern the types of evidence or presence corresponding both to the nature of the correlates and to the mode of intentionality; here it distinguishes between sensory intuition, which intends and discovers the perceived object, and eidetic intuition, which intends and discovers the ideal object (which can be either a generality, the object of a concept, or a state of affairs, the object of judgment). Secondly, as "genetic," it returns to the pre-predicative and discloses the immanence of the ideal object in the real object, of eidetic intuition in empirical intuition. Now, these two results are equally valid and equally applicable to the *a priori,* for both attitudes are possible with respect to the *a priori.* On the one hand, reflection can be Kantian (consciously or not) by isolating the *a priori* as formal and making it explicit in apodictic propositions. In principle this kind of reflection involves an eidetic intuition of the *a priori,* although in fact this eidetic intuition is perhaps never free from some compromise with empirical intuition. The mathematician, for example, does not think of geometrical space without perceiving the blackboard and the space on the blackboard; yet at least the truth of his reflection is independent of the empirical and linked instead with eidetic intuition. On the other hand, pre-reflective thought experiences the *a priori* in the *a posteriori:* the *a priori* is given to it implicitly, in perception, in the perceived object; it is totally immanent in the *a posteriori,* and is totally material as long as reflection does not attempt to formalize it. In other words, the *a priori* can be given in two very different fashions. One way, though it occurs only if sought for, is through an eidetic intuition which verifies its *a priori* status by the pregnant character of this intuition more than by the rigor of the propositions spelling it out. The other way the *a priori* is given, though without being sought and without being identified, is by an empirical intuition—in which case it constitutes the meaning of the perceived object. Therefore, the *a priori* is given as evident when there is logical evidence, and as immediate in the case of sensory evidence. It can be given in the former sense only on the condition of being given first of all in the latter; it can be essentialized only on the condition of appearing first as the essence of the perceived object.

But how can this be, how is its status as *a priori* justified? Before answering this question more explicitly in the next chapter, we must introduce two further remarks which will perhaps prevent certain objections. First of all, when we say that the *a priori* is immediately given in perception, we avoid evoking (as we have said before) a constitutive activity of the transcendental subject—i.e., an activity by which the subject would introduce a form into matter or, less naïvely, by which the subject, posited as the unity of apperception, would perform syntheses installing in the object a unity required by his own unity and thus constituting the world as a world for a subject. For the world, even if it is in harmony with the subject, is always the other of the subject; and if there are unities in it—that is, identifiable objects or sequences —allowing the subject to apprehend it, these centers of meaning are present in perception without being elaborated by syntheses.

Yet this does not signify in any way that we deny all activity on the part of the subject. Although we do not intend here to study this activity, which is inseparable from work understood as practical action and hence involving perception, we can at least say that it is employed in building upon what is given. And from this point on it may take either of two directions. Either it may isolate the *a priori* with the aim of making it explicit through the construction of a pure science, in which certitude equals truth; this can be done without ever completely annulling the subjective factor implied by this certitude, because the *a priori* refers to a subject and because certain *a priori* are clear without being distinct. Or the activity of the subject may plunge itself into the given, including all that it involves of the *a posteriori,* and construct an empirical science capable of producing probable truths by enlarging upon and ordering the perceived world. In both cases the activity of the subject is realized by judgments issuing from the understanding. In both cases the deciphering of the given—i.e., the mediation of the immediate, for the *a priori* is immediate before reflection isolates it—is accomplished by defining essences and relations; and essences are themselves defined by the relations for which they are poles.

Although the two operations are formally identical, there remain differences which may be invoked in order to distinguish the *a priori* from the *a posteriori*. In the first case, we could say, without using the Kantian sense of the terms, that judgment is reflective; always referring more or less distantly to sensory knowledge, this kind of judgment deepens our knowledge of the object by a process of self-inflection, of turning into oneself. Consciousness discovers in itself what it already knew implicitly: the *a priori* which perception reanimates. The geometer possesses a primordial consciousness of spatiality and does not have to search in the external world for the means of making it explicit. He returns to this consciousness in order to fathom its secrets; he does not need to leave it to formulate judgments which, though *a priori*, are synthetic, because moving from the implicit to the explicit represents a discovery at each step. In contrast with all this, we find in the second case that reflection seeks to provoke new experiences, to apply the concepts resulting from the discovery of new determinations or new relations: judgment expresses here an *a posteriori* synthesis. We may speak of formalization in the first instance without implying that every *a priori* is formal, since reflection determines its own object without recourse to anything other than what is given to it in a privileged experience. In the second instance we may speak of generalization, without limiting thought to the elaboration of general ideas, because reflection strives here to expand the field of experience, draw forth a new given, discover new objects and new laws. To the extent that perception is only a means here, the aim of this activity is the determination of empirical essences—e.g., the definitions of mammal, induced current, uranium, or the proton—with the understanding that these essences are defined in a certain context of theories, as well as through the relations or the system of laws, expressible according to this context, which manifest and constitute the object in experience.

Yet whatever its orientation, whether the synthesis is *a priori* or *a posteriori*, judgment finally displays its authority everywhere. There can be no question of contesting it. We may even suppose that this authority is already found in perception. How then can we assign it a limit? Though challenging the idea of a constitutive activity, we do recognize the activity of the understanding. The notion of perception that we have suggested is a limiting case: if the *a priori* is given—and this is what matters to us—and if perception is primarily receptive, a total passivity is not implied. The corporeal activity to which perception is usually joined when it is not pure contemplation is similar to and already implies an intellectual activity; and consciousness remains alert, even when our body rests. This intellectual activity, however, is limited to exploiting the given—perhaps to searching in it for a new meaning or striving to make a given meaning resound with new implications—and it never imposes meaning on something formerly without meaning. The given is always already meaningful, and perception places us in the presence of the world. Even if we must learn to perceive, and even if the adult's perceptions are in some way nourished by the imagination and commanded by the understanding, perception always teaches us something; if this instruction did not already involve meaning, we could not invent meaning for it. This is why we must suppose an original passivity at the root of perception. But this presence of the world is a presence for me; the openness of perception is the fact of a subject: the world is made known, is revealed as world to someone capable of knowing it; this defines the *a priori*. For the *a priori*, as we shall have occasion to say again, is also the fact of the subject; and if perception is passivity, it is the subject who is passive and for whom perceptual meaning is significant: a meaning given and not created, a meaning which is *for* me and not made *by* me. In other words, it is not the subject who is *a priori* or who introduces the *a priori* into the given; it is rather the *a priori* which introduces itself into the subject. The subject himself is given, and on this condition, as we shall see, the empirical and the transcendental may be conjoined in the subject.

The immanence of the objective *a priori* in the perceived object poses a second problem: if the *a priori* is given in this way, is not every given an *a priori*? Is there anything that is *a posteriori*? How can we recognize it if we cannot classify the various *a priori* and *a posteriori* in terms of subject and object? At what point can we ascribe a limit to the *a priori*? This kind of difficulty continues to concern us (as it first did in this form: is every essence *a priori*?) and will reappear when we attempt to survey all of the *a priori*. Moreover, it raises the Kantian problem: how do we distinguish between activity and passivity? Activity always takes place in relation to a given, and we must reconsider the distinction between activity and passivity from the standpoint of the given and the subject. Hence the Kantian problem arises again with respect to perception; we shall become clearer on this when

we better understand how the *a priori* is constitutive in the perceived object without the intervention of a constitutive activity.
For, if we refuse to subjectify the form, we must still introduce the
distinction between matter and form; even the material *a priori* is
a form without formal being. The matter is the *a posteriori* element, but all that we need say—here at least—is that there *is* an *a
posteriori*. Now, if the *a priori* is given, it is given as immanent in
the given. Meaning is not any more self-sufficient than the Hegelian *logos,* which must determine itself and then deny itself as
Nature: meaning belongs to something in itself meaningless. The
a posteriori is this meaningless matter: the sensory which calls
for and immediately finds meaning. Yet in a sense it already possesses meaning beforehand; it is as if it had always already found
it. This is why the *a priori* and *a posteriori* elements are indis-
cernible in the act of perception itself. On the basis of reflection,
however, we can begin to distinguish between them. The *a posteriori* is what I can learn, the given which instructs me. As Hume
pointed out, it is perfectly intelligible to say that all trees flourish
in the winter.[21] But I must *learn* that in fact most trees thrive in
the summer. The same thing holds for everything that has to be
explored, completed, and, above all, objectified—all that becomes
the object of a mediated and probable knowledge, and is continually being put into question by further experience. In certain
cases I can directly perceive the *a priori* meaning of a thing: for
example, I can perceive that this tree before me is an indivisible
object in a world of objects, or that it represents an achievement
of the vegetable kingdom, or that it offers itself to me as the
mythical form of the tree, as a captive power and mediation
between earth and sky. But other things are only known *a posteriori:* for example, that a tree's leaves are red because it is autumn,
that sunlight plays on it in a certain fashion, that it is an oak
rather than a pine, and all that biology can tell me about it. In
sum, all things that I have to discover and learn on the basis of
their presence are *a posteriori.*

This is why we can say that in a certain sense everything is *a
posteriori:* everything that perception points out to me is irreplaceable and new, and the exploration of the world is infinite. For
the character of perception is to be always both complete and
incomplete. It is complete because a meaning appears immediately, even if this meaning involves the ambiguity of a certain

21. David Hume, *An Enquiry Concerning Human Understanding* (New York,
Washington Square Press, 1963), Sec. IV, Pt. II.—Trans.

form—e.g., the obscurity of a landscape—or even a lack of meaning; perception is complete because it thrusts me into the world immediately. It is incomplete because imagination may incite understanding and because I always undertake active syntheses on the basis of the given, testing the *a posteriori* taken as *a posteriori* by forcing the given to offer itself more explicitly. The *a posteriori* is therefore the content; hidden by the indeterminable totality of things, it renders the world inexhaustible.

Husserl's notion of satisfaction or fulfillment [*remplissement*] acquires all of its meaning at this point. One kind of fulfillment can occur when the mind isolates the *a priori* and makes it explicit. The primary kind of fulfillment, however, proceeds from perception. Thus when I open my eyes, it is the visible which fills them; even when I am very attentive at a concert and am able to enter into the world of a musician, I discover the music first of all as something *a posteriori:* although I may be in contact with a form, what is given to me is the form of a content. Moreover, I may understand the music only partially the first time I hear it or I may never understand it: is the sonorous confusion, the brute *a posteriori* that I then perceive, totally formless? To be without form is still to have a form, even when something is distorted, vague, and nameless. Seeming not to have an essence is itself an essence; and it is an *a priori,* though not the *a priori* of the music to which I am listening: the world of the incoherent into which I sometimes drift is not the world of Mozart. In attempting to perceive this world better, I may discover the *a priori* which, defined now as constitutive of the object, is the real *a priori;* if so, I perceive the object itself and not its caricature. Here my perception undergoes a transformation, and a new immediate—the real *a priori* of the music—is gained through the mediation of understanding and habit. Yet this *a priori* is always immanent in an *a posteriori,* and must always be given as the form of a content. The activity of the subject striving to improve his perception does not aim at the content independently of the form or the converse: this activity directs itself to the object, the object whose form and content are revealed simultaneously. This immanence of the *a priori* in the *a posteriori* establishes that the *a priori* is itself given: that is, it is perceived and resides in the given. But it is perceived as the form of a content, as a meaning, or, if one prefers, as an essence. That which characterizes the *a priori* and justifies its name is its essentiality: its being essential both to the subject and to the object.

So far, we have been considering only the object, and to complete our consideration of the objective *a priori* we must show further how the *a priori* justifies its name, as well as its status as an essence. We shall elucidate how it is constitutive with respect to the object—i.e., how in the order of knowledge, insofar as the object is an object for me, it is necessary and not contingent. In this way we shall establish that the *a priori* is truly objective both because it is perceived in the object and because it is constitutive.

5 / The *A Priori* as Constitutive

THE *a priori* GIVES ITSELF with the same evidence as an essence. It appears not only when essentialized by being made explicit—as is particularly the case with the formal *a priori*—but also when apprehended in the object as the meaning of the object, as in the case of the material *a priori*. The apprehension of such an essence does not necessarily require an eidetic intuition, for this essence is the essence *of* an object. Thus the *a priori* designates something essential to the object as perceived, and in being essential it is constitutive. For Kant, the *a priori* signifies a condition of experience; this is a logical condition because of being a condition of intelligibility: the possible is the thinkable; to render experience possible is to render it thinkable; and thought alone can make something thinkable. This is why the *a priori* initiates a constitutive activity which constructs the thinkable, but which is itself difficult to understand, as we have seen. May we, in the light of our preceding remarks, dispense with it? Can the *a priori* be constitutive without being the instrument of some constitutive activity? If it can, what happens to the activity of the subject?

First of all, we should avoid making a serious error. If we admit that constitution is not performed by transcendental subjectivity, we must not allow ourselves to identify it with an act of creation by making the *a priori* a power of instauration. The constitutive character of the *a priori* signifies only that it is present in the object as the meaning inhabiting it and apprehended in it. In itself, the *a priori* is not pure knowledge, at least insofar as it is still implicit; nor is it a condition for knowledge, a condition which exists before the object is known; rather, it is the object of knowledge, since it is the structure of the object as known. Furthermore, the *a priori* is not an essence demanding or explicating existence; it manifests what the object is, not why it is; it does not remove contingency from existence. The essence here is not a *conatus*—i.e., the mark of substance on the modes, or rather, its presence in the modes; the essence furnishes the key for appearance and not for being. If the *a priori* is to lose its logical meaning, it should not automatically acquire an ontological signification.

Instead, its transcendental function must appear. To say that the *a priori* is formal—even when it is material—is to say that it informs the experienced object; it is a form by means of which this object acquires meaning. How then is it constitutive? By the fact that it is expressed: the object reveals it as its own being; thus Kurt Goldstein says that the meaning of the organism is its being, the immanent idea developing in it.[1] This conception of the *a priori* first arose for the present writer in a discussion of the affective qualities involved in aesthetic experience;[2] these qualities are manifested not only as the ultimate form of the sensory— the schemata organizing the sensible are only means to this manifestation (the same holds for the explicit meaning of the objects represented in the figurative arts)—but also as the truth itself of the object: thus joyfulness constitutes a Bach fugue, and the tragic pervades Van Gogh's paintings. The whole structure of the object revealed by critical analysis is at the service of this expression. This is why such an analysis may be performed only in the light of what is actually expressed—even if its aim is not to render the expression[3] explicit, but to discover the technique used in its creation. Moreover, the spectator fails to perceive the real aesthetic object if he is insensitive to this expression. The same thing can be said for the values experienced by feeling or the meanings apprehended by imagination: when the object appears as something good or evil, a value or a group of values constitutes its being; when the object appears as sacred, a mythical meaning is similarly constitutive: for the imagination, youth is the truth of springtime, just as happiness is the truth of the Enchanted Isles, and life the truth of fertile earth.

Certainly we must continue to maintain our distinction between the formal and the material *a priori*. The formal *a priori* is constitutive because it gives a form to the object, or at least it

1. See Kurt Goldstein, *The Organism* (New York, American Book Co., 1939), *passim.*—Trans.

2. See the author's *Phénoménologie de l'expérience esthétique* (Paris, Presses Universitaires de France, 1953), II, 543 ff.—Trans.

3. The term "expression" should not be understood here as the manifestation of something inward, such as an emotion; it designates something more objective and closer in meaning to a term like "appearance."—Trans.

designates the form according to which the object is the object of experience. Yet this being-as-object signifies a predicate rather than an essence—that is, an exterior form rather than a soul. For example, the temporality of a musical object [4] characterizes it as an object in general, while its expression makes it a unique object. This temporality is essential to the musical object without being its essence, as is the matter which also enters into its constitution. Here temporality is a matter with respect to a higher form, for the object has a way of relating itself to its own temporality—a manner of organizing or simply manifesting it which serves to define itself (the object) more profoundly. Thus a piece of music possesses a certain way of appropriating and mastering time according to rhythmical schemes which helps to produce its own expression; rhythmic movement is inseparable from harmonic structure and melodic themes, co-operating with them in achieving the full expression: in short, the essence of the musical work appropriates its essential predicates, subordinating them to itself. To say that temporality is an *a priori* is to say that time belongs to the essence of every object as a matter that the essence integrates and appropriates, if not determines.

Consequently, the *a priori* is constitutive in two different ways, depending on whether it is formal or material. The formal *a priori* is constitutive because it is a general condition of the being of the object; if it is a condition for the intelligibility and possibility of the object of experience (as Kant thought), this is because, from within the object itself, it determines the object as an object of knowledge; but it does not determine it as a singular object, animated by a meaning unsubsumable under the norms of objectivity. This meaning, which is not exactly singular as we shall see, is constituted by the material *a priori*. And it can be made explicit in terms of several material *a priori* because of its inherent richness, and because what is expressed is to a certain extent inexpressible. Yet the diversity of formal *a priori*—according to which the object is at once spatial, temporal, substantial, real, necessarily related to others as part of a whole or as a link in a causal chain, etc.—does not possess the same signification as the diversity of material *a priori*. It signifies the multiplicity of conditions for an object to become an object of knowledge; these conditions are fulfilled by the object of knowledge without being compelled to do so by the understanding.

---

4. By this term Dufrenne refers to a piece of music considered as an object.—Trans.

This duality in the nature of constitution leads to a paradoxical exchange of roles between material and formal *a priori*. Since the formal *a priori* designates only the being in general of objects, it is in the object as if it were matter ready to receive form: it designates the nature of the object insofar as this nature is determined only with respect to knowledge and relative to a formal ontology. Of course, it is not a question here of the empirical matter, which constitutes the being of the object in terms of the facticity of existence but does not constitute it as meaningful and inhabited by its essence; for this reason, the empirical matter can be known only *a posteriori*: as the given by and in which the meaning is revealed. By contrast, formal constitution does not introduce the object into the realm of existence; instead, it introduces meaning into the object. As a result, the formal *a priori* represents [5] a matter only in the formal order. And conversely the material *a priori* represents a higher form; it is a meaning which is more authentic—more personal, if you like—than the general structures assuring the objectivity of the object; the material *a priori* constitutes the object more profoundly, and in this sense we are tempted to say that it presents a stronger claim for being truly *a priori*.

But what about essence? Once again we encounter the problem posed by our examination of Husserl above: if the *a priori* is an essence, is not every essence an *a priori*? If so, the *a posteriori* would be thoroughly eliminated. We have already distinguished, from the noetic point of view, between an essence and an authentic *a priori*. Now we must show that, insofar as it is different from a material *a priori*, an essence is not constitutive. An essence in the classical sense—e.g., the equinity of a horse—is not an *a priori* inasmuch as it claims to be an objective truth, elaborated through observations by eliminating the accidental element and collecting together all specific characteristics, hierarchically if necessary. Conceived in this way, the essence is not constitutive because it is already constituted. It is not the truth *of* the object but an abstract truth *about* the object; thus nominalists are able to claim that "man" is not *in* Socrates. The essence is not essential to the object. This statement may be interpreted as opposing a general idea to a singular being, and as making the inadequacy of the essence—its inability to constitute the object—proceed from its generality alone. In following this line of thought, one might come

---

5. "Represents" [*figure*] should not be understood in the sense of representing something else, but as "being" or "forming."—Trans.

to say that matter is constitutive because it individualizes. But for us it is not a question of constituting existence, or the object as existent. In our effort to challenge the *a priori* character of the general essence, we must refrain from invoking the singularity of the object. Instead, we should contest giving a monopoly of meaning to this essence, which in fact states only an abstract truth: when I have defined the essence of the horse, I certainly possess the means of recognizing horses and of classifying them in a zoological hierarchy, but I do not yet know why they merit being called "man's most noble conquest," or why they may receive prestigious names like Pegasus or Bucephalus, or why they may be combined with men in centaurs. Similarly, even if I learn the rules of counterpoint, I do not know what is responsible for the joy [*allégresse*] characterizing a Bach fugue.

Does all this suggest a return to the singular? Yes, insofar as the essence, like the *a priori*, possesses a meaning transcending the individual object and apprehensible in other objects. Yet is not the joy to be found in Bach's music unique and different from that discoverable in the music of Mozart? Assuredly: the expert distinguishes between them easily, just as the horse breeder distinguishes between the "nobility" (i.e., the purity) of two thoroughbreds. Therefore, we must not oppose the general idea to the *a priori* as the general to the singular in an effort to grant to one the constitutive power refused to the other. The *a priori* is general too, both because it belongs to subjectivity as virtual knowledge and because it may be found in different objects: joyfulness belongs to spring, Dufy's watercolors, certain poems by Apollinaire, and certain landscapes in Provence. Hence the general idea and the *a priori* should be contrasted in terms of their modes of appearing and their constitutive power.

As opposed to general ideas, the *a priori* constitute the object, and they do so without provoking the nominalist objection. The material *a priori* can here be understood in terms of the formal *a priori*: if the latter are also obtained on the basis of experience, experience in turn is obtained by starting from them. Thus the formal *a priori* are universal, or at least rule all objects and events belonging to a region. They are constitutive by being forms determining the structures of an object or event: temporality is a structure of objects, just as causality is a structure of events. This structure is general in the sense that it is common to many objects, but it is not something general in those objects; it is a structure of their being, given in their appearing as an objective condition of appearing—or, if you like, as an essential predicate.

Thus temporality is not part of a horse in the same way that equinity is. Neither is nobility: we also discover the material *a priori* in the object as its form, and this discovery is in no sense inductive. But this form determines the object more specifically than the formal *a priori*. We cannot say that it determines it as unique, but it does determine it in the depths of its being: the *a priori* does not need to be absolutely singular to be constitutive. In order to be the form of the body, the soul does not have to be the "singular soul" evoked by the poet [6] (i.e., the soul of a dead person whose irreplaceable character is exalted by the force of memory; by contrast, the living, in their very effort to live, cannot escape generality). Uniqueness is certainly what we admire in another person, but it does not constitute him, at least with respect to our knowing him; this uniqueness evades all apprehension and definite meaning. Meaning becomes unique by coming into existence [*s'existentialisant*], not by exercising its constitutive function. The unique is the object as it exists—by chance or free choice—and not as it appears. Must we then understand constitution to be a function of appearance? Yes, to the degree that constituting is not creating, but structuring and making meaningful.

In consequence, the *a priori* is not for us a condition of objectivity which, proceeding from subjectivity, would form a screen for an in-itself and thus justify the distinction between phenomenon and thing in itself; it is objectivity itself, since it is present in the object as constituting it. It is a law *of* the object, not a law *for* the object. Yet, through the object, it may be known in itself as a primary meaning. It is, however, still general: the singularizing *a priori* still possesses a certain generality, not only because we may attempt to define it as a result of already knowing it implicitly, but also because it can constitute different objects. Its constitutive power is not exhausted with one object; as a meaning, it remains available [*disponible*] in spite of its many involvements. Hence to apprehend the *a priori* in the object it constitutes is, in a sense, to surpass this object and to discover a truth transcendent to the various objects in which it is immanent, and indifferent to the objects it differentiates. Thus we are invited to search for a primordial state of the *a priori*—i.e., of the constitutive as distinct from the constituted. This is where perception, insofar as it is intuitive, enters the picture: when perceiving intuitively, we are more sensitive to the *a priori* than to the *a posteriori,* and directly

6. This contains an allusion to a line from Paul Valéry's "Le Cimetière marin": "Où sont des morts . . . les âmes singulières?" (*Oeuvres,* Edition de la Pléiade [Paris, Gallimard, 1957], I, 150).—Trans.

grasp meanings in the world. Perception, then, finally guarantees the priority of the *a priori* essence over the general essence. Since the latter is elaborated in the realm of the *a posteriori*, it does not constitute the perceived meaning; rather, it reconstitutes and rediscovers this meaning, and thus transforms it more or less profoundly. Perhaps we should even measure the constitutive power of the *a priori* by the immediacy of its appearance: the equinity of a horse appears only after a series of operations whose completeness is never assured, while a horse's nobility appears immediately. Constitution is therefore the operation of the immediately sensible meaning, which animates the object and lends it a language *for* us—not a language *by* us. The object is meaningful in itself, and its meaning is *a priori* primarily because of being immanent in the object.

Furthermore, the object expresses this *a priori* meaning. Our examples indicate that the *a priori* (at least the material *a priori*) is to be found above all in what is expressed. The various material *a priori* appear as expressions belonging to the objects they inhabit—whether these *a priori* are affective (e.g., the joyfulness of a fugue), imaginational (e.g., the quality of youth), or perhaps even intellectual (e.g., unity or necessity when it appears, before any formalization, as a quality of a thing or an event). This shows that the *a priori* is first of all perceived. For the apprehension of an expression by feeling is the highest moment of perception, the moment when perception is fully achieved and when the subject somehow becomes the perceived object—at least experiencing the object to the point of losing himself in it. Here we must understand the necessary relation of object to subject in terms of perception, for what is expressed to us or before us somehow involves us, calling for our connivance through our power of comprehension. Most importantly, however, the phenomenon of expression illuminates the constitutive function of the *a priori*, for expression manifests the object itself. Beyond its partial and accessory meanings, expression is the total meaning unifying the being that expresses itself: to express oneself is to be completely present in one's expression.[7]

This is why not every expression sets forth an *a priori;* only the

7. At least when it is a question of expressing *oneself*. The Leibnizian sense of expression—as presence of the other and as reflection of the universe—is different. It implies a pre-established harmony between all monads—each considered as absolute, but also as an object from the viewpoint of the whole, i.e., of the monadology. To express oneself also implies a pre-established harmony, as we shall see, but one between two interlocutors or between an object and a subject: an earthbound and mutual understanding, not a theodicy.

authentic ones do so: those total and spontaneous expressions appearing in rare moments of communication. We must insist on this spontaneity; a premeditated expression is an artificial language striving to realize itself as language, to convey a meaning; this occurs when I "put on" a menacing, furious, or tender air; but the roaring ocean does not feign anger, nor does a mother rocking her child become tender through an explicit effort. To put on an air is to "act" and to choose a mask instead of a manner of being. It is also to act *upon* the other person instead of offering oneself to him. Authentic expression does not *intend* to say something: it *says* it; and the other is only a witness to whom this expression appeals in an uncompelling way, just as a work of art calls out to the spectator. (The work of art betrays its vocation when it ceases to be pure language and aims at provoking emotions or decisions.) Moreover, meanings voluntarily or artificially transmitted are not *a priori* because they are not total; they articulate a passing idea or a partial aspect of the person. These meanings are *too* expressive in that they concentrate all of their expressiveness on a particularity instead of extending it to the totality: such is the case in expressionist art, which forces the expression by accenting certain extremely emotive aspects of it. The same holds for particular emotions like fear, anger, or desire; they are forceful, but they express only singular episodes in our psychological life—its accidental and not its essential aspect. (This is why we must define and study the emotions empirically, as Sartre has shown.) Yet, if one's disposition to anger or fear is somehow the fundamental dimension of one's behavior—i.e., the point of convergence for all one's character traits—the expression of this disposition will then be *a priori*: violence or cowardice are apprehensible in a face as well as in things.

In things: this is important, for the *a priori* cannot be radically singular, as we have just seen. We shall verify this thesis presently by showing that the *a priori* must also be known *a priori*; this is possible only on the condition of its not being totally coextensive with a singular object. Thus an absolutely particular expression—that is, the peculiar style by which I recognize a face, a work of art, or a culture—cannot be considered an *a priori*. For this putative *a priori* would be somehow *too* constitutive to be known *a priori*; that which adheres closely to the thing, making it easily discernible and recognizable, is precisely what is indefinable; it is outside all categories and cannot be apprehended by means of a virtual knowledge. If I wish to explain why a particular expression is constantly recognizable and thus possesses a certain unity, I would have to proceed empirically by trying out certain approaches, such as those provided by psychoanalysis or Marxism. It would be less a matter of apprehending a unity than of accounting for it; at the level of perception, this unity would not be grasped as a truly meaningful and informing form; it would be a "description" rather than an expression. For the object here does not signal to us or express itself; it manifests its individuality without saying how it is incomparable. Moreover, even if required by a Leibnizian principle of indiscernibles, incomparability may be the effect of chance or circumstance: to invoke an *a priori*, we must locate singularity in a dominant trait to which everything else is subordinated—as everything is subordinated to a certain effect in a work of art. Then, instead of being only the totality of its particularities, the object expresses itself by this singular trait, which really unifies it and thus is an *a priori*.

Still, this trait must also be a universal recognized by thought and known *a priori* as a principle of unity capable of exercising the constitutive function in other objects as well. Such is the paradox of the expressed: it is immanent in the expressive object, yet knowable and thus able to maintain a certain independence from this object. Hence whatever expresses itself is worthy of being termed a "self"; it expresses itself because it is a self, and it is a self to the extent that it is more than a self—i.e., to the extent that the self is no longer a mere empirical particularity, but the positing of a universal. Expression implies *self*-expression, the act of a subject who solicits the attention of others and also presupposes them within himself. This is why we may say that an expressive object is a quasi-subject;[8] it partakes of humanity when we participate in it; this is especially true of a work of art, though also of any object that "speaks" to us. To express oneself is therefore to raise oneself to the level of universality because what is expressed is a universal, and the *a priori* is this universal which manifests the singular and offers it to perception. The singular becomes universal by revealing itself. It does not become general, for the general is a meaning constructed on the basis of the object, not furnished directly by it; it requires an intellectual operation to abstract it from the particular—i.e., from that which lacks meaning. Let us say again, then, that the universality of the tragic, for example, has nothing in common with the generality of a genus: the tragic is totally present in one of Van Gogh's olive trees, or in

8. For the concept of the quasi-subject, see *Phénoménologie de l'expérience esthétique*, I, 197, 256, 291, 306, 365, 409; II, 476, 478.—Trans.

Ophelia's madness, or in a certain Beethoven scherzo, or in a fetish belonging to the New Hebrides tribesmen. Is this the case simply as a result of generalizing hastily without being attentive to differences or without being capable of attaching a precise meaning to words? No: the word has a content that we experience quite vividly and clearly; even if we cannot make this content explicit, we do know it in some sense. This knowledge apprehends the universal because it grasps the meaning constituting the singular object. The universality of this meaning is shown by our ability to discover it in objects empirically very different; the distinction between universality and generality is thereby shown, for generalization cannot be achieved with objects so different.

The phenomenon of expression thus reveals the *a priori* as a universal. But we should not overlook this fact: just as not every expression reveals an *a priori,* so not every *a priori* is expressed. In fact, the more formal it is, the less expressible it is. Objectivity in general, spatiality, unity, even causality are certainly perceived, but they are not expressed. This is because formal *a priori* are less constitutive than material ones; they are structures of the object, necessary to its apprehension, but do not compose its real meaning. The object manifests them without expressing them. And because they are less profoundly attached to the object, the intellect can more easily make them explicit and elaborate a rigorous science starting with them. Yet when we say that they are not expressed, do we not imply that they are not universals in the sense adopted above? Yes, for the most part: the formal *a priori* usually give rise to generalizations, and their universality is in inverse ratio to their generality. Perhaps, however, they do retain a certain aspect of universality, for even if the structure designated by the formal *a priori* characterizes the object as an object in general rather than as a singular object, and even if this structure does not involve a dialectic of universal and singular, it is nevertheless already a meaning, as well as the condition for more pregnant meanings.

Therefore, we can maintain the distinction between the material and the formal even within the constitutive character of the *a priori.* We can also consider the more general question posed by the diversity of the *a priori:* why is it that, although there are different *a priori* in one and the same object, ambiguity or contradiction is not introduced by this fact? Joyfulness is an *a priori* for a Bach fugue, yet so is beauty. These two *a priori* are distinguished by the knowledge which isolates them, placing the former in a table of affective categories and the latter in a scale of values.

In the fugue itself, however, they are not distinct: the musical work expresses joy and appeals to an aesthetic value [9] with the same gesture, as it were; and similarly it is at once temporal, unified, substantial, and so on. These various *a priori* can be distinguished precisely, thanks to their universality: they do not adhere so closely to the object (which they nevertheless constitute) that they cannot be separated from it. They are, however, first of all apprehended *in* the object; they do not possess the autonomous being of a category or ideal form in relation to an empirical nature; but they retain with respect to the object a distance sufficient to confer universality on them. Moreover, although making these *a priori* explicit depends on the subject considering them, we must not invest this subject with a constitutive function: his activity is limited to emphasizing—according to the direction or character of his interest—one aspect of the object at a time, and to discovering a meaning without creating it.

Our present problem assumes the following form: if meaning does indeed belong to the object, how can it be diversified? Will the object not lose its coherence as a result of this diversification? The latter question presupposes that the object is unique and objective before the conditions of objectivity are applied; and it is perhaps futile to attempt to measure the efficacity of the transcendental in terms of the transcendent considered as a norm. The object does not exist independently of what constitutes it. Thus, for example, if we fail to recognize the expression belonging to an aesthetic object, it ceases to be this kind of object for us. It is true that the being of the aesthetic object imposes itself on the person perceiving it as an end in itself—i.e., as a norm for whoever participates in its epiphany—and hence seems to claim an autonomous existence; but the aesthetic object is still a perceived object, and its full truth requires the correct perception of the spectator. Does this mean that perception constitutes the object? In answering this question, we must not go as far as Kant does; for him, the in-itself of the object is only an idea, and the objectivity of the object comes from the *a priori* informing it. If the *a*

9. This claim to value involves an *a priori* even for something whose beauty we deny and that does not please us; similarly, the delicious is an *a priori* for a dish which we may not like but which remains a good [*un bien*] incarnating deliciousness: proof that the object does not await our judgment. Instead, judgment articulates a meaning given *in* the object by means of which we decide to judge a thing or situation in a certain way. When I say that a mountain is unconquerable, this judgment does not furnish the meaning *of* the object; but when I discover the mountain as an aesthetic or mythical object—as an Eiger or Jungfrau—I do not judge: I *know* by experiencing a meaning.

priori is constitutive *in* the object itself and if objectivity does not proceed from an objectification, the truth of the object does not depend on us for its being, but only for its recognition. This is why the truth of the object proposes itself to us as an absolute demand determining the truth of our perception. We must therefore impute to the object itself the diversity of its objective aspects, for different points of view or intentions serve only to record such an objective diversity of aspects or meanings. This diversity does not destroy the unity of the object; it attests only to its inexhaustibility. Hence the object may be differentiated without losing its coherence. Various *a priori* constitute it without compromising it and without becoming themselves blurred: none of them is a singular affirmative essence, and none of them defines the meaning of the object so exactly and exclusively that it could claim a monopoly over the others or forbid them altogether. Even joyfulness cannot define the meaning of a Bach fugue by excluding all reference to temporality or unity. The object is constituted by the joint composition of all the relevant *a priori*. This would not be possible if these *a priori* constituted the object as unique and singular in its very being: their diversity would destroy its uniqueness. The *a priori* are only a mediation between the object and the subject; they constitute the object as an object for a subject by manifesting what is universal, not unique, in it.

Therefore, the different *a priori* constituting an object do not introduce contradiction into it. Yet a definite ambiguity remains in the object's relation to the subject. We are obliged to say both that we possess *the* truth and that a truth is only true for us. If the transcendental is no longer a subjective condition for objective knowledge, and if it is elevated to objectivity and integrated with the object, the object involved here is only the object *as known*. This restriction has three implications. First, it warns us that the *a priori* cannot appear to us without being subjected to knowledge [*connaissance*], though knowledge is not the measure of being. Secondly, the *a priori* also refers to subjectivity; although it is present in the object without being introduced by subjectivity, it must also be present in subjectivity itself. For subjectivity is not absolutely receptive; what it does contribute is not, however, a systematic framework of rules, but a fashion of seeing—that is, the possibility that what it sees has a meaning for it, and consequently the possibility of failing to know or to recognize a truth when not responding to an objective *a priori* by means of a corresponding subjective one. Thirdly, the above restriction supports our view that the *a priori* must not be given an ontological meaning immediately, since being is first of all perceived and realized [*accompli*] in knowledge. Yet we are not forced to keep the distinction between phenomenon and thing in itself. The *a priori* does not construct the phenomenon as if it were the impoverished offspring of the thing in itself—which in turn would not be constituted by the *a priori* because it refers to an intuitive understanding. Since the object no longer has its constitutive norms outside itself in the structure of subjectivity, its truth can no longer be defined in relation to a thing in itself. The object as known is the object in itself, and the *a priori* is its truth as well as its meaning: the *a priori* is itself objective and not a condition of objectivity.[10] Certainly, the being of the object is related to my knowledge of it, but I know it as it really is; at least I have no reason to doubt this knowledge, once it has been gained. The function of the thing in itself for Kant is to assign limits to idealism; from our perspective, however, there is no need to safeguard against the vertigo of idealism. Appearance and being may be identified without implying a return to the belief that *esse est percipi*—as Sartre has forcefully shown [11]—nor even a return to Hegel, since truth is not identity. Of course, my knowledge may be partial or incomplete, but this does not imply that it is primarily subjective or subjectifying; its action on the object consists in realizing it, not constituting it—inasmuch as the object is a perceived or conceived object.

As a result, reflection cannot raise itself up to a point where the world would not be a world for a subject; it must respect the close co-operation found in perception, where sensation is the common act of feeling and felt: there is a world only for a being in the world. This is why the *a priori* constitutes the object insofar as it is an object for a subject; but the object is not created by the subject's initiative. The co-operation of subject and object requires from the subject only that he be present as himself in-formed by the *a priori* that forms the object. This co-operation does not exclude a dualism; it gives the object its own role by considering the *a priori* as a truth belonging to the object which the subject may recognize but cannot found. The object requires nothing from the subject except the knowledge by which it is realized. Yet the subject can say nothing about the object except insofar as he does realize it in knowledge; he can speak of meaning only to the

10. When we discuss the ontological meaning of the *a priori* below, it will be in this sense alone.

11. See *Being and Nothingness*, trans. Hazel E. Barnes (New York, Philosophical Library, 1956), Introduction, *passim.*—Trans.

extent that he discovers it, and truth is revelation [12] only when it is adequation—i.e., when the subject is equal to what he finally *has* to see, and is able to recognize what is thus seen. In the chapters that immediately follow, we shall examine this subjective aspect of the *a priori*.

12. The word "revelation" [*dévoilement*] has Heideggerian rather than theological overtones in this context; Heidegger's basic notion, as set forth in the essay "The Essence of Truth," is that truth is a process of unveiling. See Laszlo Versenyi, *Heidegger, Being, and Truth* (New Haven, Yale University Press, 1964). —Trans.

Part II
The Subjective *A Priori*

6 / The *A Priori* as Known *A Priori*

THE TRANSCENDENTAL CHARACTER of the *a priori* also means that it is known by the subject before he experiences objects: it is both given *to* him and given *in* him. Consequently, we must pair the subjective aspect of the *a priori* with its objective aspect. The former aspect is essential for Kant: since the *a priori* determines the object of experience, it is anterior to experience; as such, it can be situated only in transcendental subjectivity; even if we reject the notion of a constitutive subjectivity, we must retain the idea that the *a priori* belongs to subjectivity: the *a priori* is known *a priori*. In other words, we are not merely receptive in our relation with the world; we go out to meet it, and always anticipate it. There are things we do not learn; we know them from the beginning, as if we had always been familiar with them—as if comprehension [1] implies connaturality. We learn about the calendar, but we do not learn what time is; we learn harmony or counterpoint, not the joyfulness of a Bach fugue; we learn zoology, not the horse's nobility. In considering concrete subjectivity, we shall discover the *a priori* in its brute or virtual state; this kind of *a priori* is not so much set forth by subjectivity as given in it—given as constituent and truly *a priori* because it is anterior to the experience belonging to this subjectivity.

The *a priori* is not a rule possessed and applied by subjectivity. It is first of all objective—that is, constitutive of the object independently of the subject, even though the object is always an object for a subject. What the subject does possess is the aptitude for comprehending the *a priori* proffered to him and, once given,

1. "Comprehension" here translates *co-naissance,* which literally means co-birth but which may be seen as a variation on *connaissance*—knowledge or comprehension.—Trans.

recognized by him. As subjective, the *a priori* is just this aptitude, this pre-given comprehension of the given, without which the meaning of the given would appear—as in the case of the *a posteriori*—only at the end of a more or less detailed investigation. Furthermore, such a process of elaborating empirical knowledge requires the pre-existence of a primordial knowledge. The *a priori* is what I already know, just as the slave boy in Plato's *Meno* already "knew" geometry. Yet how can we reconcile this character of the *a priori* with the fact, emphasized by Scheler, that it is given in a specific kind of experience? How can it be a given which is already given? And if it is given, how can it belong to the structure of subjectivity?

We should first observe that the slave boy does not know that he knows geometry. His knowledge is a possibility that could remain dormant indefinitely, unless some event comes to awaken it; thus geometry as a science was latent until, as Kant remarked, there occurred "a revolution brought about by the happy thought of a single man." [2] Our example of the slave boy may, however, be misleading: the advent of geometry only represents the making explicit of an *a priori* spatiality, the transition from the prereflective to the reflective stage. But spatiality is first experienced according to a kind of natural geometry [3] immanent in perception, thus before the creation of a formalized geometry; at this stage, distance is revealed by the relative remoteness of objects, and the dimensions of space by the intercourse between my body and the world. Hence I have always known what the far and the near, the high and the low, the long and the broad are, even if I am incapable of defining these notions objectively and of constructing a geometrical figure by myself. Similarly, when the expression belonging to an object reveals an affective quality or a value to me, I have the impression that I am already familiar with the meaning thus revealed, and that I can give a name to its content, subsume the affective quality under an affective category, or place the value in a hierarchy of values—even if I cannot define the category or lay out the hierarchical system. An implicit knowledge appears as present in me without needing to be formulated; this is why it is important to distinguish the *a priori* from the pure knowledge which makes it explicit and which is not always attainable (or at least is never complete): whereas a primordial certi-

2. Immanuel Kant, *Critique of Pure Reason*, trans. Norman Kemp Smith (London, Macmillan, 1933), p. 19 (B xi).

3. "Géométrie naturelle" is an expression coined by Malebranche to designate our primordial perception of space.—Trans.

tude is always present. In order to be actualized, this certitude does not have to equal truth; it suffices that it found truth.

The above remarks imply the virtuality of the subjective *a priori* in its being, as well as the historicity of the objective *a priori* in its appearing. How may we elucidate this idea of a virtual knowledge of meaning? We shall not hesitate to psychologize such knowledge by assigning it to a concrete subject. First of all, however, we shall deal briefly with its metaphysical overtone. The ultimate meaning of this overtone will be examined later: the indication of a pre-existing accord between the subject and the world; at the present, this metaphysical aspect will be seen in its relation to the subject. It signifies that something exists in him before his personal history; thus it tends to rehabilitate the theory of innate ideas. As we have seen, this theory has been accused of naturalizing the transcendental, but the moment has now come for us to accept this accusation by renewing the bonds between the transcendental and the psychological. The theory of innate ideas is above all a metaphysical affirmation—even if it is bad metaphysics—because it absolutizes the subject. To say that the subject bears the *a priori* in himself—i.e., bears the virtual knowledge of the meaning constituted by the objective *a priori*—is to affirm that he depends neither on his personal history nor on the external world; he would be dependent only if he had to acquire what he already possesses. Therefore, so far as he possesses this virtual knowledge, he is unengenderable, as we have already hinted; he is always already there. Of course, he is born, but the upsurge of the for-itself as a being capable of revealing the world to itself is not merely an historical event. The immediate is here nontemporal. History arises from a nonhistorical ground, from a beginning which, though situated in time, inaugurates time.[4]

In one form or another, this idea is found in philosophies never accused of psychologism. Even in Kant we might find a certain support for it: does he not deny that empirical psychology has the last word? Doubtless it is the transcendental which for him is nontemporal, since it represents a system of logical conditions which cannot be compromised by the psychological. But in addition to the transcendental subject, and apart from its mysterious link with *Gemüt*, Kant maintains the idea of the thing in itself, not only in order to combat the temptation of idealism, but also to designate the moral subject who acts according to an

4. This relation of the subject to time prefigures the relation of man and world which we shall discuss in Part III.

intelligible causality. For the Kantian subject is also a moral agent, and reason is also practical reason. This moral subject is no longer purely logical; his free actions insert themselves into the temporal web, and the kingdom of ends to which he belongs must be attained within history. Now this subject, who is already a person, is not wholly temporal: not only because his free actions are absolute beginnings, but also because his moral destiny proceeds from a radical choice. Kant's *Religion within the Limits of Reason Alone* clarifies this notion of an original affirmation within the subject.

Is there not an echo of such an idea in Sartre? His existential psychoanalysis is both a genetic theory of personality and a search for a fundament for the personality. Going back beyond the explanations that psychology is content with and that "refer ultimately to inexplicable original givens," [5] he discovers the finally irreducible element in man to be an "original project" in which the for-itself determines its being and by which it unifies itself freely. Having all the unpredictability of a free act and being both completely contingent and irreducible, this "original choice of our being" is really pretemporal or nontemporal. Sartre attributes this choice to freedom and attempts to guarantee its nonsubstantiality by saying that "the structure [constituted by this choice] can be called the *truth* of freedom." [6] But it is significant that he should introduce the notion of person here: freedom "is not to be distinguished from the choice of freedom; that is, from the person himself." [7] We shall say instead that the person, considered as the subject defined by the *a priori* proper to him, is given to himself; we shall not designate a specific giver in this action. Thus the subject has a nature: he is affected by a contingency which is not necessarily the mark of freedom. Yet, whether the subject is responsible for his nature or not, what we want to affirm is the idea that he is rooted in the nontemporal—even though he manifests and realizes himself only in time.

The nontemporal is the *a priori* as virtual in the subject. In other words, the virtual can be the principle of an individual history to the extent that it actualizes itself or merely tends to actualize itself; perhaps, even at the level of consciousness and of life, there is history only through the solicitation of the virtual. All genesis or authentic development which is not simple repetition is

5. *Being and Nothingness,* trans. Hazel E. Barnes (New York, Philosophical Library, 1956) pp. 559–60.
6. *Ibid.,* p. 568.
7. *Ibid.*

perhaps an actualization of the virtual: as we have granted to empiricism, there is in this sense a historicity of the *a priori*. Though a condition of history, the virtual in itself is nevertheless not historical; only the circumstances of its actualization are. As innate, the virtual is born *in* and *with* the individual. This has the paradoxical implication that the virtual has no birth date, since birth, in any case, has a date only so far as events are dated in relation to it or so far as it too is considered as an event in the world. The virtual is the principle of genesis, not its effect. And, as imbued with the virtual and constituted by it, the subject is unengenderable.

Such is the primary significance of a theory of innate ideas for us. To the extent that it concerns what is foreign or anterior to facts, this doctrine does not have to be submitted to a factual test. Yet it calls for facts in two ways. First, as we have already seen, it does not discredit a genetic theory. For the virtual commands the actual; the anteriority of the virtual—of the *a priori*—is not only logical, but also real, for the virtual institutes a chronology. Time does not await logic, but logic must imprint itself upon time, wherein it retains its autonomy by appearing as an origin, as a beginning which has no beginning: the logical and thus nontemporal anteriority of the *a priori* is expressed in the temporal order as a radical anteriority. Moreover, we should accept the idea of a logical anteriority only with caution. As objective, the *a priori* is contemporaneous with experience because it is perceived in the object; thus its actualization takes place in history. Only as subjective—hence virtual—can the *a priori* claim an anteriority that could be called logical in order to express its absolute character, but that still has to be translated into the language of temporality by such an expression as "always already there." It is this "always already there" that a genetic theory may bring to light: by showing how the virtual is actualized, such a theory manifests the primordial character of the virtual. The value of a theory of learning, for example, lies in its showing both what is learned (including how one must learn it) and what is not learned. Thus one learns that certain foods are agreeable, but not what the agreeable in itself is; or one learns that something is an object, but not what constitutes the object as object. Similarly, psychoanalysis can show that the libido is attached to a certain object throughout its vicissitudes, but not that the patient learns what the lovable or the hatable is, or what another person is insofar as he is similar to the patient. By a sort of method of residues, the subjective *a priori* can be detected as being always already known—just as the objective *a priori* can be distinguished from the *a posteriori* as that which is immediately known. More generally speaking, a genetic theory of personality can show how an individual has been open to certain meanings or values, and closed to others, since his childhood: his personality may be defined by the several *a priori* which it conceals [8] and which, taken as a whole, form what we may call his existential *a priori*.

This brings us to the second reason why a theory of innate ideas must proceed from the metaphysical to the empirical and accept the reproach of being a psychologism. It must do so because the virtual is actualized only if it belongs to a concrete subject, capable of activity—a subject who can put it to work and who is for the virtual what *das Gemüt* is for the transcendental in Kant's eyes. A concrete subject is a subject who is born and possesses a nature. This nature is constituted as much by transcendental as by empiricial determinations, just as birth is both a metaphysical and a physical event. Yet the transcendental exists, even as virtual, only by incarnation in the empirical. Does it risk being compromised by this incarnation? No, for we shall discover that new guarantees for its transcendental character are found precisely in this return to the empirical. In the meanwhile, our view of the virtual allows us to make the subjective *a priori* appear in the psychological life of the subject, and perhaps to describe it, with certain reservations, in psychological terms. Phenomonology can aid us here to the extent that it does not deny being a psychology and employs intentional analysis in developing a genetic theory. In support of the notion of virtual knowledge, we could invoke what Heidegger calls the pre-ontological comprehension of the world: *Dasein* is a *lumen naturale*, and its fundamental project is to disclose Being by projecting its own possibilities since it carries in itself the pre-comprehension of that which it discloses.

8. Of course, every genetic theory will try indefinitely to postpone stating what this residue is and may even refuse to describe it at all, for its ambition is to apply a genetic procedure to everything. This refusal is easy, since one is always tempted not only to confuse the *a priori* and the *a posteriori*, but also to overlook the subject as subject, that is, the original act of comprehension revealing a virtual knowledge. When the given is manifestly given—and the *a priori* is just as much given as the *a posteriori*—one forgets that it must be received and that no one would search for anything if something had not already been found. One forgets to be amazed that a child is sensitive to so many things: to the atmosphere of the family, to the irreducibility of living beings, to the flight of time, to the demands of justice—all *a priori* meanings that can be grasped immediately. Yet it is still the case that a genetic theory is perfectly acceptable, and is even perhaps the ultimate recourse in explanation. Criticism of the type practiced by Kant has never discredited empirical psychology.

In *Being and Time,* where Heidegger is perhaps still under the influence of Husserl's doctrine of regions, this pre-comprehension is sometimes given a differentiated content—e.g., when it is claimed that every science brings forth an *a priori* in the very act by which it puts itself in the presence of its object, disengaging and delimiting it.[9] In Heidegger's later works, however, the world tends to be identified with Being, and pre-comprehension is conceived as an indeterminate openness to Being, a transcendence oriented by a single possibility; thus pre-comprehension has become an *a priori* of the *a priori* that is no longer *a priori* at all.

Hence we shall refer ourselves to Husserl instead. His phenomenological analysis takes account of a certain marginal element of conscious experience: all consciousness involves a zone of potentialities, an unthematized background designating the horizonal structure of all experience. The nonactualized element may of course have been actual and simply have fallen into the background from lack of attention. Yet it may be that the present nonactualized was never actual; it may be the possibility of a later experience rather than the result of an anterior experience. When phenomenology becomes genetic and reflects upon the foundations of experience (even if Husserl never completely mastered this kind of reflection, as Quentin Lauer claims [10]), what it first discovers, according to Husserl's fourth *Cartesian Meditation,* is the *habitus,* the weight of the acquired and sedimented. The genesis by which knowledge acquired through previous acts is drawn together and by which the object appears as "ready made" [*tout fait*] is a passive genesis. This kind of genesis operates in us without our conscious participation, and we can only register its results. Without wanting to be, the ego is constitutive of "a world with an ontological structure familiar to us." This problem of prepredicative experience is developed at length in *Erfahrung und Urteil*—to the point that Husserl's idealism seems to turn into an empiricism, as Jean Wahl suggests,[11] or to give free reign to an historical materialism, as Tran Duc Tao has shown.[12]

Yet one wonders whether a *habitus* sedimented from this prepredicative experience must be understood only as an acquired

9. See *Being and Time,* trans. John Macquarrie and Edward Robinson (New York, Harper and Row, 1962), p. 414.

10. *La Genèse de l'intentionnalité dans la philosophie de Husserl* (Paris, Presses Universitaires de France, 1954), p. 213.

11. See his "Notes sur la première partie de *Erfahrung und Urteil* de Husserl," in *Revue de métaphysique et de morale* (January–March 1951), pp. 6–35.—Trans.

12. See his *Phénoménologie et matérialisme dialectique* (Paris, Editions Minh-Tan, 1951), *passim.*

disposition or whether it might be a primordial disposition as well. In other words, is the *a priori* not responsible for the pre-constituted meaning which a genetic approach discovers as present and active in myself, and which assures me that I have some knowledge [*intelligence*] of the world before being explicitly knowledgeable [*intelligent*] concerning it? Husserl writes that "the culminating point of a theory of evident judgments (thus even of a theory of judgments as such) is to reduce in a genetic fashion predicative evidence to the non-predicative evidence that is called experience." [13] Is not this latter kind of evidence the experience of the *a priori* in its brute state, as immanent in perception and as irreducible? Still, insofar as Husserl considers such experience as the present effect of past knowledge and designates transcendental subjectivity as the only *a priori*, he grants both too much and too little to the ego, especially in its relation to time. He allows the transcendental ego to be constitutive not only of the world but also of time; yet he refuses to consider it as involving anything nontemporal, since its present is always the beneficiary of a past. Moreover, attempting to grasp the nature of time through the inspection of the ego (if not in fact deducing time from consciousness), he does not really do full justice to time: it becomes only the compossibility by which the ego's unity is assured and which assures in turn the constitution of time as totality on the basis of the present. To render justice both to time and to consciousness, perhaps we must realize, first, that time is a destiny for consciousness (as is attested by the flux of conscious experience) and, secondly, that there is in consciousness—we would prefer to say in the subject—something nontemporal (as is attested by the unspecifiable anteriority of the virtual). This anteriority is unspecifiable because the past involved in knowledge is an absolute past.

This we had first expressed by speaking of a logical anteriority. But this *de jure* anteriority in the thinking life of the ego is also an anteriority *de facto*. May we not confer on the subjective *a priori* a psychological name and attribute it to memory—an originary memory? What does the virtual in fact signify? It signifies what is not known at first, what I know only afterwards when I say: I already knew it, or I have always known it. In principle, the virtual is the presence of self to self: in Bergsonian terms, the immanence of the past in the present—an immanence that cre-

---

13. E. Husserl, *Formale und transzendentale Logik* (Halle, Niemeyer, 1930), p. 186.

ates the profundity of the self. The virtual is what I am because I am essentially memory, full of my past; this plenitude is not, however, specified into images, but determines the meaning of my being in the present. Thus virtuality must be understood in reference to being rather than in relation to knowing. Knowledge may also be referred to, if it is defined not as a process of aiming at, but as one of coinciding with: if, that is, it is a manner of being and not a manner of acting or of preparing for action by the elaboration of concepts. In this sense, we can say with Jeanne Delhomme that "the past is wholly knowledge, or more exactly, self-knowledge." [14] It is knowledge to the extent that it is not yet known— i.e., detached from the self in order to be represented—because knowledge here is nothing other than presence to self, a co-birth [*co-naissance*] with the self. Therefore, so far as the virtual is concerned, knowledge can only be self-knowledge, on the condition that the relation between self-consciousness and self-knowledge instituted by Sartre be reversed: for here knowledge is less, not more, than consciousness. If such an opposition is established between actuality—consciousness of the world—and virtuality— consciousness of self—we must add that the latter consciousness is really an unconsciousness, for virtual self-knowledge is a knowledge that I *am* and not a knowledge that I *possess*. To actualize the virtual, to give the unconscious access to consciousness without causing it to lose its being as unconscious (contrary to the aim of psychoanalysis) is generally to realize in another perspective what Kant took to be impossible: a nonobjectifying knowledge of the self. And it is also to claim to combine two very different senses of self-relation: the relation to oneself as negation of the self, thus as the emptiness which defines self-consciousness for Sartre, and the relation to oneself as presence to self, hence as the plenitude which defines self-consciousness for Bergson.

Is this possible? We shall return to this question shortly, but first we must see if the virtual, when it characterizes knowledge, can be referred to self-knowledge. If so, this would seem to prevent a virtual knowledge of the *a priori*—so long as the *a priori* are considered as visages of the world, hence as turned toward the world, not toward the self. But upon looking more closely we perceive that if virtual knowledge is limited to the self the reason is that apparently only the self can exist with itself in the relation of presence which here defines knowledge [*connaissance*]. I am

14. Jeanne Delhomme, *Vie et conscience de la vie* (Paris, Presses Universitaires de France, 1954), p. 156.

not related to things as I am to myself; when memory is pure, I remember only myself. But what happens when memory begins to become representative and transforms itself into conscious intuition? Or, if you like, what occurs when intuition is produced with the aid of memory? Should we not say that in this case knowledge also relates to the world? For here the human monad can no longer be said to be self-enclosed and condemned to knowing only itself and the world considered as a mere well-founded phenomenon. Knowledge of the self becomes knowledge of the world as well. We must not, however, understand this statement in a Hegelian sense: to know the object is to know it as other, but this knowledge, instead of limiting itself to general and stable opinions about the object which ignore its singularity and development, may involve an intimacy with it, because I am myself present, with the totality of the self, to it. It is in this sense that I know myself: I do not know myself as identical with the object, but as present to it with all my past, and the object is present to me with all its present. The verb "to know" [*savoir*] indicates both a dimension of my being and a form of my knowledge [*connaissance*].[15] It is true that this knowledge is no longer virtual. Yet can we not find on the plane of the virtual both a knowledge [*savoir*] of the self (a knowledge which insofar as presence to self is not in fact consciousness) and a knowledge [*savoir*] of the world with which this self-knowledge would be solidary? This knowledge of the world must also be presence to: presence to the world, pure memory of the world. Without knowing it explicitly—i.e., before experience reawakens this knowledge in me—and by just being myself, I am linked with the world. I possess a certain knowledge [*connaissance*] of the world, concerning not its reality, but its meaning, the meaning that allows me to find my way about in the world. Thus equipped, I am in the world through memory—though not as a thing among things, open to all contacts and always determined by the exterior; instead, I carry a latent preconception of the world within myself; if consciousness is awakened in me, it means that I already know; and if I invent, it means that I discover within myself.

Of course, by attributing the *a priori* as virtual to memory, we seem to make it into something *a posteriori*. Yet a metaphysical

15. Wherever appropriate, I have indicated which French verbs are employed for "know" or "knowledge." *Savoir* usually means to know in the sense of knowing how to (do something); *connaître* implies acquaintance with (something or somebody). In the present context, however, Dufrenne does not always contrast these primary meanings in such an obvious manner. Where this is the case, I omit giving the French equivalent.—Trans.

meaning may be retained for memory. With Bergson, for example, it has at least a cosmological meaning: duration is concentrated and brought together in memory, and duration is creative. By means of memory I am not only an heir, but bear my heritage within me: the history of the world; and this is why I am linked with the world. Naturally it is not a question of bearing a résumé of creative evolution that has been imprinted upon me; but in my consciousness, at the pure point where it is unconscious, life knows itself, is present to itself, and is ready for new adventures. Since memory offers to duration the means for achieving itself, the life manifesting duration is brought together in me, and the world produced by this life is in a certain sense interior to myself.[16] The meaning that I know is basically the direction that is taken by life, which expects to be prolonged by me; I know this meaning because I am its terminal point: a witness who is perhaps also responsible for it.

Now this cosmology may serve to justify the metaphysical meaning of memory—a meaning for which memory is not only the recollection of my own history or the résumé of my own experience, but also the very possibility of experience: the *a priori* as virtual. To say that memory is the "messenger" of an experience older than myself is to say that it always anticipates and conditions what my experience will be. This prepersonal memory, which is not merely the seat of particular memories, but an implicit knowledge, does not belong to me; it is the echo of a past which is not mine or anyone's: the echo of the world so far as I appear in it. Perhaps we must say both that it founds my personal memory—in the sense that my past can remain present to me only within a broader field of presence having the dimensions of the world—and that memory, as Hegel suggests, can essentialize only because it bears within it essences that are preconstituted meanings. In any case, if personal memory, understood as implicit knowledge, is first of all knowledge of self and then knowledge of the object, the converse is true of my prepersonal memory: it is first of all virtual knowledge of the world, a singular disposition to recognize and orient myself in it. And we can say that it founds the person, if "person" is defined in terms of a receptive power possessing the *a priori* and opening the individual to a particular world or to certain aspects of the world at large.

Consequently, when the *a priori* is considered in its constitu-

16. This is why man, unlike animals, may feel responsible for his individual life—and be conscious of death as a radical event.

tive function with respect to the object, we must say that it is virtually known; and in its relation with the subject, it is this virtual knowledge itself. Such knowledge is virtual in two ways: it waits for experience in order to be put into operation—as for instance we await the apprehension of a succession of events to apply the notion of causality—and it waits for transcendental reflection to be systematized and made explicit, as the categories are specified by the principles of understanding. And this knowledge, according to its formal reality, i.e., in its being as virtuality, is a structure of subjectivity. In this sense it is, like Bergsonian memory, self-knowledge; at the same time it guarantees for the self a profound being at once universal and singular, and it promotes intersubjectivity (understood as the communication of similar subjects), as we shall see later.

This suggests a return to the difficulty that we pointed to above: how can the subject interpreted as consciousness possess a profound self conceived as a constellation of subjective *a priori*? How can self-knowledge in the sense that we have taken it accompany knowledge of the world? In other words, how can consciousness make room for an unconscious? Even with Husserl the status of the *habitus* is problematical. For clarification, we must in fact return to the Husserlian notion of intentionality. Intentionality is the capability possessed by consciousness of aiming at or "meaning" [*viser*] an object, or rather it is the being of consciousness insofar as it is an opening onto the object. In its virtuality, the *a priori* appears then as an unconscious intentionality, in which consciousness is founded as intentional. Unconscious, yet also already specified: may we not define intentionality in terms of the objects toward which it is projected? If intentional consciousness is consciousness *of*, may we not speak of intentionality *toward*? And may not such an intentionality carry its own determinations within itself as virtualities? If it does, we run straight into a triple objection inspired by Sartre.

First, if consciousness is defined by intentionality, how can we speak of an unconscious intentionality? We cannot. But intention is not understood here as consciousness abolished, repressed, or crepuscular; it is a possible consciousness, the possibility itself of consciousness—that is, a possibility which appeals to nothing exterior to consciousness, but which orients consciousness in its very being. Unconscious intentionality is a direction toward certain objects of which consciousness is not yet conscious; it is a project not yet revealed, a look [*regard*] not yet aware of what it is looking for because it has not yet found it.

The objection may, however, reappear in a second form: if intentionality is an opening, an opening cannot have an interior. Sartre would reject virtuality just as he rejects Husserl's notion of *hyle* as a "hybrid being." Intentionality implies that consciousness is nothing more than the nothingness in which being is reflected, the nothingness at the origin of freedom: "To say that consciousness is consciousness of something means that for consciousness there is no being outside of that precise obligation to be a revealing intuition of something, i.e., of a transcendent being." [17] Thus consciousness cannot in any way participate in the being of the in-itself, and precisely because it maintains relations with the in-itself: "A 'pure' subjectivity disappears. . . . Absolute subjectivity can be established only in the face of something revealed" [18]— that is, something that it does not constitute. This intentional relation presupposes an ontological relation: "Consciousness is born supported by a being which is not itself. This is what we call the ontological proof." [19] In fact, if Sartre has pushed the theory of intentionality to its limit—to the idea of consciousness as a pure relation, hence as non-being—nevertheless he has not adopted Husserl's apparent idealism: the notion of the constitutive power of consciousness, of the constitution of the transcendent in immanence. This is why he will be able, as we shall see, to make room for the idea of the *person:* subjectivity is not for him, as absolute subjectivity is for Husserl, a subjectivity in general or a universal which "natures." [20] Does this mean that it is "natured"? If consciousness is indeed born, may we not assign a nature to it? If it is "supported by a being" because it is directed toward being, does it not possess a personal manner of directing itself toward the in-itself and of bringing itself into accord with certain of its aspects? Actually we should attribute this self-direction to subjectivity, not to consciousness, for in its very act consciousness is never more than a pure grasping of something transcendent. Yet should we not say that this act is founded on subjectivity, interpreted not as consciousness of consciousness, but as the possibility of consciousness and a possibility for consciousness? Naturally one grants a being or nature to consciousness indirectly by making it into the pure act of a subjectivity, and in a sense not

17. *Being and Nothingness,* p. lxl.
18. *Ibid.,* pp. lxi–lxii.
19. *Ibid.,* p. lxi.
20. Dufrenne here alludes to Spinoza's notion of *natura naturans*—the creative aspect of Nature or Substance in which Nature is "naturing." By contrast, *natura naturata*—Nature "natured"—is the fixed and already-created aspect of Substance.—Trans.

differing greatly from Sartre when he writes: "Consciousness is a being such that in its very being, its being is in question." [21] For the virtuality by which subjectivity is granted a nature is itself, we might say, a being-in-question, and in no way the opaque and transcendent being of the in-itself: a virtuality is not a state of consciousness, but the mode of being of a being that is complete only as consciousness. Far from tarnishing the transparency of intentionality, virtuality prepares for it and annuls itself in it.

There is admittedly something perfect in consciousness as such: the purity of the void, the rigor of absolute zero. For consciousness is nothing more than an opening onto the world, and its intentionality is total. It does not receive and assimilates still less; nor does it constitute—which would still be a subtle form of assimilation. Instead, it "bursts toward" [*s'éclate vers*]; Sartre's description seems faultless. Yet if consciousness manifests a Mallarméan splendor of non-being, this is because it does not *exist*. That which exists is not consciousness, but the subject as concrete.[22] The consciousness which is project is only its own project; I am never consciousness completely. My body signifies not only my contingency, but also my impurity. There is thus an opposition between consciousness and subjectivity, to wit, that consciousness *is not*, while subjectivity *is*, yet without being an in-itself. But we must add that subjectivity is the real [*réelle*] possibility of consciousness, or that consciousness represents subjectivity in its possible aspect: its project, though a project destroying itself at the very moment of realizing itself; as Sartre would say, the for-itself is constantly being swallowed by the in-itself. Subjectivity is precisely this perpetual project of becoming pure project.

By now it should be clear that subjectivity is not absolutely different from consciousness and that they may easily be confused. Subjectivity is intentional to the extent that it tends to be consciousness, and hence is already transcending itself toward the world. Yet this movement is not a pure movement without any cause or motive; it is a movement originating in the in-itself. Thus it may involve a "metaphysical" meaning, a meaning which is in

21. *Being and Nothingness*, p. lxii.
22. In this we do not mean to endorse Heidegger's critique and substitute existence for consciousness under the pretext that consciousness does not adequately express the essential transcendence of *Dasein*. It seems to us on the contrary that consciousness as described by Sartre meets this demand and that, moreover, philosophical reflection must start from it; such an analysis of consciousness casts the necessary light upon the subject. We cannot, however, stop with consciousness, but must advance to the being of the subject, that is, to the person.

fact taken into consideration by Sartre when he wonders whether physical movement might not be an attempt on the part of the in-itself to found itself, and thus whether this movement might not be a preliminary sketch of the for-itself: a still hesitant transcendence toward the absolute event represented by the upsurge of the for-itself. In affirming this, we would again be not so far from Bergson, since consciousness would be prefigured by life and somehow even by matter. We shall keep this thesis in mind—one which remains for Sartre in the stage of an hypothesis—when we attempt to understand how the *a priori* can be both subjective and objective. For the moment, we are only attempting to conceive of an intentionality which is *someone's* intentionality and which is expressed by the acts of a singular person characterized by an existential *a priori.*

The third objection is that to personalize subjectivity in this manner is to introduce surreptitiously the concept of predestination; the person would not make himself open or closed to the objective *a priori,* which he would receive unwillingly: such is the implication that results from interpreting the transcendental as innate. Involved here is the problem of my capability of conversion, that is, of opening myself to certain *a priori*—e.g., to moral values or to formal significations—previously inaccessible to me. Perhaps we should say that, even if I succeed in discovering them, this discovery is a function of a personal perspective and I cannot help relating them to a system which constitutes the basis of my personality—the ground for all my achievements—and which remains immutable. Thus the artist discovers aesthetic categories only through his own style. In any case, we must not deny that the subject has a nature to begin with. I am myself given: *aus mir* and not *durch mich*, as Jaspers says when he speaks of the contingency of the for-itself, of the facticity of its upsurge.[23] This facticity defines the fundamental relation of the for-itself with the world. It means that a world exists as a totality of things, but also that I am compromised by this world. The choices expressing the spontaneity of my various motivations also express myself as not having chosen myself. But this indicates nothing other than my contingency. It does not mean in addition that I have been chosen as one possibility among others in a system of compossibilities; nor does it mean that I am enclosed in my own formula and destined to follow the thread of a metaphysical necessity. This formula defines my openness, my existence in the world as ca-

23. *Philosophie* (Berlin, Springer, 1932), II, 383.

pable of acting in and knowing the world; I am caught up in a system only so far as the system is related to me. I am "natured" only as much as I am "naturing," and vice versa.

"Naturing" but not constituting: the only constitutive activity I can practice consists in apprehending the *a priori* in nature, not in introducing them into nature. The *a priori* orient the experience of the subject; they determine the aspects of the world to which the subject is made sensitive, as distinct from those to which he is closed and blind. They measure the amount of the subject's openness. I am not constitutive; rather, the *a priori* considered now as subjective constitute me. They define my constitution in the traditional sense of the word: as a structure of being, not as a condition of possibility. For I am these virtualities: *nosse* implies *esse*. Through them I have a nature, though not the nature acquired during my life-span as a result of the experiences I have; my nature here is composed of a set of dispositions which are present in me from the beginning and which make me sensitive to certain aspects of the world, as a body is sensitive to the actions of other bodies. Such a view of the subject perhaps avoids the impasse represented by a transcendental subject equipped with various *a priori* and yet incapable of rejoining the personal subject: for to be a transcendental subject is also to be a personal subject. The transcendental is personalizing only because it is somehow psychologized and because, instead of engendering a pure activity, it assigns a double passivity to the subject: on the one hand, the passivity implied by the fact that the transcendental is perceived in the object it constitutes; on the other, the passivity implied by the fact that the transcendental exists in the subject (which it also constitutes) in a state of virtuality.

7 / The Subject as Incarnate

WE MUST PURSUE further the path leading back to the concrete subject. In so doing, should we not equate the subject now personalized by an existential *a priori* with the empirical subject, or, more specifically, with the body? Can we, then, place the *a priori* in the body conceived as the seat of virtualities as well as of habits? Let us examine the first question. The body presents a considerable problem for all philosophies of the *cogito*: how can they take account of it and conceive of an incarnated consciousness? There must, however, be a point of departure for philosophical reasoning.[1] It is tempting to begin with the body. Yet it is *thought* that would make such a decision. Moreover, could one arrive at consciousness starting from the body? Materialism is not false, but it can be a trap; nevertheless, it may be used as a safeguard against the inverse trap—the idealist snare—which characteristically menaces a philosophy of the *cogito*. But then we must detect the body *in* consciousness, and not simply join one to the other in Cartesian fashion.

For Descartes, the "substantial union" of body and soul is attested by nature: "Nature teaches me nothing more expressly or clearly than the fact that I have a body, that this body feels out of sorts when I am in a bad mood, and that it needs food or drink when I feel hungry or thirsty. . . ."[2] This voice of nature is feeling, the experience of obscure and confused qualities; it has to be guaranteed by divine truth and appear as being itself the voice

---

1. This demand for a line of reasoning attests that our thought exists in the image of our condition: as contingent and temporal; logic does not completely escape chronology. Even for Descartes—for whom truth appears in an immediate intuition—the continuity of thought requires a certain temporal economy.

2. Descartes, sixth *Meditation*.

of God. Yet what Descartes discovers in the *cogito* is a reason for the union, not its being. The union needs a justifying reason because, even if it is directly experienced, it is not immediately clear to reflection: for the understanding, the soul is really distinct from the body, since it is an autonomous substance. This precludes interpreting the union as a unity (as Aristotle thought) or as an identification (as Spinoza maintained); it can only be a conjunction. Descartes does, however, make as much progress toward unification of the two substances as is possible. He recognizes that the soul is compromised by the body; feelings are not the pure thoughts of a soul distinct from the body, and the body in its turn is structured by the soul: its functional indivisibility results from its union with the soul. Apart from this union the body exists as a mere collection of mechanical parts without a nature of its own; such a machine gains purposiveness only when the soul bestows finality upon it, and "turns a purely mechanical assemblage into a whole, teleologically related to all of the body." [3] As a result, the body is both divisible and indivisible: if on the one hand it participates in the indivisibility of the soul, on the other hand the indivisible soul participates in extension without being itself an extended substance. In sum, Descartes accurately describes the effects of the union of body and soul, but he admits that this union is unintelligible in itself.

Furthermore, he believes that unintelligibility is a good thing, since it provides a reason to celebrate God for having created this union, and to exonerate Him for having made man fallible. Yet this unintelligibility would perhaps diminish if the duality within the subject appeared as a first approximation only, and if the effects analyzed by Descartes were used to testify to the unity of man, not to the union of two substances. This would not mean that we should cease to consider soul and body as distinct; for in the reflective experience undertaken by Descartes at the beginning of the *Meditations* [4] or in the contrasting experiences of sacrifice and abandon, their separation possesses a meaning as fully

3. Martial Guéroult, *Descartes* (Paris, Aubier, 1953), II, 185.
4. Is the discovery of the soul as distinct really an experience? Yes and no: the doubt which reveals the self as having a thinking *nature* is a philosophical experience. It results from a bias toward rationality and systematically breaks with ordinary experience; yet it is expressed in the first person and is presented as a test or trial undertaken by an individual philosopher. A chain of reasoning is nevertheless built upon this doubt when it is depersonalized and when one passes from experience to the concept, from the *cogito* to the *res cogitans*. Experience by itself does not reveal the soul as distinct from the body; it simply manifests different possibilities of the subject: the vicissitudes of his life.

lived [5] as their union. But we should at best cease to substantialize them, and cease to found the idea of a real distinction upon the real experience of a distinction. Instead, we should conceive the idea of a real unity, lived [*vécue*] in diverse experiences, though without these experiences being able to introduce a principle of dissociation into this unity. When the vicissitudes of this union— e.g., the soul acting on the body and vice versa, or the soul trying to cut itself loose from the body—are invoked to illustrate fully lived experiences, they are usually of the order of the "as if" because they presuppose dualism (as in the case of the pineal gland, which was invented to express the more particular union of the soul with a part of the body). Of course we may speak of the soul: certain moral codes invite us to, as do certain actions; but we should realize that we are then abstracting from the concrete subject, and thus making only a nominal distinction. The same holds for the body, which is all the more easily spoken of because we also speak of "physical bodies" and perhaps because the technique-oriented mind is spontaneously materialistic. Nonetheless, whenever I say "my body," I prevent myself from considering it as any body whatsoever, as a machine. And I should not think, either, of a body linked with a soul, but of an animated body; nor of a soul linked with a body, but of a corporeal soul.

Yet I can do this only by starting from either the soul or the body alone, since reflection requires a certain detachment from experience, even if it is for the sake of systematizing it. Thus one could start from the body, as Merleau-Ponty did in *The Structure of Behavior*.[6] We shall start from the soul. This would, however, lead us nowhere if "consciousness" were not substituted for "soul," as is so often done in modern philosophy. For to speak of the soul in the technical sense is already to adopt substantialism and hence dualism. Therefore, we shall start from the *cogito* interpreted as consciousness. But again we must be careful; we cannot plan to find the body as if it were already there, existing independently of the soul, and ready for a kind of pact with it. And we cannot deduce the body: either in the Cartesian sense of the word, according to which it is subordinated to consciousness both in the order of being and in the order of knowing (for if the body has a

5. *Vécue*—current English has no ready equivalent of this past participle of "live" [*vivre*], which implies more than verbs like "experience" or "feel." I have used the somewhat awkward "lived" in keeping with recent discussions of Merleau-Ponty's concept of the "lived body" [*le corps vécu*]. The noun form, *le vécu*, will generally be translated by "lived experience" or "experience."—Trans.

6. *The Structure of Behavior*, trans. Alden L. Fisher (Boston, Beacon Press, 1963).—Trans.

meaning, it is to be always already there, thanks to causes, not reasons), or in the Kantian sense of deduction, since the body is unjustifiable: it is neither a right [droit] nor a possession. I do not possess a body in the way that I own a coat; instead, nature teaches me that I *am* my body. I do say that I have bad eyes, as I say that I have a stomach-ache; but in holding my body at a distance in this manner, I affirm that I am more than a body, not that I am not a body. We must, then, find the body in consciousness, and conceive of consciousness as a body.

Doubtless one may say that consciousness bears witness to the body by the very fact that the body is present to it. Consciousness is naturally consciousness of one's body; here it is not a question of the body-as-object: we are on the plane of consciousness, not of knowledge, and shall soon have to show the relation between self-consciousness and body-consciousness. As Scheler has indicated,[7] corporeality (rather than the multiple and divisible body) is immediately given to consciousness. The child is conscious of all his body, of his body as a whole, before exploring and recognizing the diversity of its parts: consciousness of the body is anterior to the distinction between external and internal perception, and does not result from a co-ordination or interpretation of sensations. The body is given as a primary unity which is the expression of a corporeal being, not as the result of a synthesis or as the conclusion of a judgment of finality. Only in this way is it a principle of identification for the self.

Scheler does not, however, orient his analysis in this direction: for him, "I" or self—*Ichheit*—and corporeality are independent in principle, and corporeality is the principle of diversification rather than of identification. If the internal perception of the individual self and of its lived experiences [*vécus*] implies a corporeal mediation, the function of the body is (as it was for Bergson) to "select psychological experiences according to their importance for its activity," [8] to distribute them in time, and to transform their pure *Ineinander* into an *Ausser-* and *Nacheinander*.[9] In its own right, the self involves only the diversity of the *Inein-*, so that the body's intervention is necessary for classifying intentional acts according to present, past, and future, and for differentiating the

7. Max Scheler, *Der Formalismus in der Ethik und die materiale Wertethik* (Bern, Francke, 1954), pp. 408–9. (Hereafter this book will be referred to as *Der Formalismus.*—Trans.)

8. *Ibid.*, p. 421.

9. *Ineinander* means within each other; *Ausser-* and *Nacheinander* mean respectively outside of and following each other.—Trans.

various lived experiences [*vécus*] given to perception. The "explan-atory psychology" [10] which determines concrete psychic facts must therefore invoke the dissociational power of the body. What phe-nomenology reveals, however, is the fact that the identity of the "self" as such, as independent of the body, is a basic given attested by a "consciousness of continuity" which is not necessarily a continual consciousness: the totality of the individual self, which grasps itself as living in each experience, is immanent in each act of consciousness. The immanence of this unity assures "unity of meaning" and founds the relations of meaning that bring together all of the significant aspects of a total life. Thanks to these as-pects, different acts—memories or perceptions—have the same object, or at least the given object is related to the nongiven, as when we think in terms of the "same as," the "different from," the "more than," etc. In comparison with this unity of the self, the body is a factor of dissociation. At the same time, the modes of association (resemblance and contiguity), which presuppose dis-sociation, call for corporeality: there can be no resemblance for a mind without a body—only identity and difference; resemblance "expresses the essence of a self linked with a body," and conse-quently constitutes "an *a priori* form of experience for a corporeal being." [11] These principles of association restore the fundamental unity of meaning by schematizing the succession that corporeality introduces into the life of the self. In a sense they are thus the *a priori* of knowledge [*connaissance*], since they are "the material *a priori* of an explanatory psychology," and because we must invoke them in order to comprehend the reproduction of the object and the unification of meaning at the level of the corporeal self. To say that the same causes have the same effects implies a conscious-ness of the "same as"; and this consciousness implies that tempo-rality is first introduced into the self's experiences, and then mas-tered.

There is obviously some confusion in Scheler's thinking here. After describing our original body-consciousness as a total and indivisible corporeality, he tries first to make the body into a principle of dissociation and, secondly, into one of association for psychological contents, without invoking the body as an object. As

10. The distinction between "explanatory" (i.e., causal) and "descriptive" (i.e., roughly phenomenological) psychology is clarified in Karl Jaspers' *General Psychopathology*, trans. J. Hoenig and Marian W. Hamilton (University of Chi-cago Press, 1963). The distinction appears to have originated with Dilthey.— Trans.

11. *Der Formalismus*, p. 421.

if he were not assured of the immanence of the body in the self, he discovers in temporalization the catalyst capable of disclosing the presence of the body: corporeality is verified by a genetic analysis of time (and, secondarily, of space, as we might see in his investigation of contiguity). This test is well chosen: there is a close correlation between being temporal and being corporeal. But Scheler's use of this test may have backfired. For as a result of presupposing that the self is incorporeal in principle and of assuming that phenomenology can grasp it as such, Scheler also presupposes that lived experience as *Ineinander* is nontemporal at the level of the self. But is it really? Are we not obliged to understand objective time on the basis of duration, and to assign duration to consciousness? Scheler in fact must acknowledge this: if, immanent in each experience, there is a totality of the self that is the condition of the unity of meaning, this totality cannot be anything but temporal: it contains a certain density of duration, and gathers into itself "the three spheres of the present, the past (immediate memories), and the future (immediate expectation)," especially since unity of meaning is always manifested by the relation of a given with a past or future nongiven. Furthermore, this totality, which is also a continuity, flows: the *Stromphänomen* [12] belongs to all experience [*vécu*]. Scheler does, however, offer an amendment to this Husserlian doctrine: "Only the lived life [*la vie vécue*], not the living of this life, is in flux"; [13] the intentional acts in accordance with which experience is lived [*le vécu est vécu*] do not belong to the flux. But does this make sense, unless one considers acts as abstractions having only a logical signification, or unless one adopts a Cartesian philosophy of the instant which is rejected by the whole of Scheler's phenomenology?

Now, if time is more closely bound up with the subject, so is corporeality. This inference might be disavowed by a philosophy which looks for the root of time in consciousness—e.g., in the unity of its projections [*extases*]. [14] But in saying that time is *a priori*, we do not claim that it is a form projected by consciousness onto the world—a form to which consciousness is not itself subor-

12. Literally, "stream-phenomenon"; this concept of time as a flowing stream is found in William James, from whom Husserl may have borrowed the notion.—Trans.

13. *Der Formalismus*, p. 474.

14. Dufrenne refers here to Husserl's theory of time-consciousness, although the term *extase* is Heideggerian and means the way in which *Dasein* extends itself toward past, future, and present. See Heidegger, *Being and Time*, trans. J. Macquarrie and E. Robinson (New York, Harper and Row, 1962), p. 375 ff.—Trans.

dinated; instead we are claiming that both the world and the subject are temporal. The subject can understand time because he experiences or lives [*vit*] it. Temporality for him is a destiny manifesting his passivity; yet this very passivity may give him the possibility of acting, since a future is always open to him, and since the past matures him, so that this passivity lends him a defense against itself; but the subject cannot evade the continuous and irreversible flow of time: time does not suspend its course for me or in me, and my experiences of eternity are only metaphorical.

This passivity in turn manifests corporeality: time has its grip on me because I am a body. This does not mean that time is an agent connatural with the body: we should rather compare it with the movement which sets a body in motion and thus presupposes physical bodies. Yet the connection between temporality and corporeality resides principally in the fact that temporality ties me down to a present that opens onto the future only by weighing me down with a past; now the body is for me both a live opening and a dead weight, the possibility of my actions and my passions, the instrument of my future and the result of my birth: to be temporal and to be corporeal are one and the same thing for me. This holds for a rock too, but the rock is neither temporal nor corporeal in the same way that I am: it possesses neither a future nor its own body, since its present is only repetition and its body is not its own because it does not open onto the world—nor is it a center of reference in the world. In other words, I *am* time as I am my body: I am not *in* time like a thing that submits to time, repeating itself and changing without changing itself, all through the force of circumstance. I am in time only because time is in me, and because it finds in me—in the way I live it or live with it—its meaning and its fulfillment (and since it needs me to complete itself, we cannot say the converse: namely, that time is a subject). Similarly, I have a body, like a load or a limit, only because I am my body; I am the limit and the achievement, the perspective and the enclosure represented by my body. We must not, however, deduce a subordinate relationship from this striking affinity of the two terms: corporeality manifests temporality, but is neither its cause nor its effect; and corporeality cannot be captured in a causal relation, because it is contingent: it expresses my contingency.

Hence Scheler was not mistaken in using temporality to detect corporeality. What is contestable is the presupposition that corporeality exists in fact, but not in principle.[15] For this presupposition implies an insufficient idea of corporeality: the body remains exterior to the self, which in itself is as nontemporal as the transcendental ego; thus the body becomes a mere condition for the self's development, mediating and not constituting it; it does not really exist in the first person since it is accidental for the person, just as existence is an accident for essence according to Avicenna. Now it is not sufficient to describe the body as lived [*vécu*]; it must be shown to be constitutive. Scheler might have seen this had he completed his project both by discovering temporality directly in the self, not in a secondary and accidental characteristic of it, and by observing that intentional acts themselves—as well as reflection on these acts, as Husserl would add—are part of the temporal flux. He would have found in this a sign of the self's corporeality, that is, the fundamental identity of self and body, or rather, the necessity of the body.

In reassessing this identity, we must begin with consciousness, and first of all discover the self in it. We have already broached this notion when we suggested that consciousness implies subjectivity, and that only a subject can become a consciousness. Now we must verify it in another way: by disclosing subjectivity as immanent in consciousness. Why is the *cogito* in the first person? It is evident that when I say "I think," I am abstracting from my concrete personality. What then does the "I" signify? It signifies that this consciousness is a self-consciousness: when I say "I think," I think that I think. Consciousness exists for the self as a presence to self. But how is the self to be understood here? It may be interpreted as the logical condition for the unity of my various consciousnesses, and on this basis as the condition for the objectivity of my representations: here the formal being of the unity of apperception is assigned to it. Yet we have seen the difficulties involved in this elevation of the self to the transcendental level, and we shall henceforth avoid them. The self may be given another kind of being: a nonformal being which is also nonsubstantial, like that belonging to a pure relation or a pure movement: "the pure nihilating movement of reflection," [16] as Sartre says. He adds that "consciousness makes itself personal" through

15. Claiming that it exists in principle does not deny the body's contingency: if the unity of the self and the body exists in principle, not in fact, the very fact of this liaison is precisely a matter of principle: a contingency which is also necessary.

16. *Being and Nothingness*, trans. Hazel E. Barnes (New York, Philosophical Library, 1956), p. 103.

this movement, although no person is involved here, since a self, if understood as something other than the expression of this pure movement, cannot inhabit consciousness. At the very most, the self involved here is "the *reason* for the infinite movement by which the reflection refers to the reflecting and the latter to the reflection; by definition, it is an ideal, a limit." [17]

Viewed thus, subjectivity designates not a being, but the mode of being belonging to consciousness, that is, to a non-being. But does not subjectivity also refer to a subject? Does not the self refer to a "myself"? Sartre does not think so, because such a self—he calls it the ego—would alter the absolute and nonsubstantial character of consciousness by arresting the movement of reflectivity. Yet this consequence occurs only if the reflective being of the for-itself is reified into an in-itself—in other words, if the self is made into a thing, not a person.[18] And the subject as a person may always be conceived as being no one in particular, as participating in the purity of the for-itself, and in any case as not necessarily possessing the being of the in-itself, which is opaque, massive, and unalterable because it lacks otherness: thus the subject would be being and non-being at once, in-itself-for-itself (as we shall say of the body).

But let us return to the subjectivity of consciousness: self-consciousness implies a relation to the self, a consciousness of being conscious. Subjectivity manifests its interiority in this relation, for it turns back onto itself only insofar as it is turned toward the object; it is self-consciousness *as* consciousness. Yet is this all it is? Is subjectivity not also a consciousness of self *as self*, so that the self of the "of self" performs a double function here: as the pronoun of consciousness and as a pronominal absolute? Actually, at the level of the pre-reflective *cogito* there is no self-knowledge transforming the self into a known object, but only an allusion to the self that can later be made explicit by underlining the pronoun "*I*"; then the self is no longer consciousness itself or its

17. *Ibid.*
18. Sartre is certainly not wrong in fearing this danger, since psychology is always tempted to reify consciousness by substituting events for acts, facts for essences, and robots or automata for persons. Moreover, so far as Sartre's own fundamental project is to summon man to his condition and responsibility, he tries to destroy all pretext for those who act and think as if they were necessary and justified: the infamous *salauds* of *La Nausée*. Thus he radicalizes Heidegger's conception of man as a creature whose very being is in question. Yet one wonders if it is a wise move to make the subject disappear behind consciousness; this involves the risk of having to reverse one's course when undertaking an anthropology. And the description of consciousness as a for-itself separated from the specifically human cannot shake the *salauds* out of their self-complacency.

movement, but the conscious subject effecting this movement. In such a process there is no symmetrical intentionality belonging to that which intends [*vise*] the object, for consciousness does not intend or posit the subject; it experiences and lives [*vit*] it. Consciousness is not so present to its object that it is not at the same time conscious that this presence is its own presence. The "I" is thus immanent in consciousness; Scheler expresses this by saying that *Ichheit* is "an immediate given of intuition," not the result of any process of introjection. We might add that we are justified in founding the ontology of the subject upon a phenomenology. As phenomenologically given and described, the self cannot be an illusion, since it is immediately present to itself. Nor is it—like the Kantian "I think"—a simple character of successive psychological or logical consciousnesses, since it is given as a self possessing consciousness, and as an active principle that makes consciousness possible (as we said above concerning subjectivity). The subject is immanent in consciousness as that which founds consciousness, or at least as that which actively *is* consciousness. (For being conscious does not signify having consciousness like a possession. To be conscious is not to possess a quality, but to perform an act. Consciousness is the act rather than the possession of the subject—an act determining his being. "Be conscious!"—this exhortation is addressed to a subject.)

This subject is active, and therefore determined. When Scheler asserts that "*Ichheit* can exist only in an individual self" and that "the experiencing individual is given in all conscious experience," [19] he inspires us to pursue our analysis of the subject yet further. In fact, the self that haunts consciousness and helps it to achieve its fundamental selfhood [*ipséité*], as Sartre would say, is a singular self. In every consciousness, it becomes conscious of itself as unique and irreplaceable. If the *sum* accompanies even the pre-reflective *cogito*, this is because the self posits itself as an absolute by force of its singularity. An impersonal consciousness

19. *Der Formalismus*, p. 388 and p. 389. But we can no longer agree with Scheler when he adds that corporeality is not necessary to individualize the subject. He says this because he is anxious to join the self to the person, and because for him the person, understood as the seat of intentional acts, excludes corporeality. Yet he does not really succeed in joining the two: in fact he hollows out a gap within the "I think" between the "I" and the "think," between *Erlebnis* (experience) and *Erleben* (experiencing), between the function which is psychological and the act which is not. Thus Scheler gives a transcendental status to the person, except that the correlate of the person becomes the world and not an object. For if the person is not incarnated, the only purity that may be assigned to him is that of the transcendental. But what then is the relation of self and person?

would be able to posit, but might not posit *itself;* only a self affirms itself and is individualized by affirming itself. Indeed we must admit with Scheler that the individual self is not the empirical self; it is not the object of observations and inductions, the self defined in relation to others and in accordance with them. In other words, to the extent that it does not give rise to a reflection— which always risks impurity—conferring properties and prerogatives on it, this self can claim neither the being of an object nor that of a subject which would somehow remain motionless in its being as a subject, and would play the double role of subjectivity and objectivity in bad faith. It has only the precarious and absolute being of the subject. But does this being not already involve, without losing its subjectivity, the determinations that empirical investigation will isolate and emphasize? In short, if the self is a non-being, is it not the non-being of a being?

We certainly agree with Sartre that "what human reality denies or nihilates in relation to itself as for-itself can only be itself" —that is, to the extent that the self "would [like to] be what it is." [20] But does not consciousness deny itself as an in-itself precisely because it is in-itself in spite of itself, or at least because it is always menaced by the in-itself as if by its own shadow? In fact, Sartre specifies that if consciousness is negation, it is not only the indeterminate negation of the self in general, but the determinate negation of a determinate in-itself, i.e., of a particular self. In refusing its particularity, consciousness admits that it is particular; it has to have a certain perspective, a certain mode of intentionality. This particularity is not at present made explicit by means of empirical, objective determinations such as age, physical build, or social role; but it is expressed by a sort of intellectual synesthesia in the very act of the *cogito:* in the experience of a living relation with an idea that proposes or conceals itself, in the feeling of effort or relaxation, or in a certain style of thought that already characterizes me as a person. When I say "I" before any reflection on this "I," I experience myself as someone, not as just anyone or as an abstract universal. My presence to a real or ideal object is a singular presence, not an anonymous and neutral one, although it may imply different degrees of plenitude or depth—for example, according to whether I think conceptually or feel affectively. Now, the body constitutes this singularity and provides this plenitude. We should not say that the body continually reminds me of its presence, or that it supports or betrays me, embarrasses

20. *Being and Nothingness,* p. 88.

or stimulates me; for then I objectify it (though its very nature invites such objectification), and I substitute an artificial relation with my body for my spontaneous relation with the world. The body is not present to me as the world is, since it *is* my presence to the world; I am not conscious of my body as I am conscious of an object because I *am* my body. If we must speak of a consciousness of the body, we should put the "of" between parentheses, as Sartre does in the case of "consciousness (of) self": consciousness (of) body expresses the fact that the body is not an object for consciousness, but consciousness itself.

Thus we have found the body in consciousness, though not as its object: rather, as consciousness itself so far as it is singular. We have followed the same path as Sartre, who warns us not to introduce a distinction between consciousness and body: "being-for-itself must be wholly body or wholly consciousness; it cannot be united with a body." [21] Sartre also points out the singularity of the for-itself when he recalls the Platonic doctrine according to which the body individualizes the soul and represents "the individualization of my engagement in the world." [22] But in coming into the world and becoming engaged in it, are we not finally captured and compromised by it? The body in fact is "the in-itself which is surpassed by the nihilating for-itself and which reapprehends the for-itself in this very surpassing." [23] Does not reapprehending the for-itself mean that through the incarnation of the *cogito* the for-itself is also an in-itself? Yes, although not in the sense that man would be the God he dreams of becoming: a being wholly and simultaneously for-itself and in-itself. Instead, the alliance between for-itself and in-itself is established on the plane of finitude and as if it were an imperfection. Sartre, however, insists on another aspect of the for-itself: its double contingency.

On the one hand, while it is necessary that I exist in the form of being-there, still it is altogether contingent that I exist in the first place, for I am not the foundation of my being; on the other hand, while it is necessary that I be engaged in this or that point of view, it is contingent that it should be precisely in one to the exclusion of others. We have called this twofold contingency embracing a necessity the facticity of the for-itself.[24]

Therefore, the body is the facticity of the for-itself, and this is of crucial importance, as we have observed in the case of birth.

Nevertheless, in spite of this, does Sartre grant the body all of

21. *Ibid.*, p. 305.
22. *Ibid.*, p. 310.
23. *Ibid.*, p. 309.
24. *Ibid.*, p. 308.

its density? Perhaps not. Without deducing it, he arrives at the body in two ways, in both of which he is expressly opposed to Descartes. The first consists in investigating the basic relation between the for-itself and the in-itself. The in-itself here is the world, not what I am myself; consequently, the body, even though not exterior to the subject, remains idealized to a certain extent: it "designates" my situation, it "is defined" as my contingency, it "represents" my individualization. All of these verbs express the ontological function of the body, not its being; and when Sartre says that "the body manifests my contingency . . . it is *only* this contingency," [25] he defines being in terms of function and replaces the body by its meaning. Secondly, the study of the body is part of the study of the for-others. The for-itself is here opposed to the for-others, rather than to the in-itself, and the for-others determines what is or is not in-itself. The body then is in-itself only for others, while by itself, for the consciousness that experiences it or rather *is* it, it is for-itself. But is the body an in-itself only as a result of others and because it is for-others? Is it not an in-itself by itself and in its very identity with the for-itself? The body does cease to appear as the object it is for others when I experience it, instead of thinking about it and assuming the perspective of others; but does it cease to be an object? To neglect the objective being of the body is perhaps a temptation for Sartrian thinking, which remains Cartesian in principle since it starts from consciousness rather than from the body.

We must now reconsider the being of the body insofar as it is identical with consciousness: the self of self-consciousness designates both the movement of consciousness and its nature—a movement denying this nature, yet affirming it in this very denial (thus displaying the non-being of a being). The body is both surpassed and posited in this process. But we must not think it undergoes this treatment passively, as if consciousness were exterior to it. The body is surpassed and posited because it is identified with consciousness; this is its very nature. It is not surpassed by consciousness as if by its other; it surpasses itself by effecting the nihilating movement that Sartre attributes to the for-itself: such is the nature of the body-as-subject. One sometimes says that consciousness opposes the body; but one might just as well say that the body opposes itself. How does it do this? To answer such a question, we must distinguish between two kinds of experience. The first kind, exemplified by such different experiences as wild

25. *Ibid.*, pp. 309–10.

abandon or "pulling oneself together" [*ressaisissement*], is mis-leading because it involves an objectifying consciousness that may produce the illusion of a dualism; but, in fact, the body pulls *itself* together or abandons *itself*, refusing to be reduced to itself, that is, to the instantaneous and meaningless status of a thing. The second kind of experience is offered by work; this is less ambiguous, for here the body is not only on trial with itself (as in fatigue or exaltation), but also with the world. Surpassing itself toward the world, it exists only in acting, and its intentionality is the same as that of the *cogito*. More than merely "forgetting itself" in its activity, it becomes identified with it. The body is here no longer an object of knowledge, but an acting subject. It is also a thinking subject; for some thinking is inherent in its acting, and in the very style of this acting it reveals the meaning of work for the subject.[26]

Thus in all activity, even intellectual activity, the body is not experienced as a body, but as an active subject; for the geometer is also an athlete. This lateral and retrospective consciousness of the body found in work and thought is the consciousness of the body as thinking, not as capable of thought. Merleau-Ponty hinted at this when he wrote that "the subject of geometry is a motor subject." [27] But did he need to add that "the body is an original intentionality, a way of relating onself to the object which is distinct from the way we know it"? Why do we hesitate to say that the body "handles" [*manie*] symbols when it is perfectly natural to say that the body handles tools? Perhaps because we see a relation between hand [*main*] and tool that we do not see between hand and concept. Yet we should not forget that a concept must be expressed and described, as a triangle must be drawn. And, above all, the hand which handles tools is not the hand which is seen and stays seen on the same level as tools and things; it is a hand transcending itself toward the world and thus transcending what it masters; considered as a for-itself, this hand, when drawing a triangle, thinks the triangle in the very act of drawing. Of course, two students may sketch the same triangle and not have the same

---

26. This is why, as Georges Friedmann has shown, the study of the physical possibilities of the body must be followed by a psychological and psycho-sociological study of the worker. This study is necessarily incomplete inasmuch as it does not respect the worker's subjectivity; it should consider the subjective being of the body as well as the corporeal being of the subject. [See Friedmann's *Problèmes humains du machinisme industriel* (Paris, Gallimard, 1946).—Trans.]

27. *Phenomenology of Perception*, trans. Colin Smith (London, Routledge and Kegan Paul, 1962), p. 387. Except for minor changes, I follow Smith's translation. —Trans.

idea in mind; this does not mean, however, that thought is always incommensurable with gesture. The gesture of the students is an objectified gesture, which verifies the distinction between consciousness and body only because it presupposes it. By contrast, an authentic gesture is a way of comprehending the triangle, and does not differ from an idea of it; what we call "ideas" differ because authentic gestures differ. Yet it might still be objected that if I write something, I have thought of it first, and that my writing is always an instrument of ideas, just as the word is often considered as a transcription of a concept; in this view to write is to write what one thinks, and not to think as such. We could answer by showing that the gap between thought and gesture is partly filled by language, which is already gesture, and that thought does not control writing from on high. Just as thought already takes shape in silent speech, so it becomes definite in the very process of writing, at least so far as I am non-thetically conscious of my act of writing.

We should, however, render full justice to the above objection: it is true that when I reflect on the act of writing, thought seems to assume a dominant position in relation to gesture, which appears as something objective. For the body and its activity call forth objectification both as a condition and as an antithesis of their being surpassed. Nothing that is ordinarily said about the body is false: it *is* also an object, and we are not unfair to it by making it into an object to be studied by science. My body enables me to be in the world, as part of it; if the world is itself an object and not only an object of consciousness, the body is an object among other objects and can be studied as such by an objective science.[28] Once again we must realize that the body is both subject and object, consciousness and nonconsciousness. Merleau-Ponty is perhaps unfaithful to his own analysis when he writes that "the objective body is not the true version of the phenomenal body, that is, the true version of the body we live by; it is indeed no more than the body's impoverished image, so that the problem of the relation between soul and body concerns only the phenomenal, not the objective, body." [29] For objectivity designates not only a

28. This point is not immaterial: objectivity is not the being-for-others of my body. There is no reason to subordinate the philosophical examination of the body to the elucidation of the for-others. Moreover, the objectification of my body by others does not necessarily proceed from a hidden ill will on their part. Similarly, objectifying myself does not necessarily imply bad faith and self-abdication. This does not, however, excuse the *salauds* who want to gain on both counts and who exploit a situation instead of assuming it.

29. *Phenomenology of Perception*, p. 432.

quality of the known that is claimed by knowledge (and that is never completely achieved), but also the being of the object. The objective body does not possess conceptual existence; it has the existence of the in-itself that concepts strive to clarify. Thus my body is both for-itself and in-itself. The eye, for example, is both a power of vision—or rather, vision itself—and an optical apparatus. These are not two different conceptions of the eye between which we are obliged to choose; they are both true, and each has the infinite task of trying to unite itself with the other while pursuing its own course. This leads us to say again that I am consciousness and body at the same time; and we should say this without attempting to cheat by conjuring away the materiality of the body: to identify consciousness with the body is also to identify it with the body-as-object. The fact that this body exists *for* consciousness does not prevent it from *being* consciousness.

This requirement of monism concerns only a determined object: the human body (to which Descartes, as Guéroult has stressed,[30] assigned a privileged status), the only body whose status as a *cogito* is assured. I am my body on the condition of not being it, since I say "I." This is perhaps a mystery, but it is a mystery in broad daylight. Or rather, it is light itself: for the monism of the thinking body, of the body understood as *lumen naturale,* clarifies the dualism of subject and object, rather than making it disappear. But should we speak of monism here? We have already remarked that the subject-object relation cannot be one of identity: Spinozist monism presupposes Cartesian dualism as well as the substantialization of consciousness into a soul and of the body into a machine. We talk in terms of consciousness or of "consciousness-self" (to use Ruyer's term [31]) simply to avoid the trap Spinoza fell into. For monism grants too much to dualism: does one have to be dualistic in order to escape dualism? We should recall that monism, though it claims to be ontological, has a primarily logical meaning; it justifies itself by saying that soul and body are two perspectives on or two languages about one and the same reality (Substance); and substantialization is already a logicizing of experience. If we look at the phenomena themselves instead of conceptualizing them, and if we take care not to extract an ontology from phenomenology too quickly (as is done when both the world, as the correlate of consciousness, and the body, as the being-other of consciousness, are confusedly classified under

30. See Martial Guéroult, *Descartes,* II, *passim.*—Trans.
31. See Raymond Ruyer, *Eléments de psychobiologie* (Paris, Presses Universitaires de France, 1946), *passim.*—Trans.

the same rubric of the "in-itself"), we perceive that the proposition "I am my body" signifies the fundamental unity of the subject. This unity is that of a process: I am always the negation of what I am; this negation is entirely spontaneous, and is made explicit only when I reflect, as, for example, when I hesitate between materialism and spiritualism; yet it occurs all the time, and is my very existence.

Thus the for-itself and the in-itself are not two modalities of being brought together and reconciled in me: I am a for-itself— i.e., both presence and opposition to myself—but only in and through my relation with the in-itself, which is what I deny in myself and which yet *is* myself. This unity of the for-itself and in-itself in me constitutes my nature as a subject, though it does not involve an identification of subject and object—if by "object" is understood not what I am in not being an object, but the correlate of the *cogito*, the world insofar as it exists for me. The fact that I am my body does not imply in any way that I am what I think; and if, as will be developed later, I am what I think, it is not in the same way that I am my body. The unity of the for-itself and the in-itself is meaningful only inasmuch as I am for-myself. Even if we have perhaps placed more emphasis on the body than Sartre has, we cannot say that the for-itself is an in-itself. A certain dualism survives intact for us: the dualism composed of both the for-itself which I am and continue to be as a corporeal being and the in-itself understood as what I am not—in other words, the dualism of an incarnate consciousness and the world. To affirm the unity of the subject is not to endorse a monism opposed to the subject-object dualism: it is the subject as a whole that is opposed to the object. Although the incarnation of the for-itself does not suppress dualism in any particular place (since the self is not a point or sector in a larger whole), this incarnation will help us to understand how it is overcome so far as a communication between subject and object may be established.

8 / The *A Priori* as Corporeal

WE MUST NOW EXAMINE the bearing of our discussion of the incarnate subject on the theory of the *a priori*. First, however, we should note that there is no basis for seeking (at least directly) the bearing of the theory of the *a priori* on the theory of the body. The analysis of the *a priori* implies and sometimes orients a theory of the subject as transcendental. We have even been led to existentialize this subject, to form the idea of a concrete subject; yet we have not ventured beyond this point. For the body cannot be deduced; and we have found it only because we have looked for it by deliberately breaking the thread of our analysis. But we can backtrack a little now to reconsider the immanence of the *a priori* in the subject as incarnate.

Must the transcendental be materialized? Must we even say that the body itself is an *a priori*? The presence of the subjective *a priori* endows the subject with a nature and characterizes him as singular. The body performs the same role: even the most exterior determinations of the body-as-object concern the being of the subject, since they are what he assumes and sometimes denies. How may we understand that the same nature is involved in both cases? Must we locate the *a priori* in the body? Should certain specific *a priori* be reserved for the body? First, we should recall that the body is not only a non-totalizable whole of objective determinations explored by science; nor is it merely a whole of organs by which action realizes its ends [*fins*]: it is also these ends themselves. Insofar as it lives [*vit*] and I experience [*vis*] it, it is not only capable of acting, but also of willing and thinking: will and thought are not externally related to it. To say this is not to refine away the body or to transmute it into something psychic; it is only to deny the right to reduce it (insofar as it is myself) to the status of an object. Moreover, we have attempted to define the *a priori* as virtuality. In its original state, it is neither explicit knowledge [*savoir*] nor a condensed knowledge put into storage. It is a power of anticipating and revealing, a nonacquired familiarity with certain aspects of the world; this power exists in the subject like a mode of being. It is a form of subjectivity, in the sense that form is formative. Yet the body is also formative: it situates subjectivity and singularizes it; outside of it, impersonal subjectivity is an abstraction like matter. Does this authorize us to bring the transcendental and the corporeal together?

They cannot be brought together by asserting that the *a priori* resides in the body. This claim has no meaning since the body is not a container. It would be better to say that as subjective the *a priori is* body. This formula may be understood in two senses. First, it invites us to consider the *a priori* as a corporeal capacity [*pouvoir*]. Yet is the body capable of understanding tragedy, space, or the "something in general"? Now, mental and corporeal do not exclude each other here: once again we must insist that the body is not a system of blindly functioning mechanisms. It might seem, however, that the body's capacities are nothing more than mechanisms parading under the name of habits. Is this so? A habit is a capacity—"know-how" (*un savoir*, as one says in French)—to the extent that it utilizes automatisms without letting itself be overcome by them. Such a capacity is manifested by the grasp it gives us on the world and by a kind of acquired spontaneity it confers on our acts. Habit transcends itself in its exercise as the body does in its actions; it is not a mere corporeal capacity, but a mode of being belonging to the subject engaged in the world. The skill of the painter or the pianist constitutes his very being, as well as his knowledge of how to paint or play the piano.

Therefore, habit is a corporeal capacity which cannot be reduced to a physical capacity—neither when it is put into practice, nor even when it holds itself in reserve. For to form a habit is not to become a robot; rather, it is to gain a being, to become capable of a certain attitude toward the world. Since Freud, we know that the merest tic may conceal a meaning which indicates more than a faulty connection of nerves; thus there is all the more reason for believing that the habits by which the subject manifests a certain style take possession of a world which is his own and comprehend it. Now, the only difference between the *a priori* understood as a virtuality and habit is that virtuality is a nonacquired habit, even if it comes to light only through experience. Virtuality is the ground from which habits arise; it determines the facility and

rapidity of their execution: on the basis of certain basic dispositions I can more or less easily acquire certain capacities which are
themselves secondary dispositions: a second nature. Thus we can
say that the *a priori* is corporeal without being unfair to it; this
means that the subject knows, or rather prepares himself to know,
according to his nature, that is, with his body. If the *a priori* is
nothing more than the expression of a certain familiarity with the
world, this familiarity requires the participation of the body. Insofar as virtual, the formal schemes which orient logical thought—
the formal *a priori*—are originally the schemes of the engagement
of my conduct in the world. Causality, for example, is first of all a
certain disposition of my body to order its undertakings by following the thread of time. Similarly, substance is a certain disposition
of my body to give credit to the object, attach itself to it, and
experience its duration.

Are we so far from Kant here? Wary of psychologizing the *a
priori* and anxious to consider it in its products [*oeuvres*] rather
than in its being, Kant certainly did not search for it in its virtual
state. But he joins the schemata to the pure concepts of the
understanding: these schemata represent the *a priori* in their
original state. For the schema is the manner in which the *a priori*
is prepared in the imagination. Certainly for Kant the schema is
the condition under which the *a priori* can perform its transcendental function—i.e., relate itself to phenomena by restricting itself to "this formal and pure condition of sensibility . . .
[that] we shall entitle the schema of the concept." [1] Yet the
schema can accomplish this mediation between *a priori* and *a
posteriori* only on the condition of being more *a priori* than the *a
priori*, of stopping short of all conceptualization and logical expression, and of rooting itself in the imagination.

Now, if the schema is the *a priori* in its original state, is it not
the *a priori* in its corporeal state as well? It is true that the
schematism is an act of the imagination uniting sensibility and
understanding—more precisely, determining inner sense in accordance with a category; it introduces the unity required by the "I
think" into the pure diversity of the sensible. But reference to
sensibility may imply a reference to corporeality. As Heidegger
has emphasized, for Kant sensibility signifies the finitude of the
subject, his receptivity: to be restricted to sensible intuition is to
be forced to open oneself to the object and above all to wait for it.

1. Kant, *Critique of Pure Reason*, trans. Norman Kemp Smith (London, Macmillan, 1933), p. 182 (B 179–A 140).

This opening is made possible only by a movement of disconnection, a withdrawal; since this withdrawal manifests [*déploie*] time (all consciousness being in the past or future), time is the form of sensibility.

Now, we can say that this rupture is effected with the body; thus for Bergson representation arises when the totality of images is broken. The body hollows out this hole in being because it is already a body-as-subject, the organ of a will or a center of indetermination, and because in it things become seen over against a freedom; the freedom implied by finitude can be assigned to the body. Therefore, even pure sensibility evokes the body, and invites us to put it at the origin of knowledge. What, then, about the imagination? For Kant, it assures "unity in the determination of sensibility." [2] Only the imagination—the common root of understanding and sensibility—can perform syntheses in the sensible with a synthetic power. (And is this not what the empirical imagination does, even in its excesses, when it conjoins wantonly the most incoherent representations?) Space and time form the region where a pure synthesis can be effected: the perpetually possible liaison of places and moments. For on the plane of the transcendental the schema is not an image, and the synthesis of the imagination has no particular intuition as its aim; the schema is only "a universal procedure of imagination in providing an image for a concept," [3] a rule for the synthesis of imagination determining inner sense according to conditions of its form (time). Now, can we not attribute this synthetic activity to the body? Does not such an activity express the way the body experiences [*vit*] time—that is, the way it structures time by relating itself to it? Schematization is an art hidden in the depths of the human body, and it is not easy to describe its operation, for to do so we should have to show how the body orients itself in time before orienting itself in the world (and *in order to* orient itself there), as well as how, in sum, the determination of time is a determination of the body according to its motor possibilities. [4] Nevertheless, Lachièze-

2. *Ibid.*

3. *Ibid.*, p. 182 (B 180).

4. Does Kant's own exposition of the schemata bear out his promises? The determination of time in accordance with categories should make the object appear, or rather the form of the object—a form that experience alone can fill out. But except for number, which is the schema for magnitude and which is "simply the unity of the synthesis of the manifold of a homogeneous intuition in general" (*Critique*, p. 184 [A 143]), the other schemata presuppose the object instead of preparing for its advent. The schemata concerning the content of time, the order of time, and the scope of time in relation to all possible objects, presuppose the temporal existence of a possible object. Kant specifies this: "The schema is,

Rey, although subordinating time to the constitutive activity, as well as the apprehension of time to the act by which the "I think" constructs its inner phenomena (so that the discrimination of temporal moments serves to organize the succession of the acts of the mind in inner sense), observes that this discrimination "is realized by a return to the motricity of the subject." [5]

Therefore, the schematism could be attributed to the body, and the schemata might be compared to corporeal virtualities. More precisely, empirical schemata lend themselves to this interpretation: what is the schema of a dog—by which "my imagination can delineate the figure of a four-footed animal in a general manner, without limitation to any single determinate figure such as experience . . . actually presents" [6]—what is this schema if not a certain way of anticipating the perception within my body of a dog, of being present to a possible dog, without its explicit image taking form? Involved in this is something like a corporeal foreknowledge of the object—a virtuality, but an acquired one. Perhaps the operation of the body is not so mysterious here: it consists in proffering a word. When I say "dog," I do not form the concept of dog, nor do I produce its image; yet I know what I am talking about, and something is awakened in me which prepares me for receiving the experience or the idea of a dog, just as a habit makes me immediately familiar with an object and attunes me to it even before I utilize it. What is thus awakened in me is neither a particular image which would be a copy of a perception, nor a generic image which would be the result of an amalgam; rather, it is an image of an image. This receptive attitude called forth by a word is a corporeal rule for guiding transcendence. [7] And, moreover, is not language the constantly available intermediary between consciousness and body? It preserves knowledge in the state of virtuality, and this virtuality is quite corporeal because the body is the speaking power [*la puissance*

properly, only the phenomenon, or sensible concept, of an object in agreement with the category" (*Critique*, p. 186 [B 186]). Thus pure synthesis does not make the object appear; not only the empirical object must be given, but also the form of the object in accordance with a category: consequently the *a priori*. We rediscover here the idea that the *a priori* itself must be given *in* the object; it does not represent the initiative of a constitutive subject, and the transcendental deduction is possible only if the object contributes to the undertaking. This deduction can express the accord of the subject and experience, not the subordination of the latter to the former.

5. P. Lachièze-Rey, *L'Idéalisme kantien* (Paris, Alcan, 1931), p. 278.

6. *Critique*, p. 183 (B 180–A 141).

7. This contains an allusion to Descartes' title: "Regulae ad directionem ingenii."—Trans.

parlante]. Yet we remain here on the empirical level: language is learned, and learning languages involves not only the pronunciation of phonemes, but also the understanding of semantemes, the sedimentation of meanings in words and of words in meanings. *A priori* schemata cannot be identified with language. They do, however, constitute a sort of pre-language, an original orientation of the body as still not speaking—an orientation by which consciousness becomes sensitive to certain experiences that language can later render explicit, but that do not refer to any particular and namable objects; instead, they concern certain forms or structures of the world which the body prepares us to experience by means of the virtual knowledge it possesses. These forms can be numbered among the *a priori* of knowledge whose schemata Kant searched for.

But a problem arises as soon as we thrust the *a priori* down into the body and identify virtuality with the corporeal capacity which actualizes itself when put into use: are there not, in addition to a general corporeal form of the *a priori,* certain *a priori* proper to the body? This would be the second meaning of the proposition: the *a priori* is body. In fact, we can, like Merleau-Ponty, speak of *a priori* of the body, designating by this the fundamental activities corresponding to the *Umwelt's* lines of force; to repeat an example we have given elsewhere:[8] the structure of the wolf in its relation with the Siberian forest. The system formed by the corporeal *a priori* constitutes a style of life for a species in a certain environment: a specific difference must manifest itself for all living creatures both in the lived and the objective body, and we apprehend this difference in behavior, even if we express it mythically before using anatomical terms. This means that instincts, which first exist as virtualities, would be *a priori.*[9] But do we not then risk confusing all corporeal *a priori,* making the body into a sort of catchall? How may we distinguish the purely corporeal *a priori* from the *a priori* whose schema alone is corporeal? This distinction cannot be realized on the basis of the body alone: a virtuality can be discovered only when it is actualized (even habits are revealed only by the traces they leave). But the authentic *a priori* are not merely corporeal; they also represent

8. In the author's *Phénoménologie de l'expérience esthétique* (Paris, Presses Universitaires de France, 1953), II, 566.—Trans.

9. Yet we could say that since virtuality—instinct—is only corporeal for the animal, it does not merit the name of *a priori.* For man, in contrast, presence to the world involves the *a priori* because it is already more than mere presence: a meaning is presented, and bodily acts already imply this meaning.

a virtual knowledge which can be made explicit and which is actualized in knowledge; thus we can recognize them in this knowledge—that is, in its spontaneity and certainty; their corporeality can only be inferred, not experienced or verified directly. In contrast, the purely corporeal dispositions are revealed when the engagement of the body in the world is observed externally, and when we realize how primitive and necessary the correlation of individual and environment is. Then the *a priori* is known; but it is not knowledge, for we cannot invoke even a virtual knowledge concerning the kind of exchange and harmony established between body and world. This relation undoubtedly foreshadows the relation of subject and object: is not the body already a subject? But this subjectivity is immediately alienated in the object, in the experienced correlate, and the perceiving body is not the thinking body.

This is why it is difficult to speak about the *a priori* on the level of presence as opposed to representation. Physical virtualities, which define animal species rather than singular men—species as individuals rather than individuals as species—are innate insofar as they are specific. They are not, however, genuinely innate, because they do not belong to a subject for whom birth is an ontological event, the advent of a for-itself. At the vital level, the pact sealed between the living creature and his environment foreshadows and can illustrate the harmony between subject and object revealed by the *a priori*, but the two pacts are not identical. Science discloses the first and can clarify it through the notion of finality, or even reduce it through the idea of causality. The second belongs to transcendental philosophy because it is knowledge and the condition of knowledge. Not all corporeal virtuality is *a priori*.

And yet does not the real distinction exist between the *a priori* which fail and those which succeed? For can we finally separate the vital from the mental? If the vital illustrates the mental, does it not also prepare for it? Can we be sure that any human dispositions are purely corporeal and do not include virtual knowledge? The crucial dimensions of behavior have a properly metaphysical meaning in reserve: to look for food is already to experience the lack which "appears in the world only with the upsurge of human reality," [10] since "human reality is a lack." [11] The emptiness of hunger is a prefiguration of the perpetually future void found in

10. Jean-Paul Sartre, *Being and Nothingness*, trans. Hazel E. Barnes (New York, Philosophical Library, 1956), p. 86.
11. *Ibid.*

the self's presence to itself.[12] To try to sleep is to posit oneself as reposing; it is to fix oneself in the world, but by consenting to its abolition, by withdrawing inside oneself through abandoning oneself—in brief, to accept the non-being of night without and within. To make love or to fight—to measure oneself against another—is to run a risk, to exercise one's possibilities up to the mortal limit, and to experience one's contingency as fragility.[13] The fact that these metaphysical meanings are realized in action rather than in thought—their actualization taking place in behavior instead of in consciousness—does not affect the *a priori* character of the dispositions which give rise to this behavior. What would throw this character into doubt would be the failure of these characteristic dispositions of the subject to be constitutive of the object as well. Yet they do constitute the object; here again the subjective *a priori* finds its correlate in an objective *a priori:* in what could be called a vital value of the object—e.g., the desirable, the reposeful, the provoking. These are authentic *a priori* forms that could be compared to affective qualities; but instead of soliciting feeling in the subject, they call forth the body itself and its vital forces: the living, not the thinking, body. In contrast with this, the various *a priori* of representation, if they are also corporeal, suggest another aspect of the body; they are virtualities oriented toward thought and not deposited by life; they are not *a priori* of presence, but *a priori* in presence, actualized by representation. Finally, the specific *a priori* which define a species as a subject or as a quasi-subject are the variations modulated by the imagination of life on the theme of the vital *a priori.*

Therefore, we can speak of the *a priori* of presence: such are the vital *a priori* by which the body expresses its living being. We hesitated to use this language earlier because we were not sure that these *a priori* determined anything other than a blind communion with the environment, or that they concealed a meaning concerning this environment which is at least virtual. This hesitation meant that we did not want to lose sight of the Kantian sense of the *a priori*, that is, of its transcendental function. Yet when we

---

12. This hardly justifies civilizations which keep certain parts of their population in famine! (The remark in the text alludes to the words "un creux toujours futur" from Paul Valéry's "Cimetière marin" [*Oeuvres*, Edition de la Pléiade (Paris, Gallimard, 1957), I, 149].—Trans.)

13. Should we say that, compared with these basic activities, work is a learned activity (which appears to result from a condemnation) that makes a social out of the metaphysical animal? If so, work, as a fact of culture, does not seem to be an *a priori*—even though culture involves certain other *a priori*. But we cannot resolve such a complex issue at this point.

insist on its corporeal aspect we do run this risk. In fact, to say that the *a priori* is incarnated invites us to say that the body is the transcendental. We can attribute a double transcendence to it: the transcendence characteristic of intentionality insofar as the body aims at [*vise*] the world, and the transcendence found in the act of surpassing [*dépassement*] to the extent that, being engaged in the world, the body surpasses itself and becomes body-as-subject. The body is both a center of reference and a center of indetermination. But it does not fulfill its task completely: it orients itself in an environment, but it does not reveal a world. Real transcendence belongs to the for-itself, the being capable of an absolute release [*essor*], of a radical withdrawal both from the world and from itself: the being that is conscious. Only a consciousness can radically open itself to the world, and become this opening and perspective; even if we refuse to give it a constitutive activity, and even though we began our examination of the *a priori* with a study of their objective aspect, we should not forget that only consciousness is transcendental. This does not prevent it from being incarnate: our openness is perspectival only because the body limits it to a certain point of view, and perhaps this openness is possible only because the body puts us in the world. Yet it remains the case that the body itself can be understood as transcendental only in reference to consciousness, and because it *is* consciousness in a certain sense.

Consciousness can be conceived only on the basis of the body. But, without passing through consciousness, could an idea be formed of the body-as-subject, which is like a corporeal duplicate of consciousness? Moreover, starting from the body and investing it with all the burden of the transcendental, we would detect only the *a priori* of presence; thus we would forget that mixed with them, when actualized, are certain formal *a priori* whose signification surpasses the body. In order to say that the *a priori* is corporeal, we must already have disclosed the different types of *a priori*, and we cannot do this by reference to the body alone—nor can we even clarify their virtual being by such a reference. The body does not aid our consideration of the *a priori*, except perhaps so far as their innateness is concerned, since the body is what is born. Yet birth is an absolute point of departure in the order of being, not in the order of reasons.[14] Here again we must remain in contact with Kant: if the *a priori* were sought after only in the relation of the

14. Dufrenne alludes here to Descartes' notion of "un ordre des raisons."— Trans.

body and its environment, we would remain in the empirical realm. But as soon as we evoke the subject as consciousness, instead of tracing his history, we return to Kant: we pose the problem of the relations of subject and object.

We must reconsider even the existential *a priori* and the being of the subject. In discovering the unity of consciousness and body, we confirm above all that what exists is the subject, not consciousness. The necessity of understanding the subject in terms of consciousness changes nothing here. As for-itself, consciousness is the sign of subjectivity; it does not constitute the subject, or, if you like, it constitutes in him only his subjectivity. For it is not an attribute, a specific difference, that is, a "having" [*un avoir*]; rather, it is a manner of being or, more exactly, of non-being. Yet this non-being implies a being: in the subject, the for-itself presupposes the in-itself, and this in-itself is the subject himself insofar as he has a nature perpetually challenged by consciousness. This nature assigned by us to the subject is the body. But how can the body be identified with consciousness, which does not have a nature? The paradox of this unity has repercussions in the subject, who is both nature and non-nature, universality and singularity. This nature is always challenged, yet real [*reélle*], for the body becomes the body-as-object whose objectivity depends not only on the objectifying look of others, but also on the matter weighing it down and making it something chemical.

Now the existential *a priori* also defines a nature. As we have seen, it is not a particular type of *a priori*, and we can speak of it only because all the *a priori* have a subjective aspect, since I carry them within myself as virtualities and since I *am* them in a certain way. The existential *a priori* is the summation of those *a priori* which (insofar as they are subjective) determine the field of my intention [*visée*] and the style of my relationship with the world: what Sartre terms the fundamental project or what Bergson calls (when he speaks of the art of painting according to Leonardo da Vinci) the "original intention, the fundamental aspiration of the person." [15] And this defines my nature. But are there then two natures, one corporeal and one transcendental? Not at all, since the transcendental is also corporeal. The existential *a priori* defines the nature of the subject, and the body does not compete with it in this respect.

It even defines the ambiguity of this nature. For "nature" may

---

15. Henri Bergson, *La Pensée et le mouvant* (Paris, Presses Universitaires de France, 1950), p. 255.

be understood in two senses: as that which generalizes and as that which singularizes. This duality is also found in the subject's nature. We have already underlined the subject's singularity as well as his selfhood [*ipséité*]. But there is also a generality of the subject: if there were not, how could one speak of the subject in general? Of *Ichheit*, like Scheler? Of consciousness in general, like Jaspers? How could Kant continue in the third person what Descartes began in the first, and so many reflections slip insensibly or deliberately from the *cogito* to the *cogitatum est*? [16]

The existential *a priori* provides an answer to these questions —more precisely, to the question of the kinship between subjects, not their plurality; to the question of the similarity of their nature, not the identity of their selfhood. For the fact that there are other subjects who are subjects like myself, that the other is the same, and that the form of the "I" is universal is an ontologically primary fact, and is just as irreducible and unjustifiable as the upsurge of the for-itself. Sartre expresses this well by saying that the other is the one I encounter, the one in whom I discover the indefinite increase of selfhood. But the question remains: how is it that among those subjects who participate in the subject's form, there is a natural [*de nature*] community, a kinship of existential *a priori*? Now, as long as the *a priori* constituting the existential *a priori* remain virtualities, the existential *a priori* is itself a nature or force which appears as singular only when actualized; it is anonymous insofar as it is indeterminate, even if this indeterminateness is also determining. Nevertheless, such an indeterminate nature does not as yet confer a real generality on the subject.

But the *a priori* are also virtual in the sense that they are not all present in a single subject; their historicity disperses them over many subjects. The subject's singularity results precisely from the fact that only certain *a priori* are present in him, combining into a unique formula drawn out of the field of the possible. Therefore, subjects resemble one another because their existential *a priori* are rooted in the same field. This totality is unspecifiable, as much so as Scheler's cosmos of persons, since history never ends; other births can occur, at the juncture of ontology and history, provoking the revelation of other *a priori*. Yet if we become capable of conceiving this totality, we can also conceive a total subject bear-

16. This generality also belongs to the body, for, if it is the means of my individualization as Plato said, it also conceals a coefficient of generality on the basis of which intersubjectivity becomes possible, as Merleau-Ponty has discerningly insisted (see his *Phenomenology of Perception*, trans. Colin Smith [London, Routledge and Kegan Paul, 1962], p. 448).

The A Priori as Corporeal / 165

ing all these *a priori*, an absolute person, absolutely human, and impersonal by dint of personality: is this not what "humanity" means? And do we not thus account for the polyvalence and seductiveness of this word, whose resonances are both axiological and ontological, as it designates both the steadily increasing number of the dead and the future we must constantly engender and invent, inviting us to consider the course of history and its transcendence [*dépassement*]? Thus all men participate in humanity, though they never fully actualize it. Yet this makes communication possible and assures that nothing human is foreign to any human being. Humanity is the *natura naturans* whose *natura naturata* (represented by individual men) is both a part and a reflection; it is the generality on which singularity is founded, the possibility in which the reality of individuals is grounded.

This possibility is, however, never wholly realized, and this generality is not generalizable; as a result of its historicity and finitude, humanity always remains a project and a destiny for a freedom. It is only virtual. Consequently, we can say that virtuality affects the *a priori* in two different ways: insofar as the *a priori* is myself, before being actualized by experience; but also in itself, since it is not even totally actualized insofar as it is virtual in existing subjects. The historicity of the *a priori* means that its totality is unspecifiable, that it always overflows the limits in which we attempt to enclose it: by means of the *a priori* we possess part of truth, but truth itself is inexhaustible; new aspects of the world can always be revealed, and new relations instituted between subject and world. Yet with what justification do we attribute this virtuality to the *a priori,* and say that there are still others? We are entitled to do so because the *a priori* is actualized in concrete, finite subjects. If it belonged to a consciousness in general, as Kant thought, it could be circumscribed and delimited.

The finite subject is the person: the universal in the singular, the transcendental in the empirical. It is because the universal is actualized in the person that the person can be considered as the sole content of a formal ethics, and that Kant can pass from the first to the second maxim of duty. In this sense the person defined by an existential *a priori* is a practical *a priori*, an *a priori* for action, and perhaps the only one. The singular is the given, the mark of contingency: the subject is not *causa sui* (self-caused), he is given to himself. This given is a certain someone, a nonnecessary somebody, and consciousness is not only consciousness of something, but also of someone. The universal is the transcendental, the condition of knowledge, the possibility of a meaning. As such, it is impersonal: constituting the universe, promoting objectivity in the given, it cannot itself be given, not even to itself. Its insertion into the singular appears to be inconceivable.

We have, however, challenged an overly formalistic conception of the transcendental: the universal is not opposed to the singular as the constituting is to the constituted. When the *a priori* ceases to be the instrument of a constitutive activity, its universality no longer has a logical meaning; it no longer characterizes an unconditioned and active being, as if it had the absolute character of a necessary condition, or the validity rendering all thought valid. As subjective, it continues to be the condition for the apprehension [*lecture*] of experience; but this is because it is objective at the same time, and because the object conceals and manifests it as its principle: the condition is not unconditional. The *a priori* does not found a subjectivity that it would define as formal; it belongs to a concrete subject whose structure it constitutes. Consequently, its universality is factual [*de fait*], and we must experience it in history. It is less universal than general. It constitutes humanity in individual men because it is common to persons and because it makes them similar to one another. Yet men do not participate in humanity as if in an absolute mind: the generality of the different *a priori* is never perfect, their totality is never achieved, humanity remains a task. Since it gives a place to the singular, the general is able to form it in a certain way: the existential *a priori* defines the extent of the transcendental in a person, the share of the general assigned to the person—in other words, the manner in which the person participates in humanity. Humanity is limited within the person, but it is humanity that is limited and that somehow limits itself in order to concretize itself. For the universal creates the dignity of the singular, and the singular produces the being of the universal: man exists only through humanity, and humanity exists only in man.

This interpretation of the universal as general is perhaps the only means of grounding the person philosophically: we must remove the transcendental factor in the person from its transcendent position (in the sense in which transcendence designates an ontological heterogeneity, not intentionality) and situate this factor in nature, or rather, comprehend that it already defines nature in the subject. Of course it also constitutes the object, but exactly as it constitutes the subject, because it is present in the subject as a structure—although we do not accredit it to a transcendental subjectivity. The subject is certainly transcendental, yet only insofar as he also partakes in nature: the movement of the for-itself does not uproot him from the in-itself; it only prepares him for humanity.

Finally, communication is possible because the person is nourished by humanity. To the extent that the *a priori* is actualized, and so far as man realizes himself by accentuating his difference from others, he also attests to his humanity. He makes himself human, though he also knows the human: for certain of the *a priori* borne by him and defining his nature as human involve a pre-conceptual knowledge of the human. And sometimes, if they represent knowledge [*savoir*] of the world, it is the world as human that is thus known. Man is not only the promoter of the human, he is doubly attuned to other men: he is similar to them, and he possesses the means of knowing them. Thus, intersubjectivity is not only confrontation, but recognition.

9 / The Subject as Social

To PERSONALIZE the self completely, we must say about society what we have said of the body. For the subject is not only incarnated, but social, that is, living among other subjects and participating with them in a certain style of life. The subject is also natural, living in the environment of a natural world; [1] we have said this implicitly in examining corporeality: naturality is a direct consequence of corporeality. But it is not exactly the same for sociality: for I am not among others as I am among things; this is so not only because the other is not a thing, but also because my relation to things is mediated by my body—whereas society, even though related to me through my body, *is* my body in a certain sense. My relation with the human environment is more immediate than my relation with the natural environment, and is experienced as such: things usually reach me only through men, and men always concern me more passionately than things. Consequently, we must compare the social milieu with my body, rather than with the natural milieu, though we should be prepared to abandon this comparison in the course of our investigation.

Now, reflection on the *a priori* can put us on the right path here, and help to avoid the solipsistic impasse to which a philosophy of the *cogito* is often driven. But we must proceed cautiously: all that we can expect to discover is the sociality of the subject; we cannot deduce society, any more than we were able to deduce the body. Sartre is right: instead of deducing the other, we encounter him; he is found outside ourselves, not within; even my equal or my neighbor is always an other. We can say of society—under-

1. That is, to the extent that the natural and human environment [*milieu*] can be distinguished; at least the relation to others can be distinguished from the relation to things, even when these things are humanized.

stood in the largest sense of collectivity: a collection of others—
what Sartre says about the body: it attests my contingency because it is an unengenderable fact, but a fact which, like the body,
affects me profoundly. Yet if society is a fact known *a posteriori,*
reflection on the *a priori* may at least indicate, within the subject
understood as the bearer of the *a priori,* the openness to others
which is the foundation of intersubjectivity—what we shall call
"sociality," corresponding to society—just as we have shown
above a certain passivity in consciousness, a certain opacity in the
subject, to which the body corresponds.

First of all, when we consider the objective *a priori* in its
constitutive role, it seems that the objectivity it manifests in the
object appeals to the attention and assent of others: when I
experience a meaning as evident, even if I do not know that the
evidence for this meaning is different from the subjective feeling
of evidence (as Husserl stresses), at least I tend to think that this
feeling is an homage offered to the objectivity of the meaning; I
appeal to others, having the impression of being in a certain sense
humanity's delegate in the experience I have. The objectivity of
the meaning compels me to be objective myself, and this second
objectivity implies a relation to others: the concern to obtain their
assent, or rather the assurance of already having it, since, if the
meaning I recognize is not created by me, it cannot be for me
alone. In other words, the logical universality of the *a priori* or the
judgments in which I make it explicit suggest a concrete universality, a society of subjects. This is why, following another path,
we were able to contest this logical universality and reduce it to an
empirical generality: this reduction is justifiable only if the second form of universality is at least announced by the first. As long
as we deal with logical universality, others are not present, but
they are presupposed, even demanded. Moreover, it is noteworthy
that this primary relation to possible others is provoked by the
experience of objectivity, and poses others as the fellow creatures
from whom I expect assent because I assume that they are capable of objectivity, or rather I assume that the objectivity of the *a
priori* will impose itself on them. This does not in any way exclude
the possibility that my relations with others may be more dra-
matic, but this possibility is perhaps founded on equality and
reciprocity: others are other only because they are also similar, as
fellow men whose co-operation is necessary for founding the universality of a judgment or the strength of the evidence for a
meaning.

But everything is possible with these possible others: they can betray my expectations and be blind to the evidence that I experience. Must I then be suspicious of this evidence? No; it is not illusory just because others fail to acknowledge it. Their failure to do so does not teach me the precariousness of the evidence, but rather its historicity and fragmentation [*morcellement*]. Certain *a priori* may escape me and others, and the comprehension of the total system of *a priori* requires a total humanity. The totality of the *a priori* implies a totality of the human, a total system of others, an end of history; and it is against such a background that the historicity of the *a priori* appears, the contingency of its revelation resulting from the diversity of subjects. Thus, the *a priori* suggests a reference to intersubjectivity in two ways: on account of its apprehension insofar as it is objective, and because of its systematization insofar as it is subjective. Its objectivity evokes the presence of others, while its historicity calls forth a history: the two dimensions of society, static and dynamic, are thereby indicated—without, of course, any real society being deduced in this way.

Moreover, the *a priori* refers to others, not just in calling them forth, but also in attesting to them: there are certain *a priori* of intersubjectivity—in Husserlian language, categories of the region "others," as distinguished from the region "thing" or even "life." This means that, as soon as we encounter men, we always recognize them as such; we always know already what is human. Once again, this does not exclude the possibility that this recognition may give way to a struggle: the other can appear as a formidable and despicable stranger, suspect because he is different: he is not of my race, and the rules governing my society do not apply to him; he is an outlaw, above or below the law, a god or a monster to be adored or enslaved. Yet we must beware of rationalizations which justify actions performed out of passion. If the other sometimes appears strange, inspiring fear or adoration, and if we have difficulty recognizing him—that is, doing him justice—this is because we have already recognized him, but refused him justice; he is the other on the basis of identity; he is different only as similar. If he were fundamentally different, action would lose this passional ambiguity whose source is perhaps already bad faith. This immediate and certain knowledge [*connaissance*] of the other as *alter ego* is what we attribute to the *a priori* of intersubjectivity. The term is undoubtedly ambiguous: can we speak of *a priori* of intersubjectivity as we speak of *a priori* of the understanding? There are two different principles for classifying the *a priori*: one concerns the faculties of the subject possessing them, the other the object for which they are the constitutive meaning; as we shall see in another book,[2] it is not easy to choose between these two principles. In any case, we mean here that certain *a priori* are ingredient in our relations with others: they do not govern or orient them, but they make them possible, as well as their affective vicissitudes and historical developments, just as the *a priori* of the object make a technique or a science of the object possible. There are categories of intersubjectivity just as much as there are categories of objectivity.

This has two implications; the first is that we possess a certain idea of man. *Homo cogitat,* says one of Spinoza's axioms—an axiom by means of which man abruptly breaks into a meditation which, up to this point, considered only Substance. We recognize this *homo cogitans* at first glance; even if we do not know what his thoughts are, or what thought itself is, we know that he thinks. He may possess a secret aspect: this also defines him; his actions are unforeseeable: we recognize him as free without imputing this unforeseeability to our ignorance. (Occasionally we can foresee his responses because we know their motives, which are not causes: because we have learned to know him rather than the universe surrounding him, or at least this universe insofar as it has meaning for him.) I do not recognize my fellow man by projecting onto him a certain idea that I have of him: I know him before knowing myself, and I learn to know myself through him. Even before saying that he is similar to *me,* I have to realize that I am similar to *him;* this is perhaps the most irritating discovery, one that we are careful to dissimulate and forget; yet it is the primary discovery, even in the order of reasons: I am made in the image of the other.

Consequently, I can speak of man, and in speaking of him say "I" or "we" with equal ease. And this "we" is not an editorial we. Here, at any rate, is one of the reasons why the *cogito* may appear to be impersonal. This impersonality represents a condemnation of solipsism, and introduces others in two ways. First of all, impersonality involves universality because its correlate is a universal: when consciousness is evident to itself—when it is the consciousness of this evidence—it appeals to the concrete universality of others. Yet it is I who think, and what we said about the passage from the impersonal to the person remains valid. Here again, however, the appearance of impersonality can be justified, for the personalization of the "I" is itself universal; the first person

2. Dufrenne refers here to the book on "the inventory of the *a priori*" which will form a sequel to the present essay.—Trans.

is both singular and plural. There are others, and they are also persons. Humanity is not a species; it is an assemblage of persons before whom I am myself a person.[3] Of course, I can subsume humanity under a general idea, but I cannot avoid speaking of man: an indeclinable, yet universal subject. We have already stressed that the dialectic of singular and universal occurs in every man. Now we must add that the *a priori* idea of man is the idea of man as endowed with the *a priori*, hence with a universal; since this endowment has limitations, and since the *a priori* is never made wholly explicit or given as a total system, singularity is a universal human trait. Moreover, just as in terms of intension [*compréhension*] universality is never rigorous because the *a priori* is not purely logical, so, similarly, universality is not rigorous in extension because it includes singularity and because particularity is not totally surpassed in singularity; the universal is still general in a certain sense. This points again to the contingency of the other, and to the empirical particularity of societies or cultures. But the empirical is present here only in filigree form. In the realm of the *a priori*, the universal is the idea of man as universal—an idea I possess before any science and thanks to which I can always recognize man as similar to himself, thus as similar to me [*mon semblable*].[4]

But the categories of intersubjectivity go beyond this idea. For man is man only on the condition of being *a* man, and singularity is universal because it is essential; men also resemble one another in that they are all dissimilar. Now, this difference can be known by the *a priori*. Not only do we recognize man at first glance, but we also recognize him as singular; this does not occur with any object whatsoever that we know as a single object, even as a monad, yet do not know as singular, that is, as having its own personality (personality being the immanence of the universal in the particular).[5] Of course, this personality of the other is made

3. This is why Heidegger's "they" (*das man*) is not necessarily inauthentic; it may designate the person that I am and that we are.

4. This idea should be made explicit as the *a priori* of a science of man; yet, as in every instance, the *a priori* can be made explicit only historically and apropos of the *a posteriori*. (The social sciences have not found their Thales. Why?) Moreover, this *a priori* is both cognitive and axiological; it is also the content of a formal ethics.

5. The case of the animal could be considered here: the peasant who discovers a personality in each member of his flock; but this occurs only after the fact, *a posteriori*. Nevertheless, he can comprehend the meaning of expressions—even if the expression conveys incommunicability, as in the case of the sphinx. The combination of men and animals in mythological creatures opens up a whole line of possible speculation.

explicit by us only little by little, through the patience involved in dialogue or friendship; it is never perfectly clear to us: the social sciences do not overcome the coefficient of otherness harbored by the personality (they say in a different way what naïve knowledge says, because they attempt to determine causes or motivations; but they do not say more).

It would be absurd to claim that we have an *a priori* idea of every man as we have an idea of man in general: to know that man is always singular is not to know *what* his singularity consists of; this singularity appears to us en bloc, yet as a problem to be solved. We can, nevertheless, attack this problem because we possess other *a priori*: the affective qualities brought into relief by expression have an immediate meaning for us. These qualities are not the projection of our emotion onto an object; instead, they excite emotion, if emotion is indeed present; they are a meaning proposed to us by the object. This object is not necessarily human: a landscape, a work of art, any object will work, if it is expressive. Yet man has priority here, for he is naturally expressive, even if what he expresses is inexpressible. Expression is so much the peculiar property of subjectivity that we can speak of expressive objects as quasi-subjects; they reveal the inner principle that unifies and singularizes a being, a principle elevating this being to the status of a meaningful totality, inhabited by a soul which is its meaning. In man, this meaning is both manifest and hidden: subjectivity, said Hegel, is infinite. Therefore, it is menacing and maddening: the other is the stranger because he is inexhaustible, even if he belongs to our race. But since this meaning is constantly offered, it helps us to identify others: for us, their identity is that of an expression which reveals to us their existential *a priori*, though we cannot at first delineate and master this knowledge [*connaissance*] that is hidden in a feeling.

Empiricism is perfectly justified in believing that experience is necessary for understanding someone, whether it is acquired in everyday relations or in scientific (or pseudo-scientific) observation. The existential *a priori* constituting the person is only revealed *a posteriori*. Yet it is itself given *a priori*, though in a very obscure way; it is given in the immediate and global experience which, in the very first glance at a face, provides me with the essence of a person and allows me to identify him from now on. Empiricism can accept this description only if it is gestaltist and if it recognizes certain *Gestalten* as constitutive meanings: in brief, if it is a transcendental empiricism. It is also true that at certain moments expression can particularize itself and make itself ex-

174 / THE SUBJECTIVE A Priori

plicit: thus we sense fear, anger, or tenderness in someone's action; and we always know already what these signify. We can create an eidetic psychology as a propaedeutic to an empirical psychology because we possess an inherent knowledge [*savoir*] of essences; this knowledge underlies the possibility of understanding the phenomena through which others are manifested and intersubjective relations are formed.

Thus, the *a priori* in its subjective aspect prepares me to encounter others: it attests to and permits sociality.[6] But sociality, like incarnation, is a destiny for the subject. Therefore, we must pass now to the empirical level, although we shall ask ourselves later if the empirical can still be understood as transcendental in certain respects. Thus we arrive at concrete society as it offers itself to the experience of the individual and the sociologist. Does this society have the same relation to the subject as the body does? However far we must push the identification of the subject and society, in comparison with the identification of the subject and his body, we must agree that the subject is his body immediately, while he is his society only at the end of a period of socialization. To be social is both to be one's society and not to be it. The second point is easier to establish first. For to be social is to be in a society. This relation implies a linkage and proximity, but also a difference of the same kind as that between "having" and "had": to belong to a society is to have a society, as we say that we have a body. Society has a definite character of objectivity which forces us to consider it as exterior to the subject; similarly, the body is also a body-as-object. Society is objective spirit realized on the condition of its particularization in history.[7] Society as such is not myself; I no more choose my society than my body, and in oppression or revolt I can experience society's otherness vividly—just as I can feel myself constrained by my body and rebel against it by neglecting or mortifying it. It is a common experience when living abroad not to feel part of the society in which one dwells. The conflict of the individual and society is not a dialectical moment

---

6. It is another matter to determine whether there are *a priori*—especially objective *a priori*—belonging to society: whether there is a pure sociology like a pure mathematics. We could say that certain social relations (e.g., *rapprochement*, domination, collaboration, competition—structures analyzed by men like Weber, Von Wiese, and Parsons) are immediately apprehensible as necessary structures of every society; we might also consider here the fact that society is a whole, having a culture like a soul, and even an existential *a priori*. Thus society would have an immediately accessible meaning, like life or physical objects. This would be still another proof of the sociality of the subject.

7. This contains an allusion to Hegel's theory of objective spirit.—Trans.

that we can easily surpass, either through the ideality of *logos* or in the reality of history.

Yet we must attempt this surpassing, though without giving the last word to an *Aufhebung* or to a movement towards the absolute.[8] On the contrary, there is no last word: the status of the subject is essentially ambiguous. But we must attempt to oppose a monism to the dualism of the individual and society. The body-as-object is also my body: the penitent flagellates his body with his own hand; he punishes himself for being a body, yet in this very act he *is* his body. Similarly, we say "my society," and the rebel denounces his society with the very language of that society; in fact, the more completely integrated into society he is, the more skillfully and perhaps ardently he will denounce it.[9] Thus it seems that I am my society as I am my body, whether I want to be or not; and this last clause is not immaterial. For my freedom is at stake here, manifesting itself in the attitude I adopt and in the action I take with respect to my body and my society. But the fact that my freedom always exists in a situation signifies that I cannot exercise it without identifying myself with my body and my society.

Moreover, there is a way to make this identification more plausible. Rather than saying that I myself am society, I should say that society is a self [*moi*]: it is a subject, insofar as it is culture.[10] Cultural anthropology, perhaps inspired in America by questions raised by logical positivism, has investigated the being and meaning of culture at great length.[11] Yet the concept itself of culture remains uncertain; this is because culture is the subjective aspect of society. It is subjective in two converging senses. First, it appears to exist only in subjects. Society has a more objective, exterior, and official existence, residing both in impersonal institutions and in statistical, demographic, ecological, and economic realities. Of course, culture also has an objective aspect: there are cultural objects, as well as a collective aspect: it can be repre-

8. This reservation neither intends to disqualify the Marxist idea of the end of a particular history within history itself, nor to question that alienation may be overcome to the extent that it is an economic fact.

9. The case of the Negroes analyzed by Sartre in his article, "Black Orpheus," differs here only in that they have or *are* two societies; they deny one only to affirm the other: to proclaim their race as an honor rather than as an object of shame. But in order to combat white society they must borrow their weapons from it—their only efficacious and available arms; thus, in order not to be this society, they must be it after all.

10. "Culture" here does not refer to taste in fine arts, but to the object studied in cultural anthropology.—Trans.

11. See the author's *La Personnalité de base—un concept sociologique* (Paris, Presses Universitaires de France, 1953).—Trans.

sented statistically. But it is above all a way of life—of experiencing social reality—and as such it belongs to the individual. Urbanization and law are social realities, but the way in which people adapt themselves to urban life or respect law is a cultural reality: culture lives in individuals. Naturally, it is hard to determine the exact boundary between society and culture: we can say with Malinowski that every institution is at once a social reality so far as it is institutionalized, and a cultural reality insofar as it is experienced; neither of these two realities can exist without the other. But since the difference between them is irreducible, the subjective character of culture is confirmed: being experienced by subjects, culture is like the soul of society; it is to society what the soul is to the body. Because individuals possess a certain way of living in and experiencing their city, there is a spirit of the city; and there is a spirit of the law because individuals have a certain attitude toward their laws. Now, when we consider culture rather than society, and society-as-subject rather than society-as-object, we can understand the sociality of individuals as an identification of individual and society. Yet how are we to understand *this* identification? Does it not lead to the affirmation of a sociologism ruinous to the concept of the individual?

This question can be clarified by answering one it presupposes: what exactly is the reality of culture? Admitting that I am coextensive with it, what is its extension? We must agree that the domain of a culture is difficult to delimit: can we say where a society ends, except in terms of geography or international law? Can we trace a boundary between the social and the natural environment, and claim that only the latter is ontologically different from the subject? Certainly not: even the stars are part of the cultural milieu, as soon as telescopes are focused on them and institutions are devoted to their study. In fact, the boundary between subject and milieu appears to be blurred as soon as we consider the body; the body's limits are more apparent than real, and it mingles with all the objects, far and near, with which it has commerce, whether to endure or master them. Thus the voice of the Pythic oracle is not so much her voice as that of the waves and woods, because "the whole universe sways and swirls on her stem." [12] Similarly, when culture is more closely examined, at one extremity it is seen to merge with the cultures peculiar to particular groups, and at the other with a culture belonging to the whole

12. This is adapted from a line of Paul Valéry's "La Jeune Parque": "Tout l'univers chancelle et tremble sur ma tige" (*Oeuvres*, Edition de la Pléiade [Paris, Gallimard, 1957], I, 102).—Trans.

species. This indeterminateness appears in the subject himself: he participates in culture only partially, usually through the intermediary of subcultures; and he participates in history only through the edge of the present expressing his engagement in the world. In the same way, at the other pole, culture is surpassed [*débordée*] by a human universal: what Comte called humanity, and Hegel termed the concrete universal. It is true that humanity is never realized, but I still *am* it in a certain sense—both because, insofar as it is a norm, I am able to contribute to its advent, and because, insofar as it is a given, I possess the means of justifying this advent. Nevertheless, in the present state of history (for we are here on the empirical level) culture seems to have a differentiated and independent reality, precisely to the extent that it can be discovered in the actions of all the members of a society, that is, to the extent that I *am* it. In addition, if it is possible to deny that culture is delimited between the superculture and the various subcultures, it is again only in reference to myself, to the exact degree that I am *not* it. But this does not signify that, determined by culture, I am also determined in other ways, as if my being were the result of a sum of determinations; it signifies that I am still something else, that I cannot be reduced to any determination, and that in one sense I am coextensive with humanity and in another sense irreducibly singular.

In fact, the *rapprochement* of the individual and society must not be performed to the detriment of the individual and to the benefit of society. This might be quite possible: does not the assertion that I am my society—or better, my culture—simply mean that I am determined by it and that I am reduced to being its effect or its reflection? Does this not represent a return to a purely empiricist conception of the subject, a return achieved with the aid of a social naturalism? No—just as asserting that I am my body is not equivalent to saying that I am only my body or that I am determined by it. Moreover, these last two affirmations are not equivalent and are in fact opposed: the first denies that there is something in me distinct from the body; the second asserts that there is something distinct, but denies its independence. In any case, we disagree with both affirmations: on the one hand, I am not reducible to my body, because I *am* it in the mode of not being it: I express it by saying that *it* is what I am. On the other hand, my body does not determine me (though it remains exterior to me in a sense) because it is too near me to act on me; at the very most I can say that it constitutes me, thus limiting me, because *I* am what it is.

Similarly, culture cannot determine me from without, and the ambiguous relation that I have with it must be expressed by always conjoining these two propositions: first, I am *it,* and to this extent it structures and limits me; secondly, it is I [*moi*], and to this extent I structure and limit it: I live in it and it lives in me. These two propositions justify the procedures of cultural anthropology or social psychology, on the condition that their reciprocity be always respected and that a determinism (if science insists on using this language) be immediately compensated and neutralized by a determinism working in the opposite direction. (In fact, determinism thrives only between a society-as-object and a self-as-object, and the self is never an object.) This limit to sociologism is also a limit to the identification of the subject and society. Insofar as I accentuate subjectivity and affirm it as negativity, or conversely insofar as I emphasize the objectivity of society and affirm it as positivity, I cannot identify myself with it. There is undoubtedly a certain excess involved in pushing the parallelism between body and society too far: after all, society is less close, less adherent to the subject. And the following question could be posed: must society be understood in terms of the body or vice versa? If we interpret the body in terms of society, we are tempted to return to dualism. In any event, when it is a question of the body, the ambiguity is found in the body itself, which is both subject and object, since it is more easily identified with the subject; when it is a question of society, the ambiguity resides in the subject himself, in the way in which he experiences his integration into this society.

We can clarify our discussion of the relation between individual and culture in still another way. For it inspires a new question, which we have already encountered when we were dealing with the body. We have admitted that culture, though difficult to circumscribe between the subcultures which it involves and the superculture in which it participates, has a certain autonomy. Must we then see in it a certain personality? In that case, if I am my culture to a certain extent, we must also say that my culture is a "myself" [*moi*]. This means that it lives in me [*moi*] as inseparable from me; but it also means that it is a self [*moi*], capable of detaching itself from me to claim its prerogatives as a person. The question then becomes: is culture a transcendental? Does it possess certain *a priori*? This question leads to two others: first, is culture itself an *a priori*—that is, does it perform the transcendental function, normally assumed by consciousness, which consists in knowing the constitutive *a priori* of the object? Secondly, does culture have an *a priori*—that is, is it constituted itself by an *a priori* or by a system of various *a priori*? Both questions seem to us to require an affirmative answer. By saying that I am society, we have been led to say that society is a self; we have even had to support the first proposition by the second. Thus we come to admit that society is itself individualized and animated by an existential *a priori*. Hence we rejoin Hegel at this point. He can speak of objective spirit only if this spirit is also, in a people, subjective, defining society as a concrete consciousness and as a universal person.

Through its observation of individual behavior, cultural anthropology also strives to grasp this personality—whether by means of Benedict's comprehensive psychology, or by Kardiner's and Linton's use of psychoanalysis and the various procedures of the psychology of personality. Even a functionalist analysis, inspired by the idea of a necessary correlation of institutions, aims at a synthesis expressing culture as a totality and defining its singular essence. The psychological language of this culturology suggests that society is considered here as a person. Therefore, it is not sufficient to say that, for the person perceiving and studying it, society is constituted by an objective *a priori* like any other object; for we must not confuse the *a priori* of sociality with the existential *a priori* belonging to a particular society.[13] Society itself experiences the *a priori* as objective, and in this way may claim to have an existential *a priori*. Society itself performs the transcendental function, it is itself a certain look cast onto the world, a certain living relation to the world, an aptitude for recognizing and experiencing certain aspects of the world. Having made the *a priori* descend into the body, we must now let it descend into society as well. In fact, this enterprise arouses less opposition than the preceding: sociological reflection has made it natural to think of society as a person.

13. Moreover, they are not necessarily different: the relation of competition, for example, can be considered as an *a priori* of sociality, just as the relation of finality is an *a priori* of vitality, or spatiality is an *a priori* of corporeality. We can say with Margaret Mead (in all deference to the objections of Claude Levi-Strauss) that a certain society is competitive, or with Ruth Benedict that the Zuñi society is Apollonian, in an attempt to name (though in an admittedly precarious fashion) the existential *a priori* of this society. Yet there remains a difference: in the first case, the social *a priori* define a possible characteristic of society in general and are only partially constitutive for a given society, just as extension constitutes the body only partially; in the second case, the existential *a priori* defines the essential aspect of a given society: its essence, to the extent that it can be defined. The existential *a priori* is more profoundly constitutive because it constitutes a subject and the way in which a subject possesses and experiences a multiplicity of subjective *a priori*.

The difficulty lies elsewhere; it stems from the individual's protest against this bold assimilation. In developing the idea that society is an "I" [*je*], it is tempting to forget that I am society; it becomes easy to overlook the individual subject, or rather to make him the instrument or the effect of society. The collective person begins to seem more authentic than the singular person, and in this way we land back in sociologism. We cannot, however, accept sociologism, even under this new form; although it is more subtle than the sociological determinism which objectifies the subject, it is no less ruinous for the transcendental being of the subject. There is a new reason for our refusal: no longer because the subject is never wholly an object determined by a society-as-object, but now because society is never wholly a subject on the same level with the individual subject and somehow substitutable for him. As subjective or existential (whether mental or physical matters little here), the *a priori* is rooted in a singular subjectivity, a first-person consciousness [*une conscience-je*]; even if this consciousness claims universality for its acts and refers itself to others, it is singular by nature. The *a priori* attributed to a society or a culture must be present and actualized in individuals; even though we may consider it as a subject, society remains an object for a subject. It exists *for* a subject, and it exists only *through* individuals. It is not exactly an object, being more than an object; but it is not a subject: it is a quasi-subject.[14]

This reservation does not in any way condemn the psychologizing approach of cultural anthropology. It simply warns us that, first of all, we must not be the dupes of metaphor, however legitimate it may be: objective spirit is never a merely subjective mind; and that, secondly, this psychologizing research must be compensated for, on the plane of science, by the objectifying research of sociology. Yet the singularity of the subject is irreducible: the transcendental function is a privilege which he possesses by right and which cannot be granted him by society. Once again, this does not deny that society may aid the individual to affirm and manifest his personality. It permits the actualization of the virtual, as does the corporeal schematism on another level. A

14. The term "quasi-subject" can also be employed in a more elastic sense to designate every expressive object: quasi-subject insofar as it addresses itself to me as an equal, not insofar as it performs a quasi-transcendental function. A quasi-subject is usually the work of an individual subject—e.g., the work of art. But such an object is known, not knowing: the pregnancy of the objective *a priori* constituting it does not authorize us to attribute to it, even metaphorically, a subjective, thus an existential, *a priori*.

feudal society does not create the sense of honor, but allows it to be manifested—just as a capitalistic society lets the sense of competition emerge. Yet if an individual in a capitalistic society possesses a compelling sense of honor, he will find, in spite of the institutions, the means of affirming it: witness Bernanos.[15] The transcendental in itself is irreducible to the historical; the existential *a priori* is, like Sartre's notion of original choice, nontemporal. Nevertheless, since the subject is also historical, the historical in its turn participates in the transcendental, and the empirical in the apriorical.[16]

The relation of the transcendental to the social must be understood in the same way—somewhat as Bergson conceived the relation of matter and life, matter being an obstacle to life, yet also life's residue. Society is an object and is first of all opposed to me as is matter to life. Yet I am open to it, experiencing it as my destiny: thus I am it; furthermore, it is at once composed, experienced, and thought by individuals: thus it is a self [*moi*]. For these reasons, it is also more than an object, just as matter, even if it were only life's waste, is more than mere matter. Nevertheless, there is an important difference between the body and society: the body can be more totally identified with the subject. When we contest the identity of the body and the subject, we manifest our fear of an ambiguity; but what is ambiguous is the identity of the body and consciousness, for the body is consciousness and it is not; yet this does not prevent the body from always being a self. Society, however, is never wholly a self: both because as object it surpasses me infinitely and because as subject it is only a quasi-subject. Therefore, we cannot translate "I am social" exactly by "I am my society." Nonetheless, it remains the case that the relation of the subject and society is close and that it exerts an inverse effect on our understanding of these two terms: it obliges us to consider *society* as a quasi-subject; and to consider the *subject* as a quasi-object, extending itself into society and finding its roots and destiny in it: yet without losing its quality as subject, without being determined by society as an effect by a cause, and without its transcendental nature or function being altered. The subject is and is not his society; even as social, he remains transcendental; but if the transcendental is thus social, the social is not truly

15. Georges Bernanos (1888–1948) was a French writer who was also an intransigent Catholic. He was the author of novels and various polemical works.—Trans.

16. *L'apriorique*—this adjectival form of *"a priori"* is also a neologism in French.—Trans.

transcendental—being so only through the mediation of the subject.

In brief, by virtue of his contingency the person must live in a society, just as he must be a body. Through the agency of its culture, this society exerts a considerable influence on him, but one which consists in allowing him to actualize certain of his *a priori* without absolutely forbidding the actualization of others; and we can say neither that the person is reducible to society nor that he is determined by it.

A few final words are perhaps in order. In addition to the quasi-spatial dimension of the intersubjective being of the subject, we should consider his temporal dimension: in addition to social being, historical being. There is little question that the subject's relation to history is quite similar to his relation with society. Above all, it can be shown that access to history is prepared for within the transcendental being of the subject, not only by the various *a priori* of intersubjectivity, but also by the *a priori* of temporality: the subject is open to the past as he is to the present. Before any explicit use of memory, I immediately apprehend that an object present to me has a past, because temporality is a constitutive *a priori* belonging to every object, as well as to the subject himself. But it is not because consciousness is in flux that, as Hume believed, the object appears as temporal, nor is it because there are permanent and nontemporal objects that, as Kant thought, consciousness discovers itself as being in flux. Instead, temporality is universal.

This, however, leads us to conclude that the subject is in history as he is in society—as the soul is in the body—but not that he *is* history. Now, history may be defined as the totality of the past insofar as it ends in my present; this totality is unspecifiable, for there is always a past for each past, and the present of every past is indefinite in its extension. In any case, the exact boundary cannot be drawn between history, properly speaking—i.e., human history—and natural history. Should we claim that natural history is only a pseudo-history? Life has a history linked with the history of matter, and to the extent that we are objects we are tied down to this history; thus it is already ours, just as the natural world is already the human world. This solidarity is one of the signs of our facticity. Admittedly, certain parts of the past can be objectively reconstituted: history as being [*être*] is inseparable from history as science, and the past for me is what I know of it. Nevertheless, even considered as the object of this knowledge and as limited to it, history infinitely surpasses me, as does society: I am not history, and my own history is only one small history within history itself. In what sense could I say that I am history? This statement can have only one meaning: I am the result of history, as it is said that I am the product of my culture. But what about my singularity and freedom? In fact, the above statement may be opposed by another: history is contained in *me*, signifying that in me history takes on its meaning and recapitulates itself. I make history, not only because my acts are immediately inscribed in it in the present, but also because they presuppose that I determine its meaning by joining the past to the future. The historian who writes history, and thus helps to make it, must conjoin these two approaches, paradoxically considering the individual both as the product of an objective history and as the author of a subjective history. This helps us to interpret in another way the idea that I am history: I carry within myself the history of which I am the heir, not the product.

This subjective history is not, however, a subject. It is not a person who would be more authentic than the individual. It *has* a meaning through the subject who relates and relives it; it *is* not a meaning. To conceive it as a subject is possible only if it is conceived as an absolute subject in Hegelian fashion; here "subject" signifies becoming, and temporal becoming is made the illustration of logical becoming, so that history realizes meaning, even if meaning is not historical. For Hegel, history is not only reason, but also reasonable. For us, this would mean that history possesses an existential *a priori* and that it performs the transcendental function. We are certainly tempted to agree; the historicity that we have found in the *a priori* leads us to attribute these *a priori* to history; they are successively revealed in history, and their totality defines a total history: humanity as history. The existential *a priori* of history, the *logos* of becoming, would be the total system of all *a priori*. History would then be the universal consciousness which becomes aware of itself through man by manifesting various *a priori*. Yet, as we have said, such a totality is unspecifiable: humanity is an infinite task.

The historicity of the *a priori* also signifies that they do not form a neat totality: each culture or each era reveals certain *a priori* only by neglecting others. History is not a triumphant reason or a meaning certain of itself because what is surpassed is not necessarily preserved in what surpasses it; the present is not necessarily richer than the past, nor is the past necessarily pregnant with the present, or the beginning with the end. There may be reason in history conceived as a quasi-subject, but history is not itself reasonable, and this reason exists only for and through men. For men, because they alone find history meaningful. Through men, because their activities alone, even when objectified and alienated as in a statistical reality, propose this meaning: migrations of peoples differ from the migrations of schools of fish, and the laws of the market place do not operate like the laws governing scales. It is man who bears and reveals the *a priori*. Historicity signifies not the infinitude of history, but the finitude of man.

Finitude: history is man's destiny. To be finite is to be in history. This is why man is not wholly history: as objectively or quantitatively greater than man, history surpasses him; yet history is not wholly man either, being subjectively or qualitatively less than man. Since history is the trace of man—as matter is the trace left by life—it is more than a blind positivity or a brute facticity. Although man continually denounces history's inhuman character, he discovers himself in it as in a familiar landscape. Thus history is already man. And man is history because he is its heir and the agent responsible for its meaning. Yet he is not its product: history proposes, and man disposes. In brief, as a transcendental subject man is irreducible. The transcendental is historical because it belongs to man, who is in history, and because it is revealed empirically; but the historical is not truly transcendental.

Part III
Man and the World

10 / The Equality of Man and the World

WHAT IS THE MEANING of this duality—the duality which has allowed us to speak of the *a priori* as objective and subjective, as a structure of the object and as a virtual knowledge in the subject? Is it irreducible or does it express two aspects of something yet to be defined? Before answering these questions, we must be assured that we have not formulated this duality arbitrarily. It is implied in the subject's being in the world, and it reflects the fundamental duality of man and world. Moreover, transcendental philosophy elaborates the notion of the *a priori* in this perspective: to account for the possibility of science, that is, the subject's mastery over the world of objects. Yet, since this philosophy bestows a constitutive activity on the subject, it does not need to locate the *a priori* in the object, reserving it instead for the transcendental subject. But at least it grants the *a priori* the power of mediation between subject and object: it always conceives the *a priori* on the basis of dualism. We must begin again with this dualism, though not so much to justify the duality of the *a priori* as to clarify it through an understanding of dualism.

Our investigation of the *cogito* indicated that the subject is one —transcendentally as the unity of apperception, existentially as the unity of consciousness and body, of freedom and nature. Now, this monism of the subject does not exclude dualism—quite the contrary. My body is the object that I am, and, because I am it, it is a subject. The identity of this singular object does not deny the alterity of other objects; rather, it confirms it, for the relations between my body and other bodies show that my body is different. The fact that I am subject and object simultaneously distinguishes me radically from objects; I am in the world without being of it. I am in the world as a part in a whole, but this part is also a center of reference, an origin, and a power. If all transcendence is privation, and if all knowledge is finite, it is because I am also an object and because only by being this object can I establish a rapport with the other objects that I am not: "Omnipotent strangers, inevitable stars. . . ."[1]

We must examine this dualism more closely; and first we should modify the terms generally used in transcendental philosophy; instead of subject and object we should speak of man and world. The first two terms imply that the subject possesses the key to objectivity and that the object is the subject's objective—i.e., what he aims at, as well as what he posits according to the norm of objectivity. The concrete subject that we have considered is man, and we may still safely call him a subject, thus emphasizing his transcendental dignity. But we must not confuse object and world: it is the world that man deals with, and the object always appears against the background of the world. How then are we to interpret the dualism of man and the world?

For this dualism to be confirmed by the monism of the subject, it must not be radical. In fact, there is dualism only if the two terms it conjoins are capable of being brought together. No relation is possible between two wholly different terms. Thus, there must be at least some extrinsic relation between them—a *rapprochement* allowing a confrontation. This proximity is, first of all, material: through his body, the subject deals with the object in space, even if space is made the receptacle for objects through a mental movement of transcendence. The proximity is also mental: focusing [*visant*] the object, consciousness is in a relation of dependence with it, as expressed, for instance, by the famous Kantian theorem.[2] Here the extrinsic relation of proximity turns into a relation of communication; but we must beware of favoring one of its terms, especially that represented by the subject. This danger is evident in Sartre: the experience of the world introduces or rehabilitates the idea of a concrete and contingent subject who is there, somewhere in the world, as a center of reference and as an origin. But this subject is immediately invested with a Husserlian prerogative; the relation of the subject to the world is (as it

1. This is a line from Paul Valéry's "La Jeune Parque": "Tout-puissants étrangers, inévitable astres" (*Oeuvres*, Edition de la Pléiade [Paris, Gallimard, 1957], I, 96).—Trans.

2. Dufrenne refers here to the "thesis" found in the section on "the refutation of idealism": "The mere, but empirically determined, consciousness of my own existence proves the existence of objects in space outside me" (Kant, *Critique of Pure Reason*, trans. Norman Kemp Smith [London, Macmillan, 1933], p. 245 [B 275]).—Trans.

was with Kant) unilateral: "From the very fact that there is a world, the world could not exist without a uniform orientation in relation to me." [3] There is communication, but it is not reciprocal: "By denying that it is being, the for-itself makes a world appear, and by surpassing this negation toward its own possibilities it manifests the 'thises' as instrumental things." [4] The Heideggerian notion of "being-in-the-world" has not yet borne full fruit; it permits us to infer the facticity of the subject, but not to establish the objectivity of the world. Yet if we do not want to have communication established for the sole benefit of the subject, we must conceive and recognize this objectivity, even though we are critical of objectification as such. We shall ask ourselves if the rapport established between man and the world can be a rapport of mutual suitability, that is, of affinity. But we must first determine if it is a rapport of homogeneity or, more exactly, of equality: is man in the world as its equal—irreducible to it, unengenderable by it, and, in short, autonomous?

This calls for reflecting on both man and the world. As for man, we have already tried to show that the transcendental individualizes him, conferring on him a nature which manifests itself throughout his development. We are therefore tempted to claim autonomy for him with respect to the world. But the reflection on the world that we must now undertake may lead us to contest this autonomy in the name of a naturalism; and a counterattack is no longer possible once we abandon the idea of a constitutive subjectivity capable of subordinating the world to itself. And yet we must above all guard against this subjectification of the world. Without being subjectified, the world should be conceived in reference to man as that which subjectivity knows; it is not the project or the product of this subjectivity. The world expresses man because man expresses himself in knowing the world.

As a first approximation, we may say that the world with which man is in relation, like a living creature with its environment, signifies the horizon of horizons and thus that in relation to which objects assume meaning: not only that on which they appear, but also that in which they are rooted, that with which they co-operate. Even the object with the most specific contours somehow extends and joins itself to an indeterminate "outside" [*en dehors*], as soon as its meaning is determined: we say "this animal lives in a certain region, which in turn . . ." or "this tool

3. Sartre, *Being and Nothingness*, trans. Hazel E. Barnes (New York, Philosophical Library, 1956), p. 307.
4. *Ibid.*, p. 306.

is employed for a certain sector of matter, which itself . . ." The world is the unity [*ensemble*] of these sectors or regions, and it is also the "beyond" [*l'au-delà*], the indefinite of possible acts and relations; the indeterminateness of the world is the indeterminateness of an "it could be" and also of an "I could," by which, as Kant saw, the "I think" affirms itself as an "I can." But this idea of the indeterminate remains undetermined; what does the possible mean here: the power [*puissance*] of being, the priority of the whole [*le tout*] over the parts, or the effulgence of something unconditioned?

The world cannot be indeterminate like Aristotelian matter, about which we can, strictly speaking, say nothing. We must look for a principle that assures the world's unity, even if this unity characterizes an unspecifiable totality. The *a priori* can aid us here. It gives us a double access to the idea of world, depending on whether the *a priori* is considered in its meaning and function, or in its very being through a comparison of the virtual and the actual. Let us consider it here in its constitutive function. It seems to propose the notion of world on its own. For it is not a structure of an object, but of a world. Such is the case with spatiality or necessity; but even when the *a priori* is somehow condensed into a mythic image, it dilates and expands; the image of childhood expresses the world's youth, and moreover, the world *as* youth: the world not only as a theater for juvenile enterprises, but as itself impatient, impetuous, and hopeful, as if something in it were associated with and responded to the virtues of youth. The world sends back our own image to us: witness the road that in the new dawn yields itself to our conquering strides, or the fortunate fate that proposes itself to the person who solicits it. Nevertheless, there are some *a priori* that designate and constitute certain categories of objects, certain particular sectors of the world: thus "thing," "living creature," "person" are the *a priori* for certain sciences and certain types of behavior. But these *a priori* again refer to the world; they suggest a world of the object in which the object manifests its meaning continuously because it appears in the midst of this world, not at its own origin as if it were a subject. Thus there is a world for the living creature, as well as a world for the thing, a world in which the thing assumes its being as thing. Here again the *a priori* is a power of a world, although only indirectly. And if the more formal *a priori*—the "something in general," the "whole and the part," etc.—do not refer so explicitly to the world, it is because they are not as explicitly constitutive, or at least because the objective and objectifying properties they designate are still formal and do not characterize the world concretely: they are structures of the world, they are not pregnant with a world.

Yet does not the world thus manifested by the *a priori* remain indeterminate, and is it not reduced to mere "forms of the world," as Hegel would say? The world is always indeterminate, but the crucial point is that it be characterized and, as it were, put together by something unconditioned. Its indeterminateness would be objectionable only if it were considered as a closed totality. But the world must be thought of in terms of unconditionality, not totality. Kant says this expressly: totality is only an illustration of unconditionality; it can form a starting point for reason, but it is not a beginning in itself; it does not contain its reason or principle within itself. Instead, its principle is found in the unconditioned, for only the unconditioned is a principle, the soul of an infinite series, and that which makes the series a series, the world a world. The *a priori* is a principle, but it need not be formal on this account. For this principle—a practical principle on the ethical plane, where it grounds in terms of obligations—is not necessarily a logical principle on the speculative plane. It cannot be derived from reasoning like the category of judgment; Kant says that "reason does not really generate any concept"; more completely: "Pure and transcendental concepts can issue only from the understanding; reason does not really generate any concept; the most it can do is to free a concept of understanding from the unavoidable limitations of possible experience . . . the transcendental ideas are thus . . . simply categories extended to the unconditioned." [5]

But is this extension the work of reason? May it not be inspired by the *a priori* itself, even by the affective *a priori*? In other words, is the unconditioned understood as a principle necessarily formal? Even the moral imperative is conceived as categorical, hence unconditioned, only because it is experienced as worthy of respect. Is it worthy of respect because it is rational? Yes, but it is also rational because it is worthy of respect. The fact that practical reason governs sensibility does not imply that reason is wholly foreign to this sensibility. Reason may also exist in feeling, as that which confers on feeling the strength of a principle, and as that which opens up the sensible to a meaning beyond the momentary and subjective impression: instead of repressing sensibility, reason exalts it, condemning the particular only to free the universal

5. *Critique*, p. 386 (A 409–B 436). Here I have changed the punctuation slightly. —Trans.

from it. Similarly, theoretical reason may express itself through feeling; the idea of world is at first a feeling of world, the feeling of a quality capable of radiating, or rather of spreading, into a world. This very quality is the unconditioned: the principle of a totality, the soul of a world. Reason is immanent in feeling to the extent that a quality demands display in a world and finds its very meaning in this manifestation. No longer, then, will we allow the notion of world to be invalidated by the world's indeterminateness, which is the correlate of the *a priori*—i.e., which is the *a priori* as a world: youth, or the tragic, or necessity as a world. If the *a priori* is constituent of objects, it is at the same time the herald of a world.

We might be tempted to ask whether the world illuminated by the *a priori* corresponds to the common idea of world. It is not yet, however, a question of an idea, but of a feeling; feeling bears or suggests the unconditioned, though it does not bring it to completion; the notion of world is not exhausted by the experience of the constitutive power of the *a priori*, however valuable this experience is for proposing a first form of the unconditioned. Moreover, which kind of world are we now dealing with: *a* world or *the* world? In fact, when specified by an *a priori*, the world comes to be particularized. There are as many worlds as there are *a priori*. Now, if we speak of a world of youth, of a happy world, or of a tragic one, we certainly do justice to the extension in meaning proper to the *a priori*, but are we equally fair to the notion of world? Does not this notion designate both the space that encloses all places [*lieux*] [6] and the universal that contains all particularities? Can we multiply such a notion indefinitely? Thus the world risks a new avatar: to be subjectified; and we must now denounce the link that often unites the particularization of the world with its subjectification. One speaks of a world of the tragic or of the joyful as one speaks of a world of Van Gogh or of Bach— and not without reason, if these affective qualities [7] in fact define the atmosphere of the works of Van Gogh or Bach; but then one substitutes the existential *a priori* for the *a priori* proper, and the world is conceived with respect to the existential *a priori* alone. Of course, a certain world manifested by their works corresponds to the *a priori* defining the person of Van Gogh or Bach. This is a

6. *Lieu* here means "place" in all its different senses; its meaning is not restricted to physical, spatial locations.—Trans.

7. For the notion of affective quality, see the author's *Phénoménologie de l'expérience esthétique* (Paris, Presses Universitaires de France, 1952), II, 543–84. —Trans.

singular world because it is the correlate and expression of a singular being-in-the world; but it is not a particular world, for it is not part of a larger whole; and instead of being defined by something more general, it carries in itself its unique and irreplaceable meaning. One is therefore easily tempted to call this world subjective, viewing it both as the expression of the person and as the work of subjectivity; the temptation is all the greater when this world is revealed in created works, as in the examples we have chosen; but, more generally, the world of the person is always revealed by his conduct in a certain milieu, as Don Quixote's world is shown through his horseback escapades, or as the world of Julien Sorel is manifested in his behavior at the seminary or with Madame de Rênal. One will then be led to oppose this singular world to the real world more as the subjective to the objective than as the part to the whole; thus the world of Van Gogh becomes Van Gogh's look directed onto the Île de France or Provence, just as the world of someone hallucinated is found in his hallucination, or as the world of a cruel person is his cruelty projected and reflected onto things; and at this point psychoanalysis enters to offer its services.

Then one comes to speak of the world of the person only metaphorically; and a real world is presupposed, the world for which the psychoanalyst, as one example, claims to possess the key. But let us look more closely. Why can we speak of a world of the person? We can do so because the existential *a priori* is itself composed of *a priori* which are constituent in both the object and the subject; thus the person is grounded in the transcendental and not vice versa. If there is a world of the subject, it is in the same way that there is a world of the *a priori*, since the *a priori* always has a double function. There is absolutely no need to assign to the person characterized by an existential *a priori* a power other than that given to the subject characterized wholly by the transcendental *a priori*: the same subject and the same *a priori* are involved here. The only difference between the two kinds of *a priori* is that the existential *a priori* actualizes various transcendental *a priori* and combines them to produce different patterns for each person. Sometimes the combination of the *a priori* composing the transcendental nature of a person is dominated by a single *a priori*; for example, it may be dominated by an affective *a priori*, causing us to mistake the latter for an existential *a priori,* as when we say that the world of Rouault is the tragic, or that the world of a certain living species is a specific environment. This confusion attests to the common parentage of the two kinds of *a priori,* but it does not authorize us to interpret the transcendental as existential, since on the contrary the existential is only the presence and combination of the transcendental in the subject; nor, least of all, does it authorize us to interpret the existential *a priori* as subjective—as if the world corresponding to it were only the product and reflection of a subjectivity. Our entire analysis of the *a priori* as constitutive protests against designating the world of the *a priori* as subjective and requires us to do justice to the objectivity of the world.

Thus, particularization does not imply subjectification. But the problem posed by the particularity of the world of the *a priori* remains open. For one might again contrast this world with the world that claims to be the only world, the real world that is both objective and universal. The opposition between objective and subjective is here reinforced by the opposition between particular and general, or rather between singular and universal. Now we cannot say that each world related to one of the various *a priori* is particular in the sense that it is part of a whole, as individuals (a particular is an individual or a private person) are part of a group or a species. Even if every world constitutes a separate ontological region, these regions are not juxtaposed like provinces to compose a universe; for Husserl, they are related logically, not materially, to the region in general, which represents a higher degree of formalization, though not a higher degree of extension. Instead, these regions divide up the world; they attest to its fragmentation; but the real world, the "encompassing" in Jasper's language, is not some vast container: if different worlds are in it, they are there not as its parts, but as its particularities or its expressions.

What then is this real world? In order to free it from the indeterminateness that still presses down upon particular worlds, one is tempted to define it as totality: the unconditioned as a principle must be realized as totality; thus Kant says that reason "adopts the method of starting from the idea of totality, though what it really has in view is the unconditioned." [8] By defining the world in terms of unconditionality, one risks making it into an idea: a regulative idea, a polar star of research, the idea of an achieved truth that would not be true for anyone in particular. But this demand is more than wishful thinking; it expresses itself through a precise idea of the world, even if the effort to make it explicit must founder in antinomies: this idea is that of the uni-

8. *Critique*, p. 391 (B 445).

verse, the world that is unconditioned because it is total, the world aimed at by the rational thought at work in science. By subordinating the unconditioned to totality, one avoids subjectifying the world. Yet the world still refers to man, and moreover, to the singular man, to the concrete subject. In fact, the idea of a total world, although inaccessible, is not illusory. But what does it mean? The immensity of the given? Astronomy claims the word "universe" and takes control of what astonishes us: galaxies beyond galaxies. Here the unconditioned is only the innumerable. But this material immensity is not large enough: the temporally limitless should be added to the spatially limitless, for nature has a history or at least may be dealt with by history, although it is not, strictly speaking, historical: its past has ceased to be real because there is no memory to retain or transmit it, but it has been real and thus may still be considered as part of reality. And why not also join mind to nature? Does not the mind represent another dimension of the world? When considered according to their psychological or cultural being rather than their truth, thoughts are real and specifiable, if not measurable; as things belong to the geographical landscape, so thoughts belong to the cultural landscape; they are part of the world just as much as things or men are.

This inclusion of thoughts among things does not compromise the thinking subject: thought in the act of thinking is irreducible to thoughts already thought out and considered as phenomena of the world (in the same way that for Spinoza the idea of body when formed in God or in the attribute of thought, that is, the soul, differs from the same idea when formed by virtue of the understanding's *vis nativa*). In other words, the region "consciousness" ceases to be the analogue of other regions when consciousness is no longer considered as an ontic phenomenon. With this reservation, there is no reason to limit the universe to what is materially extended, and in any case magnitude [*grandeur*] does not suffice to define the universe: the limitless [*l'indéfini*] is indefinable, and the Greeks were right in thinking that the true infinite is the finite, that which carries all of its determinations within itself and explicates them by itself; and when Spinoza evoked the infinite, he had to double its name: if Substance were not infinitely infinite, it would be merely limitless, and perhaps it would in fact be so if it did not include the attribute of thought, by means of which it is something other than the universe. The sphere whose center is everywhere and whose circumference is nowhere is not infinite, but limitless.[9] Magnitude is certainly a predicate of the universe so far as it is the horizon of all horizons. But it characterizes the universe absolutely only if it (magnitude) is itself an absolute—that is, only if its grandeur is felt, rather than calculated, as the majestic immensity manifested by the eternal silence. Perhaps we must finally agree with Pascal that the very principle of the universe is given in feeling; but does this mean that we must reduce the universe to the world?

In fact, the feeling of the immensity of the universe does not preclude calculation; by defying measurement, this feeling, like the Kantian sublime, calls for it. It invites us to search for an expression of grandeur in terms of material magnitude. And this search in turn has an effect: it invites us to decentralize the universe. The substitution of Cartesian extension for the anthropocentric cosmos requires both the exploration of space by conceptual and material instruments that are increasingly precise, and an effort of thought which is equal to the world's grandeur and which refuses to consider the human being as a privileged center of reference for the representation of the universe. Then the scientific consciousness somehow makes itself universal, that is, capable of conceiving a truly objective universe, where the qualities through which objects have meaning for man are devaluated: a universe that is absolute, hence free from all connection with man, and true, hence universally valid; such is the new form to be taken by the unconditioned.

Nevertheless, this universe cannot be mastered by knowledge: it remains an idea of reason. But at the same time reason conceives that through which it would be realized as a concrete universal: total humanity. The correlate of the universal is humanity, and there is the same relation between the various worlds and the universe as there is between men and humanity. Yet we must not dismiss the worlds for the benefit of the universe, nor men to the profit of humanity. Now, on the one hand, science maintains a permanent relation with perception. To think the universe is to think the universality of thought, to will that thought be universal; but it is still a subject that initiates this willing. The universal in this sense is only a project: the affirmation of the unconditioned value of thought, rather than the

9. Even Pascal's thought is indefinite [indéfinie]; as George Canguilhem observes, "it attempts paradoxically to reconcile the new scientific conception that makes the universe an unlimited and undifferentiated milieu with the ancient cosmological vision that makes the world a definite totality referred to its center" (La Connaissance de la vie [Paris, Hachette, 1952], p. 198).

thought of an unconditioned being; its idea expresses the tension between fact and value. On the other hand, since science is linked to perception and can neither deny it without being false to itself nor assimilate it without being false to *it*, the scientific universe cannot reduce or assimilate the perceived worlds that form man's lived environment. Science involves perception only by doing justice to it: by understanding it as giving access to truth and by allowing it to have its own truth. A hallucination is false in relation to perception, and it is perception, not science, that denounces it; psychology today seeks the secret of hallucination in the world of the hallucinated. As for perception, it is not a lesser truth in comparison with scientific knowledge; science does not measure its truth by its distance from perception, but by the distance, existing within scientific knowledge, between a more and a less approximative knowledge. The astronomer's sun is the truth of the sun that is naively thought to be two hundred feet away, because the latter conception of the sun, involving a quantitative determination, already belongs to science; but it is not strictly speaking the truth of the poet's sun: the perceived sun that has its truth in itself.[10] Does this mean that there are two suns? No, but perhaps there are two wholly different ideas of the same sun. To think the universe is to think that there is only one sun and that, if the poet's sun is the *ratio cognoscendi* of the astronomer's sun, the latter is the *ratio essendi* of the former.

Therefore, the relation of perception to science is above all a relation of distinction, not of subordination; if there is interchange between them, it is in the sense that science cannot dispense with perception (even though it finally transcends it), while perception can easily do without science. Moreover, this distinction seems to authorize us to classify the scientific universe as one world among others: to place the world of the scientist or of consciousness in general alongside the world of Mozart or the world of Balzac. But do we have the right here to particularize

10. Here we would disagree with Jules Lagneau, who shows that "there is a truth of each order in itself," but who fails to distinguish between presence and representation in the order of perception; for he describes representation as if it were presence when he asserts that "it is an act and implies belief but not knowledge," and that it involves only a practical truth. Authentic perception—representation—is already more than manipulation [*usage*] of the world; it is knowledge of a world, although nonscientific knowledge, and it already puts the *a priori* of representation and the affective *a priori* into play. We invoke here the poet's sun as an expression of the perceived sun because this knowledge begins with the imagination, which tears the tissue of presence. [See Jules Lagneau, *Célèbres leçons et fragments* (Paris, Presses Universitaires de France, 1950), pp. 127–29.—Trans.]

the universe in order to refuse it any priority? Can we dismiss the effort of thought to raise itself to the universal, and can we disqualify truth in its claim to the universality by which it distinguishes itself from certitude? Actually, we can no more refuse than accept the idea of a total world. The very idea of world involves the idea of totality, but this totality cannot be conceived except in reference to a total humanity for which science would be already complete.

In any case, we must no longer dismiss man on behalf of humanity. The singular subject cannot be put aside, and it is he who is the real correlate of the universe. Humanity is only an idea and a task. In conceiving the universe, man strives to promote humanity in himself. This striving is not without a meaning, even an ethical one; Simone Weil, for example, thought that mechanism could harmonize with grace because the conception of a mechanism is accessible only to a mind which has itself, by dint of attention and patience, merited grace and which has begun on the intellectual plane the enterprise of deracination and decreation that is the vocation of the human being.[11] The sacrifice of the particular to the universal, which is also the message of Jules Lagneau, must be accomplished both on the speculative and on the practical planes; and it seems to be already attained through the effort by which pure science wrenches itself away from the glamour of the cosmos: we can see how morality is here, as Lagneau wants it to be, already immanent in reflection. Science is good to the extent that it is true; it is true to the extent that the subject, raising himself up to the universal and sacrificing himself for the love of truth, expresses the idea of the universe.

Nevertheless, this universal thought is the product and decision of a subject who is always singular. And perhaps we must follow here a path diverging from that of Lagneau, who also sacrifices the particular to the universal: "The absolute subject, with apparently perfect independence, is in reality completely dependent, and this is verified by the failure in which the effort to grasp the individual subject by reflection ends: instead of coming to individuality, [this effort] ends in the impersonal and universal."[12] If God is in me, must I not exist for God to exist, and must I not decide to realize Him in me? Thus we have looked for the concrete subject in the transcendental subject. This concrete subject is already implied in the idea of the universe as quantita-

11. See Simone Weil, *Gravity and Grace*, trans. Arthur Wills (New York, Putnam, 1952), pp. 45–49.—Trans.
12. Jules Lagneau, *Célèbres leçons et fragments*, p. 60.

tively conceived, leading Pascal to the idea of the disproportion of man: for that which is out of sight is conceivable only in relation to a project of possible vision, and we can imagine the innumerable only in relation to a project of calculation.

Consequently, insofar as we retain the transcendental perspective, we can put man and the world on the same level. The unconditioned world is related to a principle whose correlate is feeling. The world conceived as a totality constitutes an idea whose elaboration is a project of reason. Feeling and reason express two ways in which man—always singular man, even if he is the delegate of humanity—relates himself to the world. In the first way, the experience of the world is given in perception, which apprehends the *a priori* because the *a priori* is already constituent of a world. In the second way, the idea of the world is controlled by reason, which claims to grasp the universe as a totality: the experience of the world reappears in the idea of unity. In both cases, there is a world only for a subject. But this "for" should not be changed imprudently into a "by." Yet this is the risk one runs if sufficient account is not taken of another feature of the world which we have to come to in any case, since the problem of the plurality of worlds is not resolved; for we may refuse to favor the astronomer's sun, but we cannot deny that there is only one sun: the real sun.

Thus we must return to the notion of world to find in it a new determination that will this time risk putting the situation of the subject into question—a situation which was not compromised as long as we considered the world as at least a spectacle, if not a project; but the world is not only total, but totalizing, since it is the real, the totality of the real. What in fact is the "true" world which serves as a foil for the other worlds? It is a true world: true on the condition of being objective, as the correlate of an impersonal thought that favors no single point of view and annuls all of them by explaining them all, like the Leibnizian God. But it is also true because it is real: integral because integrating, capable of accounting for the differences and particularities that are present in it; it is truer than the particular worlds—the perceived world or the felt worlds—because it contains them. Its privileged position lies neither in its immensity nor even in its rationality, but in the plenitude of the real. For truth is always defined by its relation with reality, and the idea of the universe expresses the fundamental character of reality: its overflowing alterity. The unconditioned is the real, the unspecifiable totality of determinations or conditions. The appeal of the idea of universe stems from this character, and not merely from the fact that it calls for a universal thought. Instead, universal thought tries to seize reality in its plenitude, just as the Leibnizian God strives to actualize this plenitude. Thus, universal thought proceeds by enunciating the most general laws or the most fundamental structures. It is also universally valid, that is, valid for all minds; but it is valid only to the extent that it apprehends the real, or at least to the extent that the form it elaborates is a form for a matter. For knowledge wills itself as objective in order to grasp the reality of the object, the object as real, thus as not belonging to anyone and as repudiating all appropriation, all subjective interpretation. Science sometimes claims the monopoly of truth because it claims to attain the real: the essentiality of the fact, a fact that is all the more real when deprived of all meaning and reduced to the mere being of a mathematical formula. The objectivity of the universe indicates not only that it is conceived according to the norms of objectifying thought, but also that its reality is not limited by any subjective signification, since it surpasses all such meanings.

Therefore, the relation of the various worlds to the universe is precisely the relation of the particular to the universal: the real is inexhaustible, and the different worlds are diverse aspects of the real. Are these aspects real or possible? It is the real which is the possibility of the possible. But can there be two truths if there is only one reality? Yes, if every truth is only an approximate expression of the real; there can be several simultaneous explanations because they are all partially valid for one and the same reality; but this can be so only on the condition that none of them claims to be exclusive: the astronomer's sun is not the real sun, and the real sun is the possibility of both the astronomer's and the poet's sun. Does this mean that universe and world are again put onto the same plane, both being reduced to the rank of the merely possible? Not exactly: we cannot ignore the effort of science to seize the real as such through [à travers] the universe as total; but what science attains, the objectivity that is its goal, is not yet the real, that is, the universe as real. The prestige science enjoys should not give rise to a confusion: it does not authorize us to confuse the scientific world and the universe, even if science terms the world that it elaborates "the universe."

If the universe is the real so far as it is overflowing [débordant], science has a hold on it, although it does not have a complete mastery of it. The fact that it is conscious of the universe and aims at it as a goal does not guarantee that it knows it. The real is both the nearest and the farthest, the already known and the unknowable; it is the world of the being who is in-the-world, that in which we are—and science also is in-the-world—and that which is always outside us, precisely because we are within it. The world as the totality of the real is represented and sought for as the universe, but it is not given as the universe. The scientific world represents an effort to translate the world into the universe; this contitutes its dignity, but it is really neither one nor the other, for *the* world is given within various worlds, and the universe conceived as the truth of the world is always beyond: once more, the real is the nearest and the farthest. It is near because perception already grasps it, even in its plenitude; but perception apprehends this plenitude differently: through feeling, that is, by intension more than by extension; and this is why it seizes *a* world rather than *the* world.

Granting that the universal signifies the real, is the relation of the particular to the universal equivalent to the relation of the possible to the real? The real is not a sum of possibilities, and the possible must be understood on the basis of the real. Moreover, when a world is revealed to me—even a mythical world, that is, one centered on a mythical image—it is given as real, not as possible. But it is not *the* real, which is reality as total and inexhaustible. Similarly, when I imagine a world that is not presently given to me—for instance, the world of the tragic when I am inhabiting the world of the joyful—I always imagine it against the background of the real, and what I imagine appears to me as a possibility of the real and not as an abstract and meaningless possible. In other words, the various possible worlds are not possibilities pre-existing the real and separated from it; they are compossibilities whose signification is more ontological than logical: they are understood on the basis of the real as its powers [*puissances*], the witnesses of its power: power is not necessarily privation and desire, for it may also signify the unconditionality of that which no determination exhausts, reality acting as a principle. For the principle can be conceived as the motor element, the source animating thought; this is why we said that a principle can be a feeling as well as a formal requirement; but it can also be conceived as what is primary, irreducible, and active in the order of being: then the real itself is the principle. The world itself is a possible because it is the real: indeterminable because surpassing [*débordant*] all determination, unlimited [*indéfini*] because unspecifiable; and the possible worlds are the expression of the fundamental possibility which forms the very character of the real.

This has two consequences, the first of which concerns the being of the *a priori*, and the second the position of the subject in the presence of the world. In fact, we could once more invoke the *a priori*, considered this time in its being, in order to make our notion of world more precise; but at present the *a priori* no longer furnishes us with the key to the world; instead, the world obliges us to reconsider the *a priori*. By introducing the possible as a power of the real, we possibilize the *a priori* itself both as constituent of certain objects or certain worlds, and as belonging to the subject and constituting him as a transcendental subject. For we must not confuse the virtual with the possible here. In the subject, the virtual already exists, even if it is not actualized or made explicit: composing the existential *a priori*, it constitutes a system in the subject, or rather it constitutes the subject as a system. It is virtual so far as it is knowledge [*connaissance*]; if it has not yet been actualized, this is because it has not yet had the opportunity. But this opportunity is proposed by the world, since the subjective *a priori* is nothing more than the comprehension of the objective *a priori*: the subjective *a priori* remains virtual because the objective *a priori* remains possible. Ontologically, the real is pregnant with the possible, which attests to its power. To speak of the *a priori* as possible is to say that it is a possibility of the real, just as the various particular worlds are possibilities of the world. Does this not subordinate the *a priori* in its being to some higher being that would be reality? Here we come to the idea of a being anterior to the *a priori* in its two aspects: what we shall term the *a priori* of the *a priori*. It is the world which suggests this idea when we conceive it as the whole [*le tout*] and the power [*la puissance*] of the real, and when the particular worlds are no longer opposed to *the* world, attesting instead to its transcendent [*débordant*] character. By the same token, the *a priori* that constitute these worlds and that have their correlate in the subject are also products. They are always conditions or expressions of objectivity, but of an objectivity which appears in the world when a possibility is realized. They represent a second state of the world at the moment of the realization of a possibility. To define the *a priori* as possible is to define it as engenderable; that which engenders it is the world defined as metamorphizable through the conjunction of the possible and the real. The *a priori* in its double aspect is inserted into a history of the relations of man and the world, but it is the world which gives rise to this history and which is always anterior to it.

But we must also reconsider the status of the subject. For the subject, conceived as the correlate of particular worlds and especially of the objective world of science, seems totally surpassed by the world here: his facticity indicates his subordination; like the *a priori* that he bears, he appears to be nothing more than a possibility of the world. His transcendental dignity does not preserve him from an ontological degradation. We must take seriously the anteriority of the world with respect to man—an anteriority which transcendental philosophies, paying attention only to a transcendental *cogito,* take lightly.

Consequently, having come to the point in our reflection where we discover the world as an inexhaustible reality, we are tempted to return to the Parmenidean naturalism we sketched above when we defined the *a priori* as a second state of the subject and object, a state inserted into a development of being. Must we not, in the contest between man and world, finally grant primacy to the world and refuse to consider the subject as unengenderable? This move is all the more tempting because, in challenging the Husserlian notion of a transcendental subjectivity and its concomitant idealism, we have placed ourselves on the very terrain of naturalism: and how can we continue to combat it on its own ground? We must admit that naturalism is also true, and that the genetic theory of man required as a complement to its cosmology is perfectly legitimate and desirable. Perhaps we should even say that the elaboration of this theory of man is the only positive task that can be assigned to philosophy—if philosophy needs a program. Furthermore, this naturalism can find credentials in the philosophical tradition: for the world to which it gives primacy— the world that engenders man, the foyer of possibilities and the theater of individuations that is always in operation—is *natura naturans* or the being whose primary predicate is reality. Nothing here warrants the distinction between the ontic and the ontological, the physical and the metaphysical: naturalism's cosmology is an ontology, and all genesis is ontological. Why should we fear a regression to a pre-Kantian, pre-critical ontology? Perhaps it is the only viable one.

Naturalism is given its just due as soon as the concrete subject is reinstated as a being present to the world: to be present to the world [*au monde*] is above all to be in the world [*dans le monde*]: there is a history of man, which fits into a vaster history, even if it is a history that man alone can write. It is useless to allege that the history of Egypt is the history of Egyptology; man is not just his own narrative, and history is not merely a meaning without an object. This history must be written, and without being diluted by a reference to idealism, as perhaps happens with Merleau-Ponty when he substitutes the term "dialectic" for "genesis" to express the relation between the three orders: physical, vital, and human. For he is not content to substitute a philosophy of structure for a philosophy of substance; he interprets structure as meaning, and when he quotes Hegel he is not far from conceiving meaning as a moment of *logos*. Thus he refuses to "remain on the plane of being." [13] But if there is a dialectic, it does not belong to being; it operates *in* being and must be understood as a genesis. The idea that man is historical before becoming an historian should be followed through to its conclusion, as should the idea that man is incarnated: it is the same thing for him to be body and history, to be caught in space and caught in time. The genetic approach is just as valid in the form of ontogenesis as it is in the form of phylogenesis; it situates man in time's indefiniteness, which is the most eloquent form in the world; it reveals both the obscurity of the past—the past of the individual as well as the past of the species —and the obscurity of the future: two aspects of something unfathomable.

Nevertheless, a genetic theory encounters limits. The first occurs within itself when it distinguishes between ontogenesis and phylogenesis. The idea that ontogenesis reproduces and exemplifies phylogenesis has been generally abandoned today (as has the idea that primitive mentality reproduces the mentality of the child, or the idea that the neurotic adult can remain a child without behaving like one). For example, in the psychology of Maurice Pradines, phylogenesis invites us to

reverse the order of ontogenesis, which seems to make the child pass from brute sensation to intelligent perception, and to discover a more secret order which in perceptive and intelligent activity reveals the *primum movens* of an organic operation that would never have been meaningful, that is, intelligent, if it had not already been so in its germ.[14]

Here phylogenesis introduces the idea of a reverse or reciprocal genesis in which a genetic theory finds its limit, so that "the word 'genesis' in the expression 'reciprocal genesis' has a wholly relative value." [15] What then about ontogenesis? We must in any case refrain from deducing man from humanity considered as a species. Bergson said that every man is a species by himself; but this

---

13. *The Structure of Behavior*, trans. Alden L. Fisher (Boston, Beacon Press, 1963), p. 158.

14. Maurice Pradines, Preface to *La Genèse réciproque*, by J. Grappe (Paris, Presses Universitaires de France, 1949), p. viii.

15. Grappe, *ibid.*, p. 39.

does not imply that the species is like a man. Humanity is not the summation of individual men as the world is the summation of possible worlds. When we retain the perspective of a pre-critical naturalism—e.g., of a sociologism—humanity may appear more real than the individual; if we refer ourselves to the transcendental and consider that the *a priori* must be borne by subjects, it is less so; intersubjectivity is here subordinated to subjectivity, and humanity is only a quasi-subject. Therefore, we cannot deduce the subject from humanity. At the most, the two are analogous in a certain way: both have a history, but the history of the individual is no more comparable to the history of humanity than the history of humanity is comparable to a history of nature (and we must still distinguish here between the history of the species and the history of institutions). Does this mean that the genetic theory, whose ambitions are curbed in the case of phylogenesis, finds its inspiration and attainment in ontogenesis? We have already answered in the negative by showing that the genesis of the subject finally runs up against the transcendental: its source is the unengenderable *a priori*.

The genetic theory of man meets with another limit in its own results. Does not the unfathomable which it discovers on the fringes of the temporal field it explores and which recalls the world's indeterminateness indicate this limit? We should not assume this too hastily, before distinguishing between *de facto* and *de jure* limits. There are clearly empirical reasons for the obscurity of the human past—reasons which, moreover, can still justify naturalism if the admission that knowledge is overwhelmed [*débordé*] by what it does not know confirms the idea that the world is overwhelming [*débordant*]. Yet it is worth noting that each new discovery in paleontology provokes rather than answers the questions: Is this a man? What is man? For humanity must have begun with actual men. It is equally noteworthy that the individual's past is also lost in the mists of memory as one goes back toward one's birth; here memory itself disappears as if a knowledge of origins were forbidden. Does this imply that a totally historical origin has no meaning at all? Perhaps so; at least it suggests that birth may involve a metaphysical meaning and that there is something irreducible in man. Of course, others can tell me about my birth, somewhat as archaeology tells us about the "first" men; I cannot deny that my birth is an empirical fact or that the appearance of humanity is situated in natural history. But the man who is born does not come into the world as its product; he comes as its equal: every man is a Minerva. The fact that a knowledge of origins is overwhelmed in science and cut off in memory signifies that the world is overwhelming; but the subject assumes this situation and changes its meaning: he lets himself be overwhelmed in order somehow to measure up to the world and to maintain an equality with it. He transforms his historical origin, to which his corporeality is bound, into an absolute beginning, inaccessible because absolute; by the same token, the subject invites us to realize that the *de facto* limits of paleontology, however far they are pushed back, attest to a *de jure* limit: the subject is not reducible to his history.

The obscurity of the future confirms this. It indicates that humanity, in the individual as in the species, is always unattained. The genetic theory cannot seize upon this obscurity as a pretext for showing that individuation is always precarious, always in question. For the meaning of the future varies according to whether it concerns man or humanity: if it concerns humanity, it is certain that the career of man is not terminated and that no one can conceive an end, metaphorical or not, of history. But the future is not open to a genesis of man; what man has produced and invented is not his own metamorphosis, but the institutions by which he will affirm and confirm himself as man (and this allows the possibility of something new under the sun). What is to be engendered is the kingdom of ends, not the person. If we consider the individual, we cannot say that his individuation is a task for him; it is already accomplished by the existential *a priori* which constitutes him. His real task is to become what he is: to actualize the virtual by confronting the world in which the objective *a priori* call to him (instead of manifesting its pre-established series like the monad), to reveal in his history the unengenderable that orients him, and to manifest his freedom as spontaneity, that is, as self-accord. The *a priori* constituting him makes him substantial: permanent through change. For it is clear that his temporality subjects him to changes; he can even—it is thus that he has a future—take the initiative in these changes, in the same way that he elaborates a science of the *a posteriori* or a technique.

Thus, a genetic theory of man encounters its limits: the subject who is present to the world [*au monde*] is not entirely engenderable from the world. The anteriority of the world in relation to humanity and to each man is evident, though not absolute; it signifies that man is in the world [*dans le monde*], not that he is radically subordinated to it: this anteriority has a chronological, not a transcendental, meaning. We might express this by granting man his revenge on the world and by saying that the world without man is not yet the world: not that the real awaits man in order to be real, but it does await him to receive its meaning as world. Perhaps it would be easier, in asking ourselves if we can conceive an *a priori* of the *a priori,* to preserve for man his equality with the world if it is interpreted as being. But the pre-critical ontology that interprets the world as reality does not reject the transcendental philosophy that gives man his prerogatives. This ontology is as necessary as it is insufficient: witness the cosmologies which, even to describe a nonhuman world which men enter, already presuppose man as the goal [*fin*] of cosmic history, an end [*fin*] that already exists in the beginning. Thus, for Bergson evolution is creative because life is already consciousness, and matter is never more than the slackening of the *élan vital;* here, at least consciousness is not a product of evolution. And doubtless we could discern in Schelling's objective idealism a transformation of Kant's transcendental philosophy into a philosophy of nature.

Nevertheless, even if the world is not, except chronologically, anterior to the subject, it does overwhelm him. Man's being-present-to-the-world signifies the impossibility of being an objective spectator, or the objectifying spectator presupposed by transcendental idealism, which situates itself outside the world in order to know it. For this kind of withdrawal is not possible: the world is precisely that which cannot be surveyed in such fashion. The biologist who studies the relation of living creatures to their environment is himself living, and his laboratory is an environment, itself situated in the world; the philosopher who considers man as a situated being is himself in a situation; he is geographically and historically localized and localizing. The *cogito* is no more pure than it is impersonal, and the philosopher who compromises it by situating it in the world is himself already compromised in the same way. The world is encompassing not only horizontally as the horizon of horizons, but also vertically, like the star that does not admit a higher point of view. The world is indeterminate because it is indeterminable and because every determination is included in it. But this condition of the subject does not disqualify him; on the contrary, it qualifies him as capable of knowing and attaining truth. Even when he strives to conceive an objective world, he can know only a particular one. But the particularity of the various worlds of man does not alter their fundamental meaning as *worlds.* The particular is one of the modes of the universal. Through [*à travers*] it, the totality of the real is thought. And the *a priori* extends itself into a world because, in its own way, it signifies the world.

This means above all that the *a priori* is objective. It is a form of the world; saying that it constitutes the object amounts to the same thing. But we might be inclined to imagine an isolated object that would be the product of a constitutive activity. Evoking the world dispels this inclination and helps us to understand our relation to the object through our relation to the world, that is, through our situation rather than through our activity, and, similarly, to conceive truth in terms of being rather than doing. In fact, so far as the *a priori* is given in perception, it is through perception that we are "in the truth" [*dans le vrai*] because we are then in the world: in contact with the real. Our relation to truth lies in this contact. Yet reflective philosophy invites us to ponder laboriously and indefinitely the truth of our judgments or the very possibility of truth, and we cannot decline this invitation casually. When we have "merely" perceived, nothing has been accomplished; neither science nor philosophy yet exists. This is true, but *everything* begins at this point. Perception *is* the beginning; it is that which puts us in the world. And there are new beginnings and perseverance only because there is *a* beginning: the astonishing revelation that the world is given to us and that a perpetually pre-existing accord has intervened. After this, conceiving or controlling the world may take place; and error is always possible, as well as lying, bad faith, or just giving up. But this is because we somehow already possess truth. And if truth is accord with the real, this is because we are always in accord with the same real. We can possess truth because it first possesses us: it exists not outside us, but *with* us, according to the pact uniting subject with world, microcosm with macrocosm.

How should the equality of subject and world be considered from now on? As an indispensable reciprocity which can be contained in this formula: the world comprehends the subject, and the subject comprehends the world.[16] But is it the same act of comprehending in both cases? Not exactly: the world comprehends the subject by individualizing him; the subject is not comprehended in the world as a part in a whole [*un tout*], or at least he is understood as the part that sees itself granted a sort of independence; this part is not homogeneous with the whole, since the individual is indivisible and since this indivisibility is both the sign and the essential character of a thought that is incommensurable with extension. The world comprehends the subject by re-

16. Here and in the following sentences Dufrenne plays upon the double meaning of "comprehension": understanding and inclusion.—Trans.

fusing at the same time to integrate him into itself; it comprehends him as irreducible: to be present to the world is not to be inserted into a whole [*ensemble*], but to be born to reality. The subject in turn comprehends the world by particularizing it: the individual is defined on this condition. To draw upon the inexhaustible is to humanize it, but it is also to make it appear as inexhaustible: the subject comprehends the world as that which cannot be comprehended; the world encompasses the subject as that which cannot be encompassed. Thus a reciprocal envelopment exists between world and subject, precisely because their dichotomy is unsurmountable. That which opposes them is that which links them together. This relation is not dialectical; it defies all logic, signifying rather the failure of any explanatory system, naturalist or idealist; the subject's being-present-to-the-world is inexplicable although it is always produced in broad daylight. And philosophy always comes up against the same impasse, even though the impasse has different names, according to the various paths philosophy pursues: antinomies if it considers the world; or, when it strives to conceive being or substance, the unity of the empirical and the transcendental subject, of body and soul, of nature and freedom, of extension and thought, of nature and idea. Even the notion of God is involved here, for God is the being who would claim to be beyond two antagonistic yet concordant terms and who would attempt to settle their quarrel; He is the finally unthinkable means of circumventing the impasse by subordinating both the world and the subject to an absolute reality.

11 / The Affinity between Man and the World

WE HAVE JUST PUT man and the world on equal terms. But perhaps the *a priori* has something more to tell us concerning the relation uniting them. It corroborates dualism because it is itself double: both objective and subjective, knowledge in the subject and structure in the world. But this double function suggests more than an equality: it points to a reciprocal appropriateness, an affinity. The fact that the subject bears in himself a virtual knowledge of the world suggests that the subject exists for the world since it attains consciousness in him, not that the world exists through the agency of a subject; conversely, the fact that the world is structured by the *a priori* suggests that the world exists for the subject, not the subject through the world, since the world manifests what the subject already knows and allows consciousness to attain science and discover truth. Thus, dualism points to a reciprocal finality, instead of a reciprocal causality: the world is for the subject, and the subject is for the world. To be present to the world is to be at home in the world: to find one's way around in it. This assertion does not condemn the preceding analyses; it does not discount the fact that in a sense the subject is part of the world, and even homogeneous with it through his body; nor does it discount the other fact that the subject is privileged and constitutes an unavoidable center of reference for the world. On the contrary, the kind of familiarity between subject and world indicated by this assertion fits in well with the fact that the subject is both connatural with the world and independent of it. But the world is no longer seen as an opaque in-itself, a radically exterior and foreign given whose secret we must force out, or rather, which we must force to be intelligible by imposing on it the law of the understanding or the law of *praxis;* meaning appears in it immediately, a meaning that the subject can understand and that he must only make explicit; in this way the subject gains truth, and thought can make its norms prevail on the basis of an indispensable contact with the real. Conversely, the world is no longer radically separated from the subject. When the object is conceived, it does not undergo a metamorphosis or a radical promotion; its own possibility comes to light in consciousness, and it seems as if it calls out to consciousness to be realized. Knowing the world is like granting its wish, since the world proposes itself to knowledge (instead of baffling it) by bearing a meaning that is already objective. This does not indicate that knowledge is limited to recording meaning, for meaning is always given as partial and precarious, and the *a priori* always has to be made more explicit. But in the operation of knowledge the world becomes clear to itself: the understanding of nature is the understanding of man. The identity of the *a priori* creates a sort of harmony between the world and the subject.

The idea of this harmony appears in Kant's philosophy in the form of finality conceived as the accord of the object to be known with the knowing subject. This philosophy remains dualistic; it admits a given: the object of empirical knowledge, which is perhaps necessary even to pure science, because it provokes the operation of the *cogito* without being interiorizable by it. The conflict of genesis and facticity—a conflict which has been shown to arise for Fichte at the point of transition between theoretical idealism and moral realism [1]—appears in Kant not only when he analyzes morality, but even in the deduction of principles, a deduction which at least appeals to the possibility of experience and conceives the transcendental object $= x$ as existing before [*devant*] the subject. But let us consider the empirical given, which provides not only the occasion, but the content, for the activity of the "I think." Kant evidently denies that this given in itself and by itself manifests the *a priori*. But does he not admit that it must lend itself to subsumption, to the act by which the understanding constitutes it as an object of experience? The first *Critique* is especially attentive to this act, whose elucidation forms its very vocation. It postpones the examination of the accord of the given and the subject; moreover, the critique of empiricism seems to dispense with it definitively, for the problem that can be raised by this accord imposes itself on empiricism only because the latter

1. Jules Vuillemin, *L'Héritage kantien et la révolution copernicienne* (Paris, Presses Universitaires de France, 1954), p. 117.

distinguishes between the connection of perceptions according to the powers of nature and the establishment of relations according to the principles of human nature. Kant's famous example of cinnabar [2] reverses the problem; as Gilles Deleuze says very aptly, "If the given were not itself submitted first of all to principles of the same kind as those which rule the connection of representations for an empirical subject, the subject could never encounter this accord except in an absolutely accidental manner." [3] In effect, Kant asks empiricism a crucial question: "As regards the empirical rule of association . . . upon what, I ask, does this rule, as a law of nature, rest? How is this association itself possible?" [4] The answer is that "the ground of the possibility of the association of the manifold . . . is named the *affinity* of the manifold . . . appearances are subject to *a priori* conditions, with which the synthesis of their apprehension must be in complete accordance." [5] The unity of association has "an objective ground (that is, one that can be comprehended *a priori*, antecedently to all empirical laws of the imagination). . . . This objective ground of all appearances I entitle their affinity. It is nowhere to be found save in the principle of the unity of apperception." [6] In accordance with this principle, the unity of all consciousness in original apperception is the necessary condition for every possible perception. Thus Hume is dismissed: he "confounds a principle of affinity, which has its seat in the understanding and affirms necessary connection, with a rule of association, which exists only in the imitative faculty of imagination, and which can exhibit only contingent, not objective, connections." [7] Hume did not see that the empirical affinity of phenomena presupposes their transcendental affinity—in other words, that "nature directs itself according to our subjective ground of apperception," [8] which thus becomes an objective principle and the principle of objectivity.

But does Kant really answer Hume? Sould he say that empirical affinity is a "mere consequence" [9] of transcendental affinity?

2. See *Critique of Pure Reason*, trans. Norman Kemp Smith (London, Macmillan, 1933), p. 132 (A 100).—Trans.
3. Deleuze, *Empirisme et subjectivité* (Paris, Presses Universitaires de France, 1953), p. 124.
4. *Critique*, p. 139 (A 112–113).
5. *Ibid.*, pp. 139–40 (A 113–114).
6. *Ibid.*, p. 145 (A 122).
7. *Ibid.*, pp. 610–11 (A 766–B 794).
8. *Ibid.*, p. 140 (A 114). I have altered Smith's translation here.—Trans.
9. *Ibid.*

Doubtless the supreme principle of Kant's transcendental philosophy is that the condition for the possibility of experience is also the condition for the possibility of the object of experience, while for Hume the principles of knowledge are only principles of human nature and make an experience possible without making objects for this experience necessary. But the object of experience so far as it is determined by the transcendental is the transcendental object $= x$: "This object cannot contain any determinate intuition, and therefore refers only to that unity which must be met with in any manifold of knowledge which stands in relation to an object." [10] This transcendental object is, as Kant says again, the object in general. How do we proceed from there to the empirical object, and consequently from transcendental to empirical affinity? Such a transition seems impossible without invoking finality: the rule for reproduction in the transcendental imagination cannot by itself produce a rule for empirical determinations; it is a necessary, though not sufficient, condition. For the empirical imagination to "find opportunity for exercise appropriate to its powers," [11] the phenomenon must submit to a constant rule that unifies the manifold into a succession or series; for example, I must be able to conceive a piece of cinnabar as a substance, hence in terms of the idea of an object in general, independently of the manner in which the cinnabar refers to intuition.[12] Nevertheless, this reference to intuition is by no means immaterial. Kant admits as much when he says: "If cinnabar were sometimes red, sometimes black, sometimes light, sometimes heavy. . . ." [13] The rule directing a synthesis must find something correspondent in the very nature of things, in the manifold of intuition; the empirical affinity of phenomena, that is, the regularity or permanence of the cinnabar's appearances, far from being a consequence of transcendental affinity—the determination of the cinnabar as a substance—is its guarantee. If there must be an objective knowledge, it does not suffice that it have a necessary relation to the object; the object must do its part, and the rule for its unity must not be made inoperative and object-less through the irreducible and disconcerting diversity of intuitions. In brief, for there to be association, the given must be associable, and this characteristic of the given cannot be the product of the principle of association. We

10. *Ibid.*, p. 137 (A 109).
11. *Ibid.*, p. 132 (A 100).
12. Kant uses a *reductio ad absurdum* argument here: *ibid.*
13. *Ibid.*

must reintroduce finality to the exact extent that Kant does not sufficiently answer Hume—i.e., to the extent that the constitutive activity does not suffice to constitute the given.

Yet Kant sets aside this finality in the first *Critique*, particularly in the last paragraph of the Transcendental Deduction, because he is anxious to avoid the accusation of subjectivism: the categories are not "subjective dispositions," because objectivity would then be illusory, and the necessity of the *a priori* would not be in the object. Transcendental, nonsubjective subjectivity alone can constitute objectivity. Nevertheless, necessity is quite logical; it informs the object without proceeding from it. Must not the object contribute its part? This is the problem posed by subsumption. In order to pass from a pure to an empirical science, from *a priori* to *a posteriori* laws, from the object in general to particular objects, a finality must be invoked: "This understanding is no doubt *a priori* in possession of universal laws of nature, apart from which nature would be incapable of being an object of experience at all. But over and above this it needs a certain order of nature in [relation to] its particular rules." [14] Thus, after showing that "all empirical laws are only special determinations of the pure laws of understanding, in which, and according to the norm of which, they first become possible," [15] it remains to establish conversely that the "accord of nature with our cognitive faculties is presupposed *a priori* by judgment." [16] The *Critique of Judgment* strives to elucidate this accord, though it does so with a certain reluctance: the principle of finality is "a subjective principle of judgment"; it is regulative and not constitutive. This is why the judgment of taste is not founded on concepts and cannot be classified as knowledge. Its fundament is a formal finality—"the form of the finality of an object"—which proceeds neither from a subjective end [*fin*], like one aroused by interest, nor from an objective end "or possibility of the object itself." This principle of the formal finality of nature is at least a transcendental principle of judgment: of reflective judgment, to which the general (rules, laws, or principles) is not given and on which it is in fact incumbent to rise from the particular in nature to the general.

Reflection here is not at first the self-reflection of the supreme principle; it is a reflection on the given which must form the

---

14. Kant, *Critique of Judgment*, trans. James Creed Meredith (Oxford, Clarendon Press, 1952), p. 24. (The words in brackets are mine.—Trans.)

15. *Critique of Pure Reason*, p. 148 (A 128).

16. *Critique of Judgment*, p. 25. (In keeping with the French translation, I have changed "adaptation" to "accord" here.—Trans.)

object of an induction. Judgment does not prescribe this law of finality to nature; it presumes it and accepts it for its own use as a presupposition of its operation, a maxim for its act. But beyond its utility for research, is this principle really verified in experience? Is finality not ascertained as a fact? Kant suggests this when he says: "Just as if it were a lucky chance that favored us, we are rejoiced (properly speaking relieved of a need) where we meet with such systematic unity under merely empirical laws." [17] Involved here is the already aesthetic pleasure that we experience with an object which is in tune with our faculties of knowledge and stimulates their free activity. Reflection is then a return to oneself because representation is related to the object, not to the subject; yet the object itself encourages this: finality is always subjective since it neither determines the object nor contributes to its being known; it is the object which manifests this finality and awakens in us the feeling of this pleasure. In this sense, finality is objective, although it does not found objectivity. And aesthetic experience attests that it has more than an epistemological meaning: an objective value, which is not measured by its utility, or which in any case justifies this utility.

Thus we might term the principle of finality the supreme principle of knowledge, if this title were not already reserved for the constitutive activity of the "I think." Are we concerned here with a principle or with a fact? Finality as understood by the *Critique of Aesthetic Judgment* [18] implies that there is a given anterior to and independent of the constructed: a thing in itself. For the thing in itself is the transcendental limit which reduces the presumptuousness of determinant judgment and confronts reflection with the particular; it indicates the given character of the given (and this must not be confused with the transcendental object $= x$, which designates the form of the object in general). Finality is the double affirmation of the reality and the accommodativeness of the in-itself. Dualism is thereby affirmed, and consequently the reality of the subject as both transcendental and concrete. It is noteworthy that the Dialectic of Teleological Judgment makes the idea of a human understanding intervene in order to clarify the resolution of the antinomy; paragraph 77 of the *Critique of Judgment* is entitled "The peculiarity of human understanding that makes the conception of a physical end pos-

17. *Ibid.*, pp. 23–24. I have changed "want" to "need" here.—Trans.
18. Kant's *Critique of Judgment* is subdivided into the *Critique of Aesthetic Judgment* and the *Critique of Teleological Judgment.*—Trans.

sible for us." [19] This title is undoubtedly intended to oppose the human understanding, as it appears in the Transcendental Aesthetic, to an intuitive understanding; the former is characterized by its solidarity with a faculty of receptive intuition which obliges it to proceed from the particular to the general, from the given to the constructed; moreover, this same paragraph returns to the idea of the thing in itself and suggests that it can be treated in terms of finality; we evoke the thing in itself, and we act as if we had an intuitive understanding every time we appeal to a final cause.

This is why Kant's very reluctance finally favors our interpretation; we should be thankful to him for having assigned finality to reflective judgment and not to determinant judgment, for had he done the latter the domain of constitutive activity would have been extended and dualism conjured away. This is also why the *Critique of Aesthetic Judgment* seems to us more enlightening than the *Critique of Teleological Judgment*. Kant's merit is to have examined purposeless purpose [*la finalité sans fin*] before ends [*fins*] as such, the adaptability of nature to our faculty of knowledge before the technique of nature in the production of organized objects which are ends. Thus it appears that the search for natural ends is justified by the idea of a finality of nature and, as Kant says, by the idea of a harmony of natural things with judgment. Teleology can baffle the understanding to the point of eliciting an antinomy; yet it completes the understanding, and is itself conceivable only if the understanding, assured of the complicity of nature, can conceive stable objects and organized beings. [20]

In contrast, Jules Lachelier runs the risk of losing the fundamental meaning of finality by starting from the teleological and situating himself immediately in the perspective of dialectic, yet without introducing the idea of the thing in itself. More Kantian than Kant, he refuses to grant any independence to the object. "The conditions of the existence of phenomena are the very conditions of the possibility of thought." [21] Doubtless he resorts to an argument very similar to Kant's concerning cinnabar when he evokes the inconsistency of a world governed only by universal

19. See *Critique of Judgment*, Part II, pp. 60 ff.—Trans.
20. We should add that for Kant, finality is equally postulated by practical reason, and in a double form: in the explicit form of the postulate concerning the harmony of virtue and happiness, and in the form of a philosophy of history according to which this world is a world that is as morally habitable as it is intellectually conceivable, and according to which history may at least promote the idea of an advent of the realm of ends.
21. *Du fondement de l'induction* (Paris, Alcan, 1924), p. 41.

mechanism: "To imagine the world before Epicurean atoms unite offers us only a weak idea of the degree of dissolution to which the universe could be reduced in no time through its mechanical power." [22] But the argument occurs within an objective idealism for which "objective existence cannot be given and somehow springs from our own existence," [23] and it serves to support the idea "of a certain harmony between the elements of the universe" [24]—that is, the existence of systems in which the whole controls the part—but not the idea of a harmony between the world and the subject:

> To say that there exists a sort of pre-established harmony between the laws of thought and those of reality is to answer the question with the question itself: how in fact could we know that our knowledge attunes itself naturally with its objects, if we did not already know the nature of these objects at the same time as the nature of our mind? [25]

Thus conceived as a teleological structure, finality appears in phenomena only because it is a condition of the possibility of thought. The finality that is conceived as the accord of subject and object also appears in the last analysis, but it is somehow absolutized, being expressed by the identity of nature and thought: "How may we represent necessity, except as a sort of blind thought poured out into things?" [26] Similarly, "movement concentrated in force is precisely perception as it is defined by Leibniz." [27] In short, "the mind exists in germinal form in nature." [28] Therefore, spiritualism opens onto a philosophy of nature; objective idealism is transformed into a monism in which nature is reabsorbed in thought; but this is the case because "what was for us at first only our thought has now appeared to us as truth in itself, as the ideal *esse* containing or positing *a priori* the conditions of all existence," [29] so that the self is only "the phenomenon of the absolute act by which the idea of being affirms its own truth." [30] It seems that, beyond Kant, Lachelier here joins forces with Schelling or Spinoza: he denies a pre-established harmony between thought and nature only to assert their speculative identity.

22. *Ibid.*, p. 71.
23. *Ibid.*, p. 53. The idea of intentionality, prefigured in Kant, disappears with Lachelier.
24. *Ibid.*, p. 72.
25. *Ibid.*, p. 40.
26. *Ibid.*, p. 53.
27. *Ibid.*, p. 94.
28. Jules Lachelier, *Psychologie et métaphysique* (Paris, Presses Universitaires de France, 1949), p. 167.
29. *Ibid.*, p. 172.
30. *Ibid.*, p. 170.

But we do not demand so much. Moreover, we find ourselves asking whether we can even conceive this identity. For Simone Weil, the most Spinozist of contemporary philosophers, such an identity appears only in an attenuated form: mechanical necessity is a symbol of spiritual necessity. Now, if the world and the person symbolize each other, there must be a link between them which in no way attenuates their difference. As Kant saw, this link is what makes knowledge, as well as moral action, possible. But is the possibility that it establishes ontic or transcendental? For Kant, the principle of finality is still a synthetic *a priori* judgment; the concept is indeed a "transcendental concept," but the *a priori* principle of the possibility of nature belongs to reflective judgment, and this is why it involves an "as if." Judgment proceeds from the particular to the general: thus the given must be already given, or at least we must presuppose a characteristic of the given which is independent of the determinations brought by determinant judgment. Yet for Kant the identification of the ontic with the transcendental is forbidden; in his eyes, this would imply a transcendent employment of the transcendental, because the notion of the transcendental is linked with the idea of a constitutive activity, although reflective judgment cannot, without losing its meaning, be as constitutive as determinant judgment. But if the transcendental and the constitutive are dissociated, we can say that the principle of finality is *both* transcendental and ontic: it makes knowledge possible, though only by virtue of the being of the known. In other words, it proposes itself here as a fact: the fact of a harmony between knowing and known, a fact not presumed, but already ascertained and experienced in perception.

If finality thus manifests the identity of the transcendental and the ontic, this identity characterizes every *a priori*. It resides in the double aspect we have recognized in the *a priori*: it is transcendental so far as it is a virtual knowledge of the object, previous to and orienting experience, and ontic so far as it is a structure of the object. In this way the mind is at home [*se retrouve*] in the world without constituting it, and conversely the world is equally at home in the mind, without producing it: idealism and naturalism are equally excluded since they both tend to abolish the duality of mind and world, while the *a priori* respects this duality. The fact that it is common to both subject and object does not erase their difference, for it is not the same in these two locales: it is knowledge in the subject, structure in the object. The *a priori* is a solution to the problem of truth only because in it the problem of adequation retains its secret.

But may we not continue further and conceive a unity of the *a priori* existing prior to its differentiation into the duality of subject and object? Or must we admit that the *a priori* is the expression and instrument of an accord which cannot be accounted for and which we can merely observe, and must we thus deny that we can rise from the affinity between man and the world to its possibility? We must approach this last problem by a detour.

If the harmony between subject and object is real and yet if neither one initiates it, must we not call it pre-established? Are we not obliged to regress from Kant to Leibniz? Kant himself leads us in this direction: as Guéroult notes, he borrowed the idea of a prerequisite for knowledge from Leibniz (metaphysics founding the possibility of science), and more specifically the heuristic use of finality which is achieved by "the maxims of metaphysical wisdom." Moreover, one could say that for Leibniz everything is *a priori*, since substance can only display its own internal series without communicating anything exterior; and the *a priori* leads us to the affirmation of a pre-established harmony whose pre-establishment is necessary for all substances to form a system in which each substance expresses all the others. But neither the *a priori* nor this harmony yet have the transcendental meaning that they acquire in Kant and that we desire to retain for them.

In fact, by becoming pre-established—that is, by receiving the guarantee of a theology that places metaphysical wisdom in God —harmony assumes a metaphysical meaning, instead of the noetic meaning according to which it must be treated as an "as if." In relation to harmony, universal interaction is only a symbol having its meaning in what it symbolizes. This is why, as Guéroult observes,[31] Leibniz' dynamic physics presupposes metaphysics: at the root of the phenomenon of change stands the intelligible law of finality which assures its total preformation according to the law of the whole series. But if the condition of the possibility of knowledge thus exists in the metaphysical law promulgated by divine wisdom, for Leibniz it possesses nothing transcendental; it makes no allusion to a structure of the knowing subject or to the relation of the act of knowing with the known: pre-established harmony primarily signifies the concomitance of substances. In fact, although Leibniz sometimes presents pre-established harmony as the most plausible hypothesis from the standpoint of science (as well as morality), usually, for example in the *Dis-*

31. *Dynamique et métaphysique leibnizienne* (Paris, Les Belles Lettres, 1934), p. 179.

course on Metaphysics and in the letters to Arnauld, he presents it deductively as a necessary consequence of his logical conception of individual notions. Then harmony is founded on the being of substance, and it expresses the total predestination that Leibniz identifies with spontaneity: if all the moments of each movement (in terms of both force and direction) and all the movements of the universe are rigorously autodetermined, substances must be in mutual correspondence, and "each substance expresses all the rest of the universe according to the viewpoint or relation proper to it, so that all substances are in perfect accord." [32] Concomitance is conceivable only when we exclude the transitive and even the occasional cause which, breaking the continuity of development, calls for a perpetual miracle; "there is coercion in substances only outside of and in appearances," since substance is autodetermined and, in Kantian language, autonomous. Even universal interaction can be, as Guéroult says,[33] only a mixed concept, partially imaginary because abstract; it is through imagination that dynamic physics retains a Cartesian aspect and has to associate two contrasting concepts: spontaneity and interaction; for this physics is concerned not with substances, but with bodies, aggregates, and closely linked phenomena, in which every new change is produced by convergent shocks. But metaphysics both justifies physics and frees it from the ambiguity of imagination by substituting interdependence—according to which, in substances, it is only the "distinct expression" that varies and that, "when one says that one substance acts on another . . . diminishes in the substance acted upon and increases in the acting substance" [34]—for interaction, according to which, in movements, action by contact and external impulsion are necessary to account for change in direction. Interaction that is still imaginary finds its truth in pre-established harmony.

Thus the consideration of physics certainly implies a reference to the subject. But the subject is not introduced as possessing a pure knowledge or as promoting norms of objectivity; instead, he is held responsible for a deficiency, a compromise between the imaginary and the real: so far as the whole is perceived [*aperçu*] only through the part, and by virtue of the essential limitation of every creature, "abstractions are indispensable for the scientific explanation of things . . . ; there is as great a difference between substance and mass as there is between things which are complete

32. Leibniz, *Oeuvres choisies*, ed. Prenant (Paris, Garnier, 1948), p. 154.
33. *Dynamique et métaphysique leibnizienne*, p. 205.
34. Leibniz, *Oeuvres choisies*, p. 154.

as they are in themselves and things which are incomplete as received by us through abstraction." [35] Leibniz opposes the for-us to the in-itself, the phenomenon to the noumenon, but only by passing from the monad to the monadology, by placing himself at the vantage point of the in-itself, and consequently by explaining, as well as discrediting, the for-us; whereas for Kant the transcendental does not permit, except on the practical plane of moral judgment and perhaps on the level of reflective judgment, a leap onto the metaphysical level, and it is not subordinated to metaphysics. Is this leap that Kant refrains from taking a *saltus mortalis*? However this is, we must gain a clear grasp of the Leibnizian for-us; it designates not a transcendental or positive condition, but a negative condition or the condition of the negative: of that which is imaginary and confused in knowledge. In the eyes of Leibniz, the genuine transcendental is precisely the in-itself, the metaphysical that founds the physical, the truth that founds and rectifies certitude. In other words, even if we can speak of prerequisites for the subject, they are not constitutive, but constituted. Moreover, the notion of prerequisite concerns being for the most part and signifies a principle or element: "The part is nothing more than an immediate prerequisite of the whole and is in a certain fashion homogeneous with it." [36] In this sense, rather than having prerequisites, the subject *is* a prerequisite. The whole [*le tout*]—the concomitance of substances—is the condition for the possibility of knowledge because it is the truth of knowledge: a metaphysical truth which reconciles spontaneity and interaction in the affirmation of the system's solidarity. And, precisely because it is metaphysical, this affirmation surpasses, as does Lachelier's similar claim, our demands: it converts the accord of subject and object into a universal interdependence. And at the same time it is closely connected with two unverifiable assertions, both of which also appear, though in sketchy form, in Lachelier.

The first assertion concerns the mentalization [*spiritualisation*] of the universe. As Guéroult says, "The universe of bodies is no longer opposed to that of minds. . . . In reality, there is only a single universe of substances, all of which, including corporeal substances, possess memory and life." [37] Being spontaneous and capable of expression, every substance—as distinguished from aggregates, which have no objective reality—is a subject in a

35. Leibniz, *Die Philosophischen Schriften*, ed. C. J. Gerhardt (Berlin, Akademie Verlag, 1923), II, 253.
36. *Oeuvres choisies*, p. 223.
37. *Dynamique et métaphysique leibnizienne*, p. 209.

certain sense. Everything within the harmonious universe is promoted to the status of a subject. The identity of entelechy with substance (affirmed in paragraph 18 of the *Monadology*), and of entelechy with soul, would allow Leibniz to adopt Spinoza's dictum: *omnia animata sunt.* But does not this elevation of the object to the dignity of a subject imply a certain degradation for the real subject, for the person? Doubtless a separate place is reserved for minds having a reasonable soul, but they can claim only a difference of degree, not of kind, from other substances. Ignoring the possibility of a Copernican revolution, Leibniz puts the priority of the *cogito* into question: is this devaluation not a consequence of the substitution of the metaphysical for the transcendental? The physical system of harmony assimilates the subject and finally alienates him. Of course, the *omne predicatum inest subjecto* ensures the spontaneity of substance, of every substance, but this spontaneity is without freedom, and Arnauld is right in opposing Leibniz here. Leibniz was not able to shatter the *fatum spinozanum,* and perhaps the monadology of the *Theodicy* imposes on the monad a servitude from which Spinoza's *Ethics* had freed it. Predetermination has at least the form of predestination.

For harmony is pre-established. By whom?—by none other than God. Thus "the mutual correspondence of substances . . . is one of the strongest proofs of God's existence." [38] If metaphysical wisdom is not located in the subject who postulates finality in the form of an "as if," it must be found in God, who pre-establishes harmony. Moreover, by effecting the transition from essence to existence, and even from the possible to the compossible, God not only institutes, according to His free decrees, the harmony of substances which is nothing more than their compossibility; He also makes substance as such appear. For the essence of that which exists or must exist is not identical with the essence which is a pure possibility considered independently of all existence, so that "God finds [this latter essence] in the domain of possibilities, that is, in His understanding": it is the *notio primitiva simplex,* concerning which Guéroult has shown that, even if it constitutes the nucleus of substance, the ground of its *vinculum,* it is, strictly speaking, different from it.[39] Essence in itself is an absolute position without physical or even logical relation with anything; concrete substance appears only in relation to the proj-

38. *Oeuvres choisies,* p. 129.
39. "La Constitution de la substance chez Leibniz," *Revue de métaphysique et de morale* (January 1947), p. 61.

ect of a harmonious creation, which puts God's will to work and introduces the consideration of compossibilities. This indivisible point becomes a viewpoint to which the whole system of compossibilities is related; the position without predicates becomes the posited unity of an infinite series of predicates which express this system: according to its nominal definition, substance is the being that accounts for the infinity of its predicates. Through this recourse to the idea of creation, and of a possible nothingness [*néant*], this definition of substance in terms of inherence differs from that of Aristotle. And since these predicates express the universe, substance is closely linked with concomitance; thus it is already mental, for it attains consciousness simultaneously with compossibility: when pure possibilities, confronted with other possibilities and undergoing a limitation as a result of the relations instituted between them and the determinations entailed by these relations, become compossibilities, they cease to exist in themselves [*en soi*], and it is consciousness (which is at least possible) that comes to contain the infinity of predicates which differentiate these possibilities and which are in the process of constituting actual substances: the principle of consciousness is the reflection of the in-itself [*en-soi*] on its difference, on the predicates assigned to it from now on. The mentalization of the universe is correlative with divine creation.

Hence the system reposes on God. Pre-established harmony implies that each substance, being a consciousness in which the entire universe resounds, expresses the whole universe, and consciousness implies the difference elicited by a creative intention. Doubtless Leibniz minimizes God's intervention in order to safeguard man's freedom: witness his refusal of occasionalism. Nevertheless, he imputes to God a more general choice which bears on the entire universe and which thus acknowledges pre-established harmony:

To proceed accurately we must consider God as possessing a more general, more comprehensive will which He employs with respect to the whole universe, since the universe is like a whole that God penetrates with a single glance; this will potentially includes other wills concerning what enters into the universe, and especially the will to create an Adam, who is related to the rest of his posterity, such as God has also chosen it.[40]

But it is not certain that Adam's freedom is saved here—or even his consciousness. For this consciousness, common to every substance, and necessarily confused since it reflects the entire uni-

40. *Oeuvres choisies*, p. 135.

verse, is not a true for-itself: it is not a consciousness *of* [some-thing], for if it expresses the universe, it does so in spite of itself; it has no intentionality since the monad is windowless; it can only re-flect its own difference. Yet it is no longer self-consciousness: it is not self-presence because it can only affirm its difference and can-not deny it: the negation which both separates and unites, and in this sense transforms the in-itself into a for-itself, belongs only to God: consciousness is here a for-itself only by proxy. Absolute reflection is not really reflection. Unquestionably, Leibniz takes notice of certain minds or "souls capable of reflection" which express God rather than the world; but these minds are inserted into a hierarchy of substances. A philosophy of subjectivity must not be sought in a philosophy of substance.

If subjectivity has no role, that is, if harmony is pre-estab-lished, this is because everything is dependent on the divine act. Is not God here a *Deus ex machina*? Moreover, like every monad, the supreme Monad, caught in the system, is perhaps not free. There seems to be an opposition between essence and existence, between understanding and God's will, between the logical laws that define substance and that preside at the calculation *de maximis* and the choice of the best; for God's will can do nothing about logical laws, and his freedom is only the acknowledgement of necessity. God is both logical and moral necessity, understanding and will. But this duality does not lead to a dialectic which would put him into question. It merely assures a double patronage for pre-established harmony in attempting to confirm its reality.

Therefore, we do not want to regress all the way from Kant to Leibniz and thus lose the double benefit of the Copernican revolu-tion: the affirmation of the subject and the denial of a dogmatic metaphysics. We must situate ourselves midway between the con-ditional affirmation of finality as a postulate of reflective judg-ment and the unconditional affirmation of harmony as a meta-physical fact. By subordinating the physical to the metaphysical, Leibniz invites us to understand that knowledge cannot found itself: it cannot be entirely deduced (in the Kantian sense of deduction) from the activity of a transcendental subject. But then he invites us to enter into God's wisdom, to place ourselves at the vantage point of the monadology, and, in brief, to assert pre-established harmony. Leibniz affirms a great deal here: pre-estab-lished harmony is the universalization of the accord between subject and object. Less ambitiously, instead of affirming the meta-physical fact of harmony, we can ascertain the ontic fact of the accord between person and world. Yet does not the mention of "ontic" deny the transcendental nature of the subject? For we cannot disregard this nature; we can even seek a confirmation of it in Leibniz: since the monad receives nothing from outside itself, and since perception is confused intellection, the *a priori* is coextensive with knowledge. But here again the best is the enemy of the good: if everything is *a priori*, nothing really is; the *a priori* is not the prerogative of a subject, but the expression of a law which integrates the subject into the system of the intelligible world; it manifests the hypertrophy of pre-established harmony, in which the subject loses his autonomy, and the person his personality, for even if predestination is total, it is still not autodetermination; when essence, the absolute position of the in-itself, attains existence, it is in turn posited by the system of existences.

But then the question recurs: if pre-established harmony is reduced to an accord between subject and object, and if this accord is conceived as an in-itself, is the subject still transcendental? He is, in that this accord, itself limited, limits and specifies him as a subject. For the world is not a system, but an inexhaustible reality. It can be conceived as a system only if one subordinates the real to the possible, conceived as logical possibility rather than as power or virtuality, and if one confers on God both the knowledge of essences and the power of elevating them to existence. When, by contrast, the world is conceived as reality, as unspecifiable totality, the subject is not in total accord with it, but merely reveals some of its aspects. We say "reveals" instead of "expresses" purposely. For the Leibnizian relationship must be reversed: it is the world which expresses, proposing itself as meaningful through the *a priori* immanent in it; it expresses itself by expressing the meaning that it bears. Of course, the subject can also be expressive so far as he is part of the world, but he expresses himself, not the world; he manifests the meaning which he carries in himself and which is precisely the aptitude to grasp meaning. But he is also the correlate of the world; he is not only an element of the system, one compossibility among others; we have put sufficient stress on the reciprocity of person and world, a reciprocity that requires us to grant the subject a being-for-himself; even though the subject possesses a certain *a priori* knowledge of the world which manifests his real nature, he is not determined from without in reference to a total knowledge of the world. In becoming aware of the world, he discloses it and bears witness to it. Still, he cannot comprehend totality; he can speak of it, but only as a limit or an ideal, and he must declare himself unequal to it. It is because totality is lost to his view that forms take shape—forms that the subject perceives against the background [*fond*] formed by the world, that is, the background of nothingness [*néant*]: from the bottom [*fond*] of his own nothingness (if by "nothingness" we mean what Leibniz sometimes called the essential limitation of the creature). The subject is transcendental through his finitude, since he is present to the world and caught up in a history. It is clear then that the dignity of the transcendental may be retained for him even when his accord with the world is reduced to an ontic fact. The subject exists as transcendental, as reciprocal with the world and as capable of bringing it to consciousness, because at the same time he is in the world: his being-there [*être-là*] is a fact. Another fact is his accordance with the world, as attested by the duality of the *a priori*. And nothing compels us to account for this fact by a theodicy, since neither the world's unity nor its creation can be fully understood and mastered by philosophical reflection.

But we must also declare that this fact is not homogeneous with other facts; it cannot be explained by them. We have not refused transcendental idealism only to accept naturalism and to demand from empiricism some means of constituting the subject. If the subject is constituted, it is only by virtue of the transcendental: he is not the result of a history, and history can only make the transcendental appear. In other words, it is the transcendental which is a fact, a primary fact on which the history of the relations of man and the world is founded: man is by nature in accord with the world; he knows something about the world, and the world that he reveals discloses itself as that which he knows. Should this primary fact be termed merely "ontic"? Or should it be elevated to the level of the "ontological"? Should we not attempt once more to rise from the fact of the affinity between man and the world to its possibility, that is, to the very possibility of the transcendental?

12 / Philosophy and Poetry

IN ORDER TO MOVE from the affinity between man and the world to its possibility, we should have to relate the duality of the *a priori* which expresses this affinity to a higher entity, even at the risk of encountering the difficulties mentioned in our Introduction—difficulties common to post-Kantian philosophies when they attempt to pass from dualism to monism. This higher entity must be a unity bearing the duality of the *a priori* within itself, not the unity of a totality (such as we find in Leibniz, whose cosmology overlooks the transcendental element). Yet even if the two terms of this duality manifest an affinity for each other, they are still not homogeneous; the *a priori* mediates rather than identifies; it confirms the duality instead of annulling it. Where may we find a common denominator between the objective and the subjective, between a structure of the object and a knowledge [*un savoir*] of this structure in the subject? Should we look for it in a first state of the *a priori* which would be anterior to its differentiation, without referring ourselves to its second state?

But in order to conceive this *a priori* of the *a priori* we cannot appeal to the notion of virtuality. We have already employed it in defining the subjective *a priori;* instead of suggesting a virtual state of the virtual, this notion refers to something actual: the subjective *a priori* belongs to an actual subject by whom it is actualized. Similarly, if the objective *a priori* has appeared to us as a possibility, this possibility belongs to the real world. Therefore, we cannot make a being out of virtuality; it is only a mode of being, or the attribute of a being.

Should we, then, return to the idea of world that we evoked before examining the affinity of man and the world? Would not the world itself be the ultimate entity from which the two aspects of the *a priori* are derived, and consequently, man and the world, which bear these two aspects? But we must now conceive the world in another way: no longer as the particular world whose correlate is the person, and no longer as the universal world whose correlate is, at the limit of history, the whole of thinking humanity; rather, we should conceive it as a world which includes every correlate without being itself included: as a world without correlate. Perhaps this is the world evoked by a philosophy of nature that thinks in terms of *natura naturans*, engendering both subject and object in a radical genesis, and perhaps we were unfair to genetic ontology when we confined it to *natura naturata*, that is, when we reduced it to an explanation of man's advent in terms of a determined state of the world instead of a determining world. But what is this *natura naturans*, this world which is no longer the world of science, and through which becoming comes into being? It is the one or the encompassing. "No matter how seriously the dimension of the subject-object relation is taken, and no matter how subtly it is developed, it will never be the unique region [*espace de jeu*] of Being. The world is more primordial [*originaire*] than any being [*étant*], than any subject or object." [1]

By naming this world, speculative thought achieves the leap to the metaphysical, or more exactly, to the ontological level; for the world is Being: "Being itself is not the vague generality that hovers above all things; it is the space-time of the world that encompasses everything that is." [2] Thus the reciprocal relation which links thought to beings, subject to objects is abolished. The world is no longer the correlate of thought; it is thought itself: "Being itself is that which is thought in all thought, if the saying of Parmenides is true: thought and Being are identical." [3] From this point on, the duality of subject and object is surpassed, and their initial unity is discovered; we might even say that a new Spinozism saves us from returning to Leibniz.

Perhaps so—but at what price? What does the identity of thought and Being mean? And, above all, what is this thought, identical with Being, which is neither the thought of any person nor the prophetic voice of waves and woods? If the world is identical with Being, Being is identical with truth; thought is nothing other than the power to disclose that makes everything

1. Eugen Fink, "L'Analyse intentionelle," in *Problèmes actuels de la phénoménologie* (Paris, Desclée de Brouwer, 1951), p. 83.
2. *Ibid.*, p. 95.
3. *Ibid.*

appear and arise:[4] the light of Being as both revealing and dissimulating. Thought is this pure movement of Being, this transcendence that designates neither a transcendent being nor the act of a being that transcends; for the self which sometimes serves to express this transcendence evokes a presence rather than an ego. Now, this free openness that conditions all appearing is also the world understood as the *Woraufhin* of transcendence, as the total space for all appearing. The identity of thought and Being does not signify the identity of thought and its object—since thought here does not think the object, but the nonobjective condition of all objects, and since it is not a thought about Being, but the thought of Being. Just as extension for Descartes is both substance and predicate, world and geometry, so light for Heidegger is both thought and world. This clearly implies that thought is dehumanized; but how far can this process be carried on? We see such a dehumanization in the notion of *Dasein,* which expresses the ascendency of Being over man, the initiative it takes in man; for the *Da* (the "there") expresses less a spatial dimension than the "openness of the open," the world toward which transcendence is directed, or in turn the very transcendence which makes the world appear. Instead of *Dasein*'s being a reality by itself, "there would be neither man nor reality of any sort without this light of Being, a light which is also the *Da* of *Sein*." [5]

The identity of thought and Being is realized in the world. And the world is no longer in a reciprocal relationship with the subject, even if he were enlarged to the dimensions of history, nor is the subject contained or included in the world. Instead, the world itself is the subject: at once light and its own light, provided that we understand by subject something analogous (except for the dialectical element) to the Hegelian self, the substance that is subject. Because *Dasein* is the *Da* of *Sein,* and because its freedom consists in letting beings be, it is in a certain sense *Sein* itself, that is, the world.

Thus, by thinking the world we are transported into a region of Being—a region which *is* Being, in contrast with Husserlian regions—where original truth dwells, where the light of the "there is" [*il y a*] appears as the nothingness of every being and does not

4. Not the understanding of nature, as for Hegel, but the imagination of *physis:* the imagination, common root of intuitions and concepts, nature and freedom.

5. Birault, "Existence et vérité d'après Heidegger," *Revue de métaphysique et de morale* (January 1951), p. 53.

allow us to discern subject or object yet. Heidegger's "way back to the ground" ends in a universal indistinctness resulting from sheer luminosity.

But are we in fact able to conceive a unity which would precede duality? We are no longer supposed to term it "substance" because we are now less attentive to totality than to unity, and because we do not consider intelligibility as primary. We should thus say that the world is meaning or light. Can we really think so? We are also told that meaning and meaninglessness, light and darkness must be conjoined: Being conceals itself; the dissimulation which provokes errancy, itself the source of error, is an ontological dimension.[6] Yet does this not impute a feature of our own thought to Being? Is not a certain theory of man [*anthropologie*] ontologized here? Heidegger denies it. He definitely refuses to say that, if Being hides, it hides from a finite knowledge, since he does not want to measure man's finitude by a divine infinitude. But we cannot help wondering if it is still not a God—a finite God—that he invokes, and if ontology does not thus become a theology.

Yet let us secularize this God: He is not hidden; self-revealing, He *is* revelation. Being is appearing: the sheer brilliance [*chatoiement*] of the necessary and sufficient image; we prefer to avoid speaking of a system of images, for this would be formalizing the formal: necessity should not be conceived as necessary, but merely as necessity: there are images. Positing a systematic whole of images would confuse a logical demand for coherence with an ontological declaration of totality. But can such a totality be conceived? Is not appearing always appearing *of* and appearing *to*?

And, most importantly, does not the identification of Being and appearing emasculate Being? Is it not then deprived of an essential dimension: reality? Does not conceiving the world as meaning deny its intransigent reality, its opacity, and its inertia— all forms of necessity? For Hegel at least, Idea is dialectically conjoined with Nature. Doubtless one grants today that Being is always the Being of beings;[7] but Being should not be compromised here: instead of a dialectical relationship, Heidegger counsels us to see a struggle between Being and beings, world and

6. For Heidegger's own exposition of these concepts, see his essay "On the Essence of Truth," in *Existence and Being*, ed. Werner Brock, Gateway Ed. (Chicago, Regnery, 1949).—Trans.

7. The French *l'être de l'étant* is a translation of Heidegger's phrase *das Sein des Seiendes*. As distinct from Being, which is treated by ontology, beings are the "ontic" entities encountered in everyday experience and explored by science and metaphysics.—Trans.

earth, day and night. But in what sense are we to understand this? Day succeeds night effortlessly. A being [*un étant*] has no negative phototropism: instead of shunning light, it seeks it; the in-itself does not will itself as opaque. There is only human struggle—a struggle in which the other is also the same, the *alter ego,* as in the struggle between ancient and modern gods, or that between philosophers, or lovers. There must be an assertion for there to be a negation; there must be a new meaning, the meaning assumed by the other, for meaning to be threatened with meaninglessness.

In other words, appearing is also appearing *to.* The image presupposes a subjectivity in which it is reflected and becomes an image; there is nothing before reflection, and we are wholly unjustified in converting this nothing [*rien*] into Being. We mean that there is no meaning here; there is indeed the light ray that is diffused toward the mirror, and there is the world as overwhelming reality, but not as meaning. There are at least beings; and Heidegger would grant that beings offer themselves to finite knowledge as already existing before being discovered, although they are not under the jurisdiction of truth. But he denies them any priority. What is primary is the image, not the object. Nevertheless, Heidegger appears to grant us more: there is meaning only insofar as there is reflection, and Being only insofar as there is subjectivity.[8] Does this represent a return to dualism? It certainly does not mean that man chooses to exist (Heidegger illustrates this by his notion of "being-toward-death," and not "being-through-birth," which would indicate the subject's contingency more eloquently, for we cannot imagine having a good birth in the sense that we may have a good death), or that man chooses or still less produces Being. We do not, however, ask for this much: we have sufficiently stressed the subject's finitude. It is enough for us if the subject, even though overwhelmed by the world, is not wholly foreign to it. Heidegger admits this when he speaks of a pre-ontological comprehension of Being, a secret intimacy with Being which is man's prerogative alone. Yet he leaves the real initiative and priority to Being; *Dasein*'s existence is also its des-

---

8. If *Dasein* is interpreted as subjectivity, Heidegger says this twice, at least in *Sein und Zeit:* "Only as long as Dasein *is* . . . 'is there' Being" (*Being and Time,* trans. Macquarrie and Robinson [New York, Harper and Row, 1962], p. 255); and: "The Being of truth is connected primordially with Dasein . . . Being (not beings) is something which 'there is' only so far as and as long as Dasein is" (*ibid.,* p. 272). (In this connection, the reader should also notice Macquarrie's and Robinson's explanatory footnote on p. 255, *ibid.*—Trans.)

tiny, its response to the call of Being; its freedom is the freedom of Being *in* it. Thus, Heidegger does not really affirm dualism.

When we attempt to understand Heidegger, we cannot help interpreting him in the light of Spinoza, although we recognize the considerable differences between the two philosophers. For both, Being is the central concern: Spinoza interprets Being as power [*puissance*] or *conatus*, and the manifestation of this power is a genesis in which chronology illustrates logic; Heidegger envisions Being as light, and this light is both its own manifestation and the manifestation of everything else. But we cannot refrain from viewing Heidegger here from the standpoint of Spinoza; both tend toward a theology of immanence, whether affirmed or disguised. For we must admit that there is a sort of immanent causality in Being understood as light: even if light can only illuminate, it requires an object to illuminate and a subject reflecting this illumination. The necessity of the Spinozist God is the same thing as the freedom of the Being that overruns *Dasein*. In both instances, the world is the origin or God immanent in the terms between which the secondary *a priori* establish communication: the *esse* which founds *nosse*. Spinoza, however, stresses the known, the object of knowledge, that is, reality understood as necessity or as history; whereas Heidegger emphasizes knowledge understood as truth or disclosedness, not as the act of a subject. Both philosophers strive to consider Being as the background [*fond*] against which subject and object appear afterwards, like forms. After what? There is no clear answer to this question; perhaps a divine deed must be invoked. This background, like the Kantian thing in itself, is unthinkable, and can hardly be named. Perhaps it corresponds to a philosophical experience enjoyed by certain philosophers, just as the idea of a divine person corresponds to a mystical experience; perhaps it takes a profound thought to experience the vertigo of this abyss [*fond*]. But what happens then to philosophy? Does it become the expression of a singular experience?

In any case, the idea of such an abyss is not amenable to human thought: it cannot be conceived as a ground [*fondement*], for we cannot return from it, as a background, to the forms it reveals. In Spinoza, the advent of man is announced in two startling and unexpected words found in the middle of Book II of the *Ethics:* "*Homo cogitat*" is an axiom that is not justified by a meditation on Substance. For Heidegger, the "way back to the ground" does not permit a return to what is grounded; the *a priori* of the *a priori* does not allow a transcendental deduction of the *a priori*.[9] Thought commits suicide; it doubtless dies in beauty, but, as Valéry said, while Pascal yields to anguish, mathematicians continue to calculate.

Must we return then to a philosophy of nature, to a pre-critical ontology for which Being is the world and the world is the real? This ontology may employ a language which does not differ greatly from post-critical ontologies; but it pursues an opposite goal: it is concerned with the way up rather than the way down; and by the same token it invokes positive knowledge [*savoir positif*] instead of challenging it. The opposition culminates in the fact that this ontology treats time seriously—the time proper to genesis—while post-critical ontologies are always in some sense philosophies of *logos* for which chronology is a mere illustration of logic: this is evident in Spinoza, but it can also be seen in Heidegger, as Vuillemin has shown.[10] Yet it seems to us that even though the project of such a pre-critical ontology is perfectly legitimate, it is not wholly viable: as transcendental, the subject cannot be engendered starting from the world; something in time escapes time here; since this something appears in time and has its career there, and since there is a historicity of the various secondary *a priori*, a genetic theory must continue its enterprise, but this theory itself discloses the very obstacle on which it comes to grief.

What can we conclude from this, except that reflection cannot, without losing its way, overshoot the point at which it discovers the duality of man and the world (symbolized by the two aspects of the *a priori*) as well as their affinity? Here is a fact which forms a ground, for it establishes that man can inhabit and know the world; but this ground cannot be further grounded. Hegel, standing before a mountain, said: "Thus it is"; we must say the same thing, but before *man* contemplating the mountain. Yet can philosophy agree to remain at this point? Can it accept the Kantian verdict that, even if the need for metaphysics is irrepressible and even if metaphysical experience is *felt*, metaphysics is impossible? If philosophy wants to advance further, and if it wants to communicate the experience of a background that would also be a radical ground, it must become poetry. But does poetry itself surpass philosophy?

9. *A priori* here is plural and refers to the *a priori* in its full variety; it is all the particular *a priori* that cannot be deduced from a common ground or "the *a priori* of the *a priori*."—Trans.

10. "A new formal ontology appears in which the reduction to time is constantly compensated for by the opposite reduction of time to eternal temporalization." (Jules Vuillemin, *L'Héritage kantien et la révolution copernicienne* [Paris, Presses Universitaires de France, 1954], p. 295.)

In fact, the history of thought attests to a close bond between philosophy and poetry; it is as if philosophy, claiming to think the unthinkable and yet failing to be self-sufficient, sensed the need to be relieved or renewed by a kind of knowledge [*savoir*] that is no longer philosophical, by a sort of discourse that is perhaps situated even beyond knowledge. Before the present era, this role often devolved upon religion. But in relation to philosophy religion *was* poetry: a poetry unaware of itself because it imagined itself to be absolute truth, as well as the truth of the actual poetry that it pressed into its service. Its central assertion represented the attainment of totality, the definitive reconciliation of idea and nature in God as existing and through God as creator: ontology is realized in the ontological proof, which connects existence to essence and suppresses contingency; the very contingency of what is created, its unintelligibility, is justified, foreseeable, and assimilated: every question has its answer, for there is, somewhere, a true idea of everything. Yet the source of this belief perhaps lies in the experience of a concrete reconciliation of man and nature: the ontological proof is perhaps a rationalization of the cosmological proof, and perhaps more precisely a rationalization of a teleology that is at first experienced: "The heavens declare the glory of God, and the firmament proclaims his handiwork." The glory of God signifies the apotheosis of man, who is glorified as a guest, not as a lord [*seigneur*]. The intelligibility of Being consists primarily in the inhabitability of the world. Is this experience mystical or poetical? The predominant feature of mystical experience is perhaps its precariousness; it tends to disavow itself to the extent that the reconciliation of man and nature is deferred, projected onto a dim future: this world is only a valley of tears whose vanity is felt by ascetics; the "I" is an other, and we are not *of* the world; our real homeland is elsewhere. Once again appearance and essence cannot be reconciled, and St. Francis of Assisi is challenged by St. John of the Cross. We feel this in Giotto's frescoes, whose rigorous composition, massive volumes, and static brilliance [*éclat*] of color point to something beyond, as if the very perfection of appearance denounced the vanity of such perfection—as if a being revealed itself as non-being, not for the benefit of movement and becoming, but in order to affirm another being: immediate being is exalted only to be sacrificed in the end. Thus, religion may not be able, at least in the experience which supports it, to attain the unity it asserts: if thought has no point of repose, neither does feeling.

In any case, we see that religious experience and poetic experience are to a certain extent similar; the difference is that poetry is the expression of an experience which refuses to be enclosed in a system and which is its own self-revelation. And we understand that when philosophy denies the idea of a dogmatically assertable truth (though not truth as such) and when it identifies truth with the movement of revelation rather than with its content, it turns toward poetry. In fact, we must first understand poetry on the basis of philosophy, even if poetry is not philosophical and even if the poet does not know that he is animated by an intent which is comparable to that of the philosopher and which extends philosophy itself. For what does the poet do? He seems to transport himself beyond dualism, leaping with all the ingenuousness of innocence: the world ceases to be the other; it is made to his measure and in his image. He invokes it and conjures it up; everything has a name, and the name is the thing itself. Language ceases to be a system of artificial and arbitrary signs; speech [*la parole*] returns to its primordial state, to the state of nature: not the nature which is reduced to objectivity like the dried flowers arranged in a collection, in a system of relations and general ideas, but the living nature whose meaning consists in being present and having an immediately perceptible sense. In this way, things have a soul and resemble us; they speak and the poet listens; his voice is indeed that of the waves and woods. From now on it is impossible to distinguish subjective from objective, feeling from the object arousing it, association from the object it controls; man is not added to nature: it is nature which is human.

Moreover, poetry is not only feeling in the poet, but also an aspect [*visage*] of the world: thus we describe a landscape as "poetic." When do we say this? When the landscape manifests a certain harmony, an accord for which painters search so passionately (though by other means, by the properly abstract means they use: colors and values). In the case of the real landscape, the accord is not only for the eye, but for the entire body as it is appealed to in various ways; real things are in accord here, as for example the palm tree with the blue sky, the sun with the sea, or the tree with the slope. It is the world itself which is poetic; in it, then, Being is opposed to appearance, and *natura naturans* to *natura naturata*. For whatever is poetic—in brief, "the poetic" [11]—attests to the energy of *physis*,[12] a measured energy which is at

11. For a more detailed analysis of "the poetic," see Dufrenne, *Le Poétique* (Paris, Presses Universitaires de France, 1963), pp. 171–94.—Trans.
12. For Heidegger's interpretation of *physis* see his *Introduction to Metaphysics*, trans. Ralph Manheim (New York, Anchor, 1961), *passim.*—Trans.

once power and grace (as distinct from the sublime or the tragic, which evoke only power, or from the pretty, which evokes only grace). This energy constitutes the soul of the world so far as it regulates and harmonizes everything that is. It regulates more than a Gestalt; as the soul directs the body, so this energy rules reality itself. Of course, not every landscape is poetic: when it rains, a Mediterranean cove loses its poetry; by contrast, the Breton coast remains poetic in rainy weather because rain there is in accord with nature; in a Mediterranean environment it represents an eruption that denatures or alters what is organic, as hiccups distort a face. According to the relative opposition of gravity and light (to use Schelling's terms), the soul of the world has its avatars. Above all, it appears only for the person who can apprehend and enter into accord with it: the poetic is another *a priori* which must find something correspondent in the transcendental structure of the subject.

This *a priori* enjoys, however, a certain primacy in that it indicates that other *a priori* bonds are possible—that is, it shows that the world is within our reach and perhaps made in our image. For the world stretching out before us and smiling is the poet here. It is undoubtedly marked by necessity, but geometry and inertia do not seem to be the last word. Its beauty is the visible image of a system, and this system is pregnant with a future: nature is not only what is born, but also that which gives birth. Here pre-critical ontology is correct: the world is in gestation as women are, though not for the sake of producing human offspring. If it is good to be in the world, and if the world is inhabitable and knowable, it is because it resembles us like a brother. Even before we control it, that is, before our industry creates a technological environment, the natural environment is in a certain sense human.[13]

This truth of nature must first be sought in the feeling of nature; perhaps science, which continually puts perception to the test, must finally justify this feeling by discovering energy *in*

13. Because of this fact, a psychoanalysis of nature is a legitimate project— provided that we psychoanalyze nature, not man, or fire, not man contemplating fire. But since this soul of inanimate objects has no individual history, that is, since fire has no childhood, the psychoanalysis of things or elements should be replaced by a phenomenology of nature. (In this note, Dufrenne has in mind Gaston Bachelard, the French philosopher and literary critic [1884–1962] who proposed a "psychoanalysis" of the four "material" elements—fire, water, air, and earth. In the five books he wrote on this subject, Bachelard always included the subjective, human relation to these elements; this remained the case even when he later turned to a more phenomenological perspective.—Trans.)

nature, if not the energy *of* nature. But poetry does not think; it feels. We have attempted to show elsewhere [14] that perception culminates in feeling. Poetry moves within the sphere of feeling. There is poetry when something is communicated to us which is communicable in this way alone: all art is poetic, as soon as it ceases to be merely sensual or didactic and as soon as feeling ceases to have a definable object. For our feelings represent multiple ways of relating ourselves to a determined object, as for example love relates us to a lovable object or hate to something despised; this object detaches and imposes itself completely only when a feeling aroused by some frustration clings to the object as if to a value which is all the more singular and precious when its possession is most compromised: the person we love appears to us as really irreplaceable only at the moment when we lose him or her, when despair changes love into passion; so far as it is happy and innocent, love overflows the other and is a love of the world through the other without betraying him, for he is the necessary go-between, the presence who makes the world present to us and ourselves present to the world. But the feeling exalted by poetry is still more pure and ingenuous: it does not represent, like love or hate, a certain means of relating ourselves to an object, for it has no object except the world, a world which sends back to this feeling its own image. In this sense it accomplishes the phenomenological reduction or the return of beings to Being spontaneously. There are no objects in the world of Van Gogh; his olive trees are not cultivatable or lovable; they do not exist for themselves, but as catalysts of a world. Yet they are necessary, for the feeling involved here is singular, and instead of being singularized by a psychic modality, that is, by a certain attitude toward the object, this feeling is made singular by the world that it evokes, and this world must be apprehended in special objects. Feeling is no longer an affair of the heart; it is an aspect of the world. Poetry purifies feeling because it retains only its noematic component, which makes feeling the principle of a world. Poetry is the grace which saves feeling from being attached to and alienated in particular objects, instead allowing it to manifest itself according to the measure of a world.

A poetic work is an expression of the poetic state, or rather of the poetic life—that is, if the poetic is not a state into which we settle, but an experience we live by virtue of openness [*générosité*],

14. See the author's *Phénoménologie de l'expérience esthétique* (Paris, Presses Universitaires de France, 1953), II, 421–81.—Trans.

when every object is a witness to the world and a pretext for saying [*dire*] this world. For poetry says nothing else through the objects that it describes, the adventures of the mind or heart that it relates. And in saying the world, it expresses the accord between man and the world: it celebrates an immanent God. But it does not name Him; instead of explicating anything, it makes us feel. Although true itself, it does not state truths. Truth no doubt implies authenticity, but authenticity in turn is defined by its relation to truth: to give feeling is to give sight. Poetry is wholly contained in this unself-conscious gift; when the pitiable vagabond Lélian confides his ill-starred love affairs—"You believe in tea-leaves . . ." [15]—everything is true about this false world in which wine is a love potion and girls are nymphs: there is a truth in errancy [16] itself as soon as it is revealed to us in the light of poetry. Truth signifies the necessity with which something gives itself to us: not the factual necessity sedimented in historical truth—e.g., it is true that there are vagabonds—but the necessity of meaning, according to which fictitious vagabonds are true by the very fact that they are witnesses of an errant world. Truth is experienced in the truth of the poem, and the truth of the poem is found in the light that it proffers, like a world whose objects exist only to reveal meaning.

When poetry says this world, it expresses the accord between man and the world. Or rather, it lives it and makes it live. For the world is nothing more than the manifestation of feeling, and feeling is the soul of the world. The world speaks the language of man, and man joins himself to the world. This would be a mere game if the world of poetry were only subjective, an arbitrary invention or the mere projection of a state of mind [*un état d'âme*]. But we have said often enough that particular worlds represent the possibilities of the real world; poetry does not lie. Yet it does not speak of the total world—the world as a totality—and thus it does not resolve the problems raised by philosophy. It aims at [*vise*] the world through [*à travers*] the world of the poet, and there is no poetry without a poet. There is no poetry of poetry either: poetry cannot lose its spontaneity; it always conjures up a world, making it seen by making it felt. This is why it cannot by

15. This is a free translation of the first line from the twentieth poem in Verlaine's cycle of poems entitled "Chansons pour elle": "Tu crois au marc de café" (*Oeuvres poétiques complètes*, Edition de la Pléiade [Paris, Gallimard, 1948], p. 540).—Trans.

16. Like Heidegger, Dufrenne plays here upon a double meaning of errancy: wandering, and a state of error or untruth.—Trans.

itself make us think a totality or unconditionally necessary entity which would be the unity of reality and appearance. And it does not allow us to surpass dualism: the accord between man and the world, poet and poetry—an accord consummated in poetry itself —is not reduced to a monism; even if the poet labors in the service of poetry, the poem is the work of the poet, and poetry is realized only through the poem.

It is understandable, however, that poetry may tempt the philosopher and appear to him as a kind of conclusion [*achèvement*] to his own work. First, because the accord that poetry reveals between man and the world is so complete that it may look like a unity. Secondly, because poetry seems in any case to be already on the way back to the ground, so far as the poet abolishes himself in inspiration and so far as the empirical content—the being that conceals Being, the object that conceals the world—is obliterated in feeling. Finally, because philosophical experience can possess the same characteristics of lived immediacy, urgency, and completeness [*achèvement*] that poetic experience involves. Yet it seems that the only relation philosophy can maintain with poetry is one that respects the specificity of the philosophical enterprise. Philosophy is reflection: it can reflect on poetry and find in it a project related to its own, even though the means employed for this project remain quite different. But philosophy should not endeavor to imitate poetry. Its proper tool is analysis, and its peculiar virtue rigor. Even when it aims at an absolute, it cannot attain it by incantation, but by making it appear, within a chain of reasons, as that which can be conceived, if not understood. Philosophy cannot imitate poetry because it cannot find its conclusion in poetry or in an experience beyond language whose description would strain language to the breaking point. For the philosopher, not being a poet, would then lapse into silence: he would no longer express himself except to denounce what is not philosophy in his eyes; his dogmatism would show itself only by pronouncing exclusions. Philosophical experience may animate philosophy, but it cannot supplant it by substituting itself for rational discourse; on the contrary, it must be put to the test in this discourse. For philosophy, philosophical experience is a lived experience that must be continually conceptualized, not relived. The philosopher must prove himself by doing philosophy: repeating or recreating in his own way the philosophical discourse in which reflection is expressed.

Bibliography

BOOKS BY MIKEL DUFRENNE

Karl Jaspers et la philosophie de l'existence. Paris, Editions du Seuil, 1947. Written in collaboration with Paul Ricoeur.
Phénoménologie de l'expérience esthétique. Paris, Presses Universitaires de France, 1953. Volume I. "L'Objet esthétique." Volume II. "La Perception esthétique."
La Personnalité de base—un concept sociologique. Paris, Presses Universitaires de France, 1953.
La Notion d'a priori. Paris, Presses Universitaires de France, 1959.
Language and Philosophy. Bloomington, University of Indiana Press, 1963.
Le Poétique. Paris, Presses Universitaires de France, 1963.
Jalons. The Hague, Nijhoff, 1966.

ARTICLES BY DUFRENNE IN ENGLISH

"The Role of Man in the Social Sciences." *Philosophy Today,* 1960, pp. 36–44.
"The Aesthetic Object and the Technical Object." *Journal of Aesthetics and Art Criticism,* Fall 1964, pp. 113–22.
"Existentialism and Existentialisms." *Philosophy and Phenomenological Research,* September 1965, pp. 51–62.
"A New Approach to Novelty." *Pacific Philosophy Forum,* February 1966, pp. 78–81.

SELECTED ARTICLES BY DUFRENNE IN FRENCH

Aesthetics

"Intentionalité et esthétique." *Revue philosophique*, 1954, pp. 75–84.

"Philosophie et littérature." *Revue d'esthétique*, July 1948, pp. 289–305.

"L'Expérience esthétique de la nature." *Revue internationale de philosophie*, 1955, pp. 98–115.

"Valeurs et valeurs esthétiques." *Actes du IIIe Congrès International d'Esthétique*, 1956.

"La Sensibilité généralisatrice." *Revue d'esthétique*, April 1960, pp. 216–26.

"L'Expressivité de l'abstrait." *Revue d'esthétique*, April 1961, pp. 210–15.

"Critique littéraire et phénoménologie." *Revue internationale de philosophie*, Nos. 68–69 (1964), pp. 193–208.

"Mal du siècle? Mort de l'art?" *Revue d'esthétique*, August–September 1964, pp. 190–214.

"L'Art—est-il un langage?" *Revue d'esthétique*, March 1966.

On the A Priori

"Signification des *a priori*." *Bulletin de la Société française de Philosophie*, June–September 1955, pp. 97–132.

"Les *A Priori* de l'imagination." *Archivio de filosofia*, 1965, pp. 53–63.

"L'*A Priori* comme monde." *Annales de l'Université de Paris*, 1966, pp. 1–15.

General Philosophy

"Brève note sur l'ontologie." *Revue de métaphysique et morale*, 1954, pp. 398–412.

"Un Livre récent sur la Connaissance de la Vie." *Revue de métaphysique et de morale*, 1953, pp. 170–87.

"La Philosophie de Jaspers." *Etudes germaniques*, March 1948, pp. 64–79.

"Maurice Merleau-Ponty." *Les Etudes philosophiques*, January–March 1962, pp. 81–92.

"Gaston Bachelard et la poésie de l'imagination." *Les Etudes philosophiques,* October–December 1963, pp. 395–407. Reprinted in *Jalons.*

"La Critique de la Raison Dialectique." *Esprit,* April 1961, pp. 675–92. Reprinted in *Jalons.*

"Wittgenstein et la philosophie." *Les Etudes philosophiques,* July–September 1965, pp. 281–306.

Sociology

"Sociologie et phénoménologie." *Echanges sociologiques,* 1947.

"Existentialisme et sociologie." *Cahiers internationaux de sociologie,* Vol. I.

"Note sur l'anthropologie culturelle américaine." *Cahiers internationaux de sociologie,* Vol. X.

STUDIES ON DUFRENNE

Barilli, R. *Per Un' Estetica Mondana.* Bologna, Mulino, 1964, pp. 271–98, 323–28.

Beardsley, Monroe C. *Aesthetics from classical Greece to the Present* (New York, Macmillan, 1966), pp. 371–72, 395–96.

Gilson, E., Langan, T., Maurer, A. *Recent Philosophy: Hegel to the Present* (New York, Random House, 1966), pp. 396–401.

Kaelin, Eugene F. *An Existentialist Aesthetic.* Madison, University of Wisconsin Press, 1962, pp. 359–85.

Levinas, Emmanuel. *"A Priori* et subjectivité." *Revue de métaphysique et de morale,* No. 4 (1962), pp. 490–97.

Morpurgo-Tagliabne, Guido. *L'Esthétique contemporaine.* Milan, Marzorati, 1960, pp. 460–68.

Ricoeur, Paul. "Philosophie, sentiment et poésie." *Esprit,* March 1961, pp. 504–12.

Ricoeur, Paul. "Le Poétique." *Esprit,* January 1966, pp. 107–116.

Spiegelberg, Herbert. *The Phenomenological Movement: A Historical Introduction.* The Hague, Nijhoff, 1960, II, 579–85.

Acknowledgments

FIRST OF ALL, I wish to express my profound gratitude to Mikel Dufrenne. He not only read the entire English manuscript, uncovering errors, ambiguities, and omissions that might have gone unnoticed, but also rendered the equally valuable service of suggesting what the proper corrections should be. To both M. and Mme Dufrenne, I owe the pleasure of many hours of their extraordinary hospitality; in addition, Mme Dufrenne retyped a nearly illegible first version of the Introduction.

I am also indebted to Paul Ricoeur for allowing me to translate and reprint his brief, but valuable, essay on *The Notion of the A Priori.* Under the title "Philosophie, sentiment et poésie," this study first appeared in the March, 1961, issue of *Esprit.*

To Messrs. Edie, Browning, Veatch, and Earle of Northwestern University I offer my thanks for their insight, understanding, and support. Dean Robert Baker of Northwestern made possible a grant which came at a crucial time.

Jack Putnam and Janice Feldstein of the Northwestern University Press were most accommodating and helpful in their difficult position as editors.

For advice and aid of various sorts, I want to thank Jean Chatillon, Hubert Dreyfus, Roy Elveton, George Downing, Alphonso Lingus, Loy Littlefield, Charles McCracken, Charles Parsons, Donald Morano, Joseph Bien, Marc Law, Simone Johnson, and especially Richard Vernon.

I owe much to the encouragement of my parents, Marlin S. Casey and the late Catherine J. Casey.

Without the perspicacious and persevering efforts of my wife, Brenda Casey, the translation would not have reached its present degree of clarity. Her suggestions, gleaned from a close scrutiny of the whole manuscript, have been invaluable, especially with respect to style.

[245]

A Priori (continued)
xiii, xv, xvi, xx, 48, 53, 55, 115,
121–22, 125–26, 136, 154, 155,
161, 166, 170, 174, 180, 187,
202, 210, 227; as virtual, 154–56,
164; as virtually known, xiii, 94,
121, 124–25, 132, 154, 187, 190,
202, 218, 227. *See also* Meaning,
a priori as
—dual aspect of, xx, 187, 202, 210,
218, 226, 227, 233
—genetic character of, x, xii,
52–55, 70
—in primary state, 80, 94, 109,
227; in secondary state, 156,
203, 227, 232, 233
—of the *a priori*, xv, xxi, xxv,
xxvii, 127, 202, 207, 227,
232, 233n
Aristotle, 138, 223
Art, 237

Bad faith, 170, 208
Bachelard, Gaston, xxiv, 236n
Beauty, 236
Beginning, 208
Being, xi, xv, xxi, xxvii, 27–30, 38,
58n, 116, 127, 157, 203, 204,
207, 208, 217, 221, 227, 228–29,
230–31, 232–35 *passim*, 239
Being in the world, 22–23, 28, 187,
193, 201, 203, 206
Benedict, Ruth, 179
Bergson, Henri, 94, 96, 128–29,
131, 135, 140, 157, 163,
181, 207
Bernanos, Georges, 181
Birth, 54, 123, 125, 126, 143, 148,
160, 162, 164, 205, 231, 236
Body, xii, xviii, 22, 52, 122, 136,
137–44 *passim*, 147–53 *passim*,
154–55, 157–58, 162, 163, 168–
69, 174–78 *passim*, 181, 182,
187, 188, 204, 209, 210; as constitutive, 144–45; as lived, 144,
159, 161; as object, 140, 151–52,
154, 159, 163, 174, 175; as subject, 149–50, 157, 162; perceiving, 160; thinking, 160, 161

Carnap, Rudolf, 50
Category, 114; aesthetic, xxv; af-

fective, xix, 113; intersubjective,
171, 172–73; Kantian, 9, 16, 156,
191; objective, 171, 190
Causality, 63–64, 86–87, 108, 113,
124, 132, 143, 156, 160, 210, 232
Cogito, 11, 21, 137–38, 144, 147,
148, 150, 153, 168, 171, 207,
211, 222; pre-reflective, 145;
transcendental, 203, 207
Cohen, Hermann, 19, 30, 36n, 70
Communication, 111, 165, 167,
189, 232, 237
Community, 164
Compossibility, 222, 223, 225
Comte, August, 177
Concept, 93, 151, 157, 158, 214,
218; *a priori*, 87; empirical, 76;
pure, 76, 156, 191. *See also* Intuition, sensible
Conceptualization, 239
Concrete, the, 76
Consciousness, 19, 21, 52, 54–55,
95, 96–97, 100, 127, 128, 132,
134, 137, 139, 140, 144–54 *passim*, 157, 158, 162, 163, 165,
169, 178, 181, 187, 188, 195,
197, 207, 210, 211, 223, 224,
226; empirical, 12; first-person,
180; in general, 64, 65, 164, 165;
intellectual (transcendental), 12,
17, 20, 21, 90; moral, 33; philosophy of, 92; universal, 183
Constitution, x, xix, 5, 14, 16, 23,
30, 31, 40, 65, 70, 77, 84, 88–89,
95, 98, 104–5, 107, 109, 110, 114,
128, 136, 166, 208, 214, 216, 218
Contingency, 143, 148, 149, 161,
169, 172, 182, 234
Corporeality, 140, 141, 142–44, 153,
155, 160, 163, 168, 206; and
temporality, 142–44
Correspondence, xi, 92, 93; of
substances, 220
Cosmology, 207, 227
Culture, x, xii, 111, 172, 175–79,
182, 183; and self, 178; as *a
priori*, 178–79

Dasein, 27–28, 36, 229, 231
Death, Being-toward, 231
Descartes, René, 21, 55, 90, 137–38,
139, 144, 149, 152, 164, 196, 229

Particularization: of universe, 197–98; of world, 194, 209

Pascal, Blaise, 196, 199, 233

Past, the, xii

Perception, xii, xxiv, 4, 22, 47, 49, 51, 52, 59, 64, 77–78, 84, 141, 158, 196, 197, 199, 201, 208, 217, 218, 225, 236–37

Person, the, 55, 124, 131, 133, 145, 146n, 147, 165, 166, 167, 171–72, 178, 182, 183, 190, 193, 206, 218, 222, 225, 228, 236, 237; absolute (universal), 165, 179; collective, 180; singular, 180

Personality, 172–73, 178, 179, 180

Phenomenology, xviii, xxi, 21–30 *passim*, 41, 51, 56, 70, 92, 96, 126–27, 146, 152; of nature, 236n

Philosopher, the, 239

Philosophy, 209, 232, 233, 235, 238, 239; and poetry, 234; reflective, 208

Phylogenesis, 204–6

Physics, 220

Plato, xii, xix, xxii, 89, 90, 122, 148

Poem, the, 238, 239

Poet, the, 236, 238, 239

Poetic, the, xxiv–xxv, xxvii, 235, 237–38

Poetry, xvi, xvii, xxiv, xxvi, 233–39

Positivism, 20, 47, 49; logical, 60

Possibility, 7, 10, 13, 14, 20, 136, 165, 200, 201, 218, 226, 227, 238; logical, 20; as power, 20

Possible, the, 200, 201, 202, 222, 225; as power of the real, 202

Power: of being, 190, 232; of the real, 201, 202; of world, xiv, 190; and grace, 236; in subject, xvii, 188

Pradines, Maurice, 204

Praxis, 210

Pre-ontological comprehension, 126–27, 231

Pre-predicative (pre-reflective), 94, 97, 122, 127

Prerequisite, 221

Presence, 90, 93, 101, 160, 229, 235; of body, 147; of self, 147–48; to self, 129, 153, 161; of world, 202, 237; to world, 148, 159n, 203, 206, 207, 209, 210,

226, 237

Psychoanalysis, 112, 125, 129, 179, 193; existential, 124; of nature, 236n

Psychologism, xii, xiv, 5, 12, 19, 21, 22, 27, 32, 64, 123–24, 126

Psychology, 174, 197; comprehensive, 179; of personality, 179; social, 178

Quality, 192, 196; affective, xix, 95, 105, 122, 161, 173, 192; ontological, xxiv

Quasi-object, 181

Quasi-subject, xiii, 112, 173, 180, 181, 183, 205

Real, the, 199, 200–1, 202, 207, 208, 211, 220, 225, 233

Realism: moral, 211

Reality, xiv, xv, xvii, 20, 66, 96, 195, 199, 200, 201, 202, 203, 207, 209, 225, 229, 230, 231, 232, 236, 239; and appearance, 236; cultural, 176–77; of history, 175; of individuals, 165; of world, 225; social, 176

Reason, 3, 6, 9, 32, 34, 95, 183–84, 191, 192, 194, 196, 199

Reduction, 25–26, 84, 91

Reflection, xvi, 97, 98, 139, 144–45, 198, 214–15, 231, 233, 239; absolute, 224; philosophical, 226, 239

Region, 190, 194, 195; formal, 75; material, xviii, 75, 80, 108, 170; of Being, 229; in general, 74, 75, 194

Religion, 234

Representation, xiii, 4, 9, 12, 13, 157, 160, 197n, 215

Revelation, 117, 230; self-, 235

Ricoeur, Paul, xxv, 6, 12, 15, 17

Sartre, Jean-Paul, xxii, xxiv, xxvi, xxvii, 18, 21–22, 95–96, 116, 124, 129, 132–35, 144–45, 147, 148–49, 163, 168, 181, 188

Scheler, Max, x, xx, 5, 57, 73–74, 83, 87, 140–44, 146, 164

Schelling, F. W. J., xxii, 36, 39, 207, 217, 236

World (continued)
sim; feeling of, 192; forms of,
191; as horizon of horizons, 207;
human, 182; indeterminateness
of, 191, 192, 194, 205, 207; natural, 168, 182; objectivity of,
193; power of, 45; as power of
real, 202; real, 193, 194, 238;
singular, 192; soul of, 236, 238;
structures of, 159, 191; subjective, 192; as totality, 199, 238;
as unconditioned, 199